Ascent of the Mountain,
Flight of the Dove

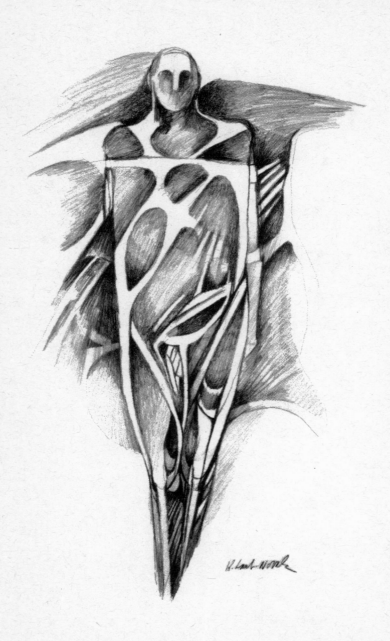

Ascent of the Mountain, Flight of the Dove

AN INVITATION TO RELIGIOUS STUDIES

REVISED EDITION

by Michael Novak

1817

Published in San Francisco by

HARPER & ROW, PUBLISHERS

New York, Evanston, San Francisco, London

LIBRARY OF CONGRESS CATALOG CARD NUMBER: 70–128050

ISBN 0–06–066322–7

The text of this book is printed on 100% recycled paper

78 79 80 81 82 10 9 8 7 6 5 4 3 2 1

For K.
climber who soars
dead-alive
knows the abyss

Contents

viii

Acknowledgments

Carol Christ made many astute criticisms of the early drafts of this book, supplied me with readings, and supervised the footnoting, particularly for the first three chapters. In the years since, she has gone on to win the wide recognition, especially in the field of women's spiritual quest, predicted for her in the first edition; and her life's work is barely at its beginnings.

Karen Laub-Novak, whose husband I am, completed the drawing which deepens these pages.

Sharon Winklhofer left her concert piano and came east yet once again, this time from UCLA rather than Stanford, to type the first draft from my cryptic handwriting. Evelyn Becker of Bayville typed the later drafts. Isabelle McKeever and Ida McDaniel at S.U.N.Y., Old Westbury, helped with several related tasks. Judy Lally typed portions of the revised edition. William Gooley assisted me in the revision of the footnotes.

M.N.

Preface to the Revised Edition

The response to this short book over the seven years since its publication has been a joy to me. Many letters have come to me on account of it, and many seminar discussions and general assemblies in schools across the country have permitted me to hear students react to it. I recognize that the book stretches beginners a little. Some of the words in it are jawbreakers (my favorite is intussuscept). But virtually everyone seems to have grasped the basic insight and learned a way of talking about the self and religion that is both accurate and helpful. That is the important point. The purpose of the book is to help each reader to find words to express his or her own religious experience in a comfortable and exact way.

In the years since the first text was being written (1970), America has lived through some vivid experiences. Some of those now using the book—I keep reminding myself—were only nine years old in 1969, the year of the "march on the Pentagon," and only thirteen or fourteen in 1974 when Richard Nixon resigned. Many have no memory of the years when John F. Kennedy was president. The hippies and even the Beatles seem very long ago. And new history is being made. The "horizon" of our lives keeps shifting.

It is a disadvantage of living in our era, in fact, that so many layers of our experience are flooded over by great public events, broadcast for our attention. It is harder now than it used to be to grow up as a private person, shielding one's inner life from intrusions by public noise. Young people spend a great deal of discretionary money, and so advertisers seek out new "styles" and "attitudes" that can attract millions of imitators. The young are necessarily insecure. The young have always been willing followers of ideals and causes—have marched in many different armies, for many different purposes—and they are vulnerable to all the public incantations and pressures. We have not learned sufficiently how to resist the public world. We safeguard too little private space in which the self can encounter itself in inner dialogue, alone and in silence.

For this reason, it is even more important than it used to be for religion to strike more deeply into the self, away from public glare. Unless Americans become more sophisticated about the language of the self, inner life will shrivel. In addition, our people will continue to be vulnerable to fundamentalist movements like those of the Reverend Moon and Scientology. Such movements take over too many innocents. They promise, and sometimes deliver, a touching happiness. But they do so by closing the spirit in a powerful and dangerous way. Because our families and our schools do not provide a large and critical vocabulary by which to express the inner longings of the spirit, the souls of many are parched and they gladly accept water, any water, from those who offer it. The liberation of the religious spirit from trivial, closed, and simplistic systems of thought can only be achieved through a kind of "cure of souls"—the development of a critical language, exercises, and disciplines that open rather than close the mind, that lead to higher viewpoints, breakthroughs, and new syntheses, in a constant enlargement of spirit. A religion which stifles the inquiring spirit is unworthy of that spirit.

In this revised edition, many small changes have been made throughout the text: Chapter Five, Section 6 has been thoroughly revised; the notes have been brought up to date; and a new epilogue has been added to provide one more in the book's series of "higher viewpoints," in order to account for developments since the appearance of the first edition in 1971. For one thing, the circle of my own work has expanded as I have tried to explore the stories, symbols, and myths hidden in several unexplored areas of American life.

Michael Novak
Syracuse University
September, 1977

Introduction: An Invitation to Religious Studies

The experience of being alive today often evokes wonder, surprise, determination, delight, reverence, risk. Understood in a certain way, these experiences are religious. This book is written for those who want to understand such experiences in their own lives or those of others.

Religious studies are to a dangerous degree personal. They call for an attitude of fresh awareness, a new sensitivity to others, to nature and to oneself, and a series of conversions in one's way of life. For what is the point of merely studying *about* religion, without also changing one's life?

Each of us must choose who he or she will be. Religious studies are an inquiry into the possible identities among which our actions gradually reveal our choices.

Religious studies are also social. They introduce us reflectively to the countless brotherly bonds which already unite us, or might more freely and profoundly do so if we wished. For human beings are more alike than different; uniqueness is a quality attained after long efforts. Through language, family, class, nationality, and other determinants our identities are social more thoroughly than they are individual.

Religious studies are also institutional. Institutions are not so much man's enemy as his natural habitat. Man is a political animal. Thus religious studies must offer insight into the way in which institutions assist, assuage, shape, and trick us.

Finally, religious studies inquire into those experiences which suggest to human beings that they live in a network of meaning that transcends their ordinary, pragmatic lives. Such transcendence appears as a unity, or purpose, or dynamism, or perhaps a terrifyingly immobile center around which their lives turn. The transcendent context of human life may be viewed as an illusion or as the really real by comparison with which all else is straw.

At times, religious studies are pursued with disciplined subjectivity: Who am I? Who should I become? At other times, they are pursued with detachment: How can one most accurately draw a map of certain areas of experience? Subjectivity and objectivity are often at war, perhaps more properly so in religious studies than in any other field. No field is wholly objective, or wholly subjective. But religious studies stand at a crossroad of the human spirit. No matter how objective one may try to be in one's knowing, sooner or later the events of one's life ask one to choose how one will act in this or that circumstance. They ask one, with eventually relentless pressure, to declare (in action rather than in words) what one most truly values, what one ultimately loves most.

Religious studies demand of each inquirer some degree of consciousness and some degree of reflective justification for her ultimate choices. In a sense, then, religious studies are nothing more than a full articulation, through systematic, historical, and comparative reflection, of a person's way of life. The assistance of many specialists is required for such articulation. There are many traditions and institutions that provide a brotherly challenge to our own prejudices and narrow horizons. It can happen that a person's specialized knowing has little to do with his actual living. An atheist may be the world's greatest expert in the history of Buddhism or Christianity. Yet perhaps nowhere more than in the field of religious studies does disharmony between a person's knowledge and his personal living invite students to be sad.

Religious studies—then called "theology"—used to be undertaken mainly in monasteries, seminaries, schools of divinity, church colleges. Theology was pursued for the professional preparation of clergymen, and somewhat more marginally for the greater sophistication of a few devout laymen. In the eighteenth and nineteenth centuries, philosophy was written within a religious context and was full of religious concern. For the past fifty years, the methods of philosophy have been so defined that a fruitful treatment of religious questions was precluded. Today religious studies are pursued at secular universities in connection with programs of humanistic studies, with departments of the social sciences (psychology, sociology, anthropology), with institutes of African or Asian or Near Eastern studies, and even with investigations in the meaning and interpretation of the natural sciences (biology, physics, ecology).

For some generations, various of the secular disciplines wrestled against the churches for their independence. In psychology, sociology, and anthropology an explicit hostility toward religion was nourished. The opposition between "science" and "religion" is a story often told—and oversimplified. Men sought autonomy both from the religious establishments of the past and from the claim of theology to be "queen of the sciences." Many persons today seem to feel that they are stifling under secular establishments and secular methodologies. The wheel has turned.

A fresh conception of religious studies has become necessary and possible. The social basis for "theology" has broken down. The denominations cannot keep their members (or their clergy) safe from the impact of other world views. The divinity school has had to explain its traditional categories in the critical eye of those who speak other languages and employ other methods. A humanistic and transcultural perspective has become obligatory. Thus, religious studies are at a creative threshold and boldness is required. So large a mountain is in labor it would be shocking if a mouse came forth.

No one would deny that the field of religious studies, before the large task awaiting it, is in creative disarray. An admiration for Eastern religions, a new respect for primitive religions, a shaken confidence in ascriptions like "higher" or "superior" when used of European or American Christianity, have altered standards of judgment and ways of perceiving. Enormous materials in history, world religions, social studies, and psychology remain to be assimilated.

Meanwhile, the classical intellectual traditions, in the East as in the West, are straining and bursting under the pressures of rapid cultural change. The future of religion, and *a fortiori* of religious studies, is hardly predictable. An invitation to this field, therefore, is not an invitation to a settled land but to open territories, where not even good maps yet exist.

My prejudices are bound to show and, indeed, I would like them to. Religious studies are primarily the taking up of successive standpoints, from which one may assimilate a fresh horizon. Progress in religious studies is not a logical progression, within one fixed and unchanging standpoint. It is a series of "conversions" from standpoint to standpoint, of breakthroughs, of perspectival shifts.

In the ascent of the mountain from standpoint to standpoint, one often proceeds by dialectic: denial, affirmation, denial, mounting ever higher ground until, at last, a desired horizon comes into range. Only then, *within* an achieved horizon, on a plain as it were, do the key terms and operations remain constant enough for the use of logic. Then a new breakthrough occurs, the old logic feels the strain, and the climb begins again.

Logic operates only *within* a horizon. But in the progress from standpoint to standpoint, quite other disciplines, quite other skills, are demanded. In *The Structure of Scientific Revolutions*,[1] Thomas Kuhn makes a similar point. Within the natural sciences, too, there are two different rhythms of progress: one normal and logical, the other revolutionary and involving a new world view, a new prior paradigm.

The student must learn to become acutely conscious from the very first of which standpoint an author occupies at any given time, for the author's logic makes sense only from the author's standpoint. If the author's standpoint is not well taken the logic of his position, however faultless in itself, is not sufficient.

The present essay is written from a moving standpoint. Sentences uttered in each chapter are true from the standpoint of that chapter (as nearly as I can make them true). But successive chapters are written from within a larger and more difficult context: one will have to mount higher in order to understand them. From the higher standpoints, what was earlier treated more simply is not so much rejected as questioned from new points of view.

I have tried to write in my own voice, not so much as an impersonal mapmaker but rather as an explorer. I have not tried to set forth all possible alternatives. I have taken up useful vantage points that are favorites of mine.[2] Ample notes will guide readers to both classical and contemporary discussions.

Over some of the ground I have passed often. In other cases, I am rather painfully a novice. In the ambition to explore the whole range of religious studies, relating all its many areas as standpoint to standpoint, I am not the only novice among my colleagues in the field; no one has yet set our entire field in order. It is the urgent need of earlier explorers to go out and send back the first sightings that has emboldened me. I would find it a great help if someone else had done it. Since no one has, there seemed nothing to do but take the risks—and to enjoy the adventure—myself.

It is possible that newcomers to the field will feel empathy the

more keenly as they sense my struggling. For the voyage undertaken is a metaphor for the field itself. Religious studies are a
journey, a descent, an ascent, a pilgrimage, a way, a trip, a voyage.
This invitation will be well constructed if it not only says but also
shows—if, in the end, the reader has made a journey, and
changed, and not merely read rapidly through another book.

Good books are almost invariably nonlinear, and artists have
always known that art lies in both respecting and defeating its own
indispensable materials. I have tried to keep before my eyes the
conviction that books are for the sake of experience; they open
up new possibilities of life. Life is not for the sake of books.

Yet even this claim should not be misunderstood. Many, hearing today (in this most rationalized and disciplined of societies)
of the need for fantasy, passion, and festivity, forget how profound a passion inquiry is, how full of fantasy creation is, how
festive is the act of making a good piece of work. Too many
Americans seem to think of passion and emotion only in their
most elementary and sentimental forms—in touch, in affective
speech, in gesticulation and inflammatory rhetoric. The quiet,
complex, and subtle passions, even when white-hot, go unrecog-
nized.

The art of writing is an exemplification (one only, among
many) of the full wedding of all one's passions and all one's
intelligence in joy. In the revolutionary social order we ardently
desire, the arts will prosper—and, not less, the passionate intelligence.

I love to write. I want the result to be a joy to read.

ONE

The Voyage

Four religious questions (there are others):

"Who am I, under these stars, with the wind upon my face?"

"Am I first of all a brother, or a self? Out of many grains, one wheat? Out of many grapes, one wine?"

" 'Who am I?' includes, doesn't it, 'Under what institutions (idols?) do I live?' "

"In the silence, in honesty, with courage, freely, living in community, may I address—who? what?—as 'thou'? If I tell a feverish child, awakened in the night, 'It's all right, Richie, everything's all right,' is that a lie?"

Silence. It is good to meditate. Wordlessly.

1. THE RELIGIOUS DRIVE

"Paranoia is true perception."[1] Sanity is a lie. Dostoevski's Christ (Myshkin) is an idiot.

What is real? Which world is true? If "pragmatic" is the same as "real," the sensitive and visionary person seems slightly mad.

"To be or not to be?" today is rendered *"Insane or sane?"*

1

We have acquired such flexibility of consciousness that nothing seems fixed. Or, rather, we can adjust nearly everything external in order to render our experiences such and such. We rearrange our external environment, move in the groups we choose, avoid situations we choose to avoid, direct out attention and perception as we wish.

Very well, then, what ought we to make of ourselves? Who do we think we are? Who do we choose to become? What do we count as real?

Such religious questions have become insistent practical questions. They are practical for individuals. Cultures no longer decide all questions for the individual. Each person seems to have today an unparalleled capacity to choose his own ultimate values, to give himself his own name, to direct his own voyage—or to surrender its direction to others.

Such questions are also practical for societies: Modern societies must decide what their loves truly are—or else technology itself will entrap them in what is merely feasible.

I understand by "religion" a root intention, an ultimate drive.[2] Religion is the acting out of a vision of personal identity and human community. Religion is constituted by the most ultimate, least easily surrendered, most comprehensive choices a person or a society acts out. It is the living out of an intention, an option, a selection among life's possibilities.

It is wrong to link religion too closely to notions about God or gods, or to religious organizations. For such notions and institutions are but one expression of the basic drive. In my sense of the word, atheists and "irreligious" persons make choices that are of equally high interest to religious studies.

The study of "fundamental" or "ultimate" questions used to be called religious, and that is the justification for the word. We have long since found out that there are secular, nonreligious answers to such questions. A drive that gives a person his own sense of how he is related to his own complex operations (his identity), to other men (his communities), and to his world (nature and history) is implicit in human acting. Watching a stranger or a friend in action, we wish to ask: "What does she mean by that? What does she have to imagine about the world and herself in order to act like that?" Adverting to our patterns of action, we ask: "What am I trying to do? Who do I think I am?" Such questions are the fundamental concerns of religious studies. An atheist is as at home with them as a theist.

I would not wish to quarrel over boundaries. It is true that one may raise similar questions in anthropology, sociology, psychology, and many other fields besides. There is, so far as I know, no absolutely airtight definition of religion, by which to distinguish it antiseptically from every other aspect of human life.[3] There are many definitions of religion which reduce religion to some other drive: for sexual fulfillment, for security, for emotional peace, for stability, etc. For the moment I am content to uncover in myself a drive to unify my own psyche, to perceive its harmony (or, in any case, relations) with others, with nature, with history.

My actions, every least one of them, involve me implicitly in such relations. Did I eat bacon for breakfast? A pig was slaughtered in my name. And did each of the men and women who worked to bring the bacon to my table receive, in creative work and in wages, what I approve as a satisfactory return? Whether I thematize such relations consciously or not, a world view was implicit in my raising of fork to mouth, implicit in my groping for the coffee cup behind the *Times*.

The drive which ultimately gives sense to all my diffuse actions is a unifying, meaning-giving drive. It is that drive which even in atheists and agnostics, I wish to call the religious drive: it ties one's life together. (L., *Re-ligio,* to tie, to fasten.) The religious drive works its way out in our actions. By our living we tell a unique personal story. Gordon Allport has emphasized in *The Individual and his Religion,* in too Protestant and Western (i.e., individualistic) a way, the need for attention to singularity:

The conclusion we came to is that the subjective religious attitude of every individual is, in both its essential and nonessential features, unlike that of any other individual. The roots of religion are so numerous, the weight of their influence in individual lives so varied, and the forms of rational interpretation so endless, that uniformity of product is impossible. Only in respect to certain basic biological functions do men closely resemble one another. In the higher reaches of personality uniqueness of organization becomes more apparent. And since no department of personality is subject to more complex development than the religious sentiment, it is precisely in this area that we must expect to find the ultimate divergences. Still, the very emphasis on individuality is a Western phenomenon; it is a social achievement of the West.[4]

Each person's life is "tied together" in a singular way. It is important, then, not to prejudice religious studies in favor of the theist, as if only the theist were capable of unity of life, harmony, reverence, community, commitment, courage unto death. By *homo religiosus* I mean the person who manifests awe and wonder before the signs of the holy in human life, an attitude of reverence, adoration, prayerfulness. The qualities of life which characterize the saint may belong to the secular person as well as to *homo religiosus*. Put another way: *homo religiosus* manifests but one type of religious behavior.

In our more secular age, the drive to unify one's psyche, and to relate oneself to all other human beings, to nature, and to history has assumed new shapes, sometimes more hardboiled (at least on the surface), sometimes more sentimental ("the world is getting better"). Substantively, moreover, secular and religious persons may appear to do the same things—like Rieux and Paneloux as their relation develops in *The Plague*[5]—but the different story each is living out almost always affects the style, significance, and bearing of what each does. Hence, one wishes to keep distinct things distinct, and not to hurry into saying either that the secular saint is a crypto (or anonymous) believer *or* that the reasonable Christian or Jew is really just an atheist who can't bear to admit it.[6]

The religious drive cuts across all phases of human life. It is not a slice of life, like a section of *Time* magazine. It is present in every part of life—present in one's senses, one's sexuality, one's emotions, one's imagination, one's intelligence, one's aspirations. It never manifests itself in its pure state, apart from other interests and desires of human life. Thus it is always highly conditioned, highly colored, by the various cultural and temperamental projects through which it exercises its shaping, unifying influence. It is virtually impossible to isolate religion purely *qua* religion in human life. Its role in human life is not to *add* something else, but to *unify* and to *direct* what is already there. The religious drive is not one more among a panoply of human drives (for self-preservation, for community, for sexual fulfillment, for progeny, for power, etc.). It is the contextual drive, as it were, manifested in all the others, the comprehensive drive through which they are related.[7]

It is, in that sense, the final secret of an individual's or a society's life, the set of keys to its intimate identity, priorities, purposes. It is not merely a resolution of those other drives named above: the passive sum, as it were, of conflicting forces. It is, in itself, the restlessness with disharmony, the dissatisfaction with inconsistency, the demand that feelings match thoughts, thoughts words, words actions, and actions the dynamism of life.

It can also be, of course, the proclamation of inconsistency, delight in anarchy, a willingness to "let it flow." In that case, too, it is a selection of a way of life. It is a drive to raise ever further questions, to venture new actions, to expose oneself to new experiences. It is the oncoming drive of life itself, as a unity. (Such an oncoming drive, we should note, does not necessarily imply that history is progressive. History may be cyclical and going nowhere. Even individual life though it is usually thought of as growth and the metaphor for it is way, journey, trip, may be lived as a magical mystery tour, going nowhere in particular.)

The religious drive, then, is dynamic, unifying, comprehensive, ultimate. It is never isolable from the concrete tissue of life.

Thinkers who like their subject matter pure are inevitably disappointed by their attempts to abstract religion from the stream of life, in order to give it a clear, distinct definition in itself.

2. WHAT RELIGION IS NOT

Before one begins to study religion, however, one usually has had some experience with it. That experience, as often as not, has a distorting effect upon further study. No one should deny his earlier experience. For, whatever its quality, it is, as experience, part of the data in the field to be explained; it cannot be wished away. Still, religious studies are the passing over from standpoint to standpoint. And the first standpoint to be brought fully to consciousness is the one within which one begins. "What until now has been my experience of religion?" "With what experiences (place, date, circumstances) do I give content to words like 'God,' 'community,' 'myself'?" "What experiences of my life give me, most vividly, the sense of who I am?" . . . Such questions as these allow one to search in time and memory down the journey which defines one's present standpoint.[8]

There are several particularly distorting experiences of religion common among Americans, and it is well to come to see clearly how and why they are sources of distortion. We have not yet proceeded far enough to give good reasons why the so-called distortions *are* distortions. We do not at this point have criteria by which to distinguish the genuine from the distorted. Nevertheless, there is a rather rough-and-ready common-sense tool at our disposal: We can point to contradictions internal to certain attitudes toward religion, and suggest that *even on their own grounds* some meanings given to religion are not likely to prove to be genuine.

In a sense, we find ourselves in a position like that of Aristotle at the beginning of the *Nicomachean Ethics:* all around him, he finds Athenians using the words "good" and "happy," praising and blaming one another for their actions, and acting in this direction rather than in that. Yet, even in so small a city as Athens, he discerned several different, competing views of ethics. He did not all at once construct an ideal model by which to condemn the ones he found in practice. Instead, he examined each available way of life on its own terms, pushed it as far as it would go, until it tumbled over into self-defeat.[9]

Thus, in the United States, there are people (especially radio preachers and politicians—these often come to the same thing) using the word "God," defending religion or claiming that Americans are, or should be, a religious people, urging that religion is the source of the nation's strength, etc. There is even a sort of civil religion in the United States. The United States is "a nation," as G. K. Chesterton put it, "with the soul of a church."[10] The American way of life is described in reverential, almost mystical, godly terms; its national competitors and enemies are described as "godless." The American nation is thought to be particularly beloved by God, its way of doing things spectacularly blessed. Its wealth and success—the number of indoor toilets, family cars, and television antennae on suburban roofs—are interpreted as proof that God is on its side, and that it was wise to win him over early by a law-abiding way of life. Attacks upon the American way of of life are taken to be, not merely pragmatic or even political, but as in some way spiritually malicious, blind, satanic.

The American way of life, in a word, is ordinarily an American's first instructor in religious experience. Pledging allegiance to the flag is a sacred act. Political celebrations—the Fourth of July, Thanksgiving, Memorial Day—would be seriously incomplete were there no mention of God in the proceedings. The awe and majesty of the courtroom are reinforced by the heavy oak paneling, the judge's robes, the formal manners, and also by swearing on the Bible. Even the manner and style of scientists and engineers, dressed in spotless white robes and surrounded by the mysterious accoutrements in their laboratories, induce in us a sense of awe before incomprehensible power, a layman's respect for those who have mastered the arcane. The screaming whine of a suddenly approaching jet jars our sensibilities: *mysterium fascinans et tremendum*—our own mystery fascinating and terror-spreading.

The American way of life is a religion, and Americans have to come to terms with that. It is not without potential profundity and sources of self-transcendence. But it is not the only, the best, highest, or most commendable of religions. It is one of many national religions. If separated from its vast economic and military power, its spiritual profundity would not command much notice.

Religion is often made to supply reinforcement to a cultural status quo. A Spaniard is Catholic to the marrow. To be atheistic is to be not quite trustworthy as an American.

Religion is often made to reinforce morality. "If I did not believe in God, then why would I keep my word, avoid drunkenness and licentiousness?" Without God, everything is permitted. "If I had no God, I would lack the strength to be good." God is made the means to my moral living.

Religion is often made the key to peace of soul, the power of positive thinking, the thrust of friendship, dynamic decision, and success.[11] Religion gives a person "get up and go," it recharges worn-down batteries, offers spiritual tune-up and overhaul. Religion is the service station of the spirit.

Religion is often made a vehicle of belonging.[12] It has buildings, memberships, rules. It gives people something to *do*, something to organize and to feel good about. It offers us *one* nonpragmatic task (to be carried out pragmatically) that has no tangible goal or profit. Its fruit is a sense of belonging to a special group. Its spice is uplift and inspiration. It "keeps a man going" by incorporating him in a privileged fellowship of healing. No matter how hectic the other six days, Sunday makes a person feel right with the world, justified.

Religion is often made to serve aesthetic purposes.[13] It indulges the appetite for refined perceptions of diction, sight, sound, awe, solemnity. Life is impoverished without such perceptions, and they are rare enough in American life. Still, the ultimate seat of the aesthetic life is the sensibility or the complacence of the perceiver. It is possible (perhaps even frequent) for the genuine aesthetic impulse to carry the perceiver beyond the aesthetic, to an enlarged sense of unity, harmony, and transcendence. It is even possible for the aesthetic impulse to carry the perceiver to a state of fear and trembling, or to a state of joy and tranquillity, on the brink of moral and religious conversion. But an aesthetic conversion, of itself, is neither a moral nor a religious conversion.

Religion, especially perhaps among certain Roman Catholics, is often made to serve dogmatic purposes. The principle of authority tends to occupy the center of attention.[14] The heart of the matter is deemed to be outward and inner assent to certain dogmatic statements: to the formulations of a creed. In the background, genuine religion is considered to be trust in God; in the foreground, genuine religion is considered to be belief that doctrines x, y, and z, as stated, are true. A subtle and hardheaded defense of clear, doctrinal articulation can be mounted, especially in these days of double talk and flaccid sentiment. Still, a religion that places all or most of its emphasis on notional assent to correct formulations runs afoul of the way words and notions change their meaning in history, and also of the way human experience and perception change.[15] Most of all, such a religion would falsify the meanings of reverence, love, and community, by making human beings the instruments of a conceptual system and not the reverse.

Religion is often made into a function of an individual's psyche.[16] If he is afraid, it consoles him. If he is restless, it pacifies him. Whatever his needs, it administers to them. But, surely, religion does not exist only in order to fill man's needs—to be a crutch, *deus ex machina,* or necessary illusion. For if religion were so to present itself, then, clearly, each man would be at the center of his universe and God would be a flunkey who supports man's ego.

Finally—and more generally—religion is often made into a cover-up. Life in itself is deemed too terrible to face. And religion is imported to cover over the abyss, to make everything right with the world, to make things appear to be sweeter than they are. Religion, in a word, is made into a means of escaping too much reality. A good man, a decent man, a religious man, looks for the bright side of things, fixes his attention on hope, seeks in religion springs of action which a naked glimpse of life would not allow him. Religion is flight from the absurd.

There is nothing human which cannot be corrupted: "The corruption of the best is worst of all." Common to all these distortions of genuine religion is the attempt to defend the placid, secure, ordered surfaces of life—to make us accept as normal and blessed the pragmatic, given, ordinary world of everyday.[17] It sometimes seems that religion functions to take our minds away from terror, mystery, absurdity, pain, madness: to domesticate the human animal. Religion seems to bless the conventional, the trite, the expected. It seems to screen out terror. Yet, surely, that is a reversal of fundamental purposes.

In the Jewish scriptures, the "people of God" could only for short periods tolerate a hidden God, a God who could not be named, a God who sent his rain on good men and evil men alike. Continually, they turned away from the Unmanipulatable, Demanding One, and fashioned for themselves gods of clay, stone, wood, bronze, gold.

So it has also been with the other great world religions. Routines, systems, bureaucracies, and the insistence on daily proprieties soon cover over the disruptive, awesome terrors of genuine religion. Even holiness, once manifest and participated in, soon suffers the jading of everyday. In our age of committees and fund drives, perhaps the favorite idol to be established in God's place is an organization. Membership campaigns—even strike-steering committees—are much easier to understand than a hidden, silent God who is not a functionary of our peace of mind.

John Cogley, the noted journalist, has suggested that genuine religion is a little like music. You either have an ear for it or you don't. And most of those who don't join religious organizations.

The cardinal principle of such a religious spirit would be: "When in doubt, build."

The religion of the poor and the uneducated, to be sure, often appears to "the enlightened" to be merely slavish and conformist. In some cases, particularly in America where social connections are mobile, shifting, and comparatively shallow, it may be true that the religion of the lower middle classes, admixed with American nationalism, functions as an emotional crutch. The test is whether persons of that class or any class recognize in practice any source of transcendence over and above the needs of the tribe. Would God ever be imagined as condemning the public, official, popular actions of the nation?

But students of religion do well to guard against rash judgments. Many who lack education are beautifully articulate and astonishingly profound.[18] Many of the inarticulate make, in acts of courage and endurance, discriminations that shame the privileged. It is among the uneducated, since biblical days, that the choicest religious witness is often found, and it is wholly possible now as then that some doctors of theology are thin of soul.

3 . WAY OF LIFE

We have so far been generous with negations, swift to say what religion is not. It is time, now, to summon energies for a far more difficult climb: toward the standpoint from which we can begin to glimpse what religion is.

Let me state it briefly. Religion is a conversion from the ordinary, given, secure world into a world of nothingness, terror, risk

—a world in which nevertheless there is strange healing and joy. Religion is a way of perceiving oneself, others, the world; a way of acting. Living comes first. Reflection comes afterward. The first religious act is to clap one's hands, to dance, to do. The second, later moment is the moment of reflection.

"Lex orandi, lex credendi," the old proverb says: "The rule of belief follows the rule of prayer." Those who pray, who have experienced internally and lived out externally the genuine impulse of religion, are the criterion which those who reflect upon the meaning of religion must follow. Experience comes first, understanding afterward.

In this perspective, religious studies are before all else a conversion in one's experience of life and, only secondly, an articulation of that conversion. To be sure, some persons are good at articulation even when they haven't had the experience. They try to put faithfully into words, and to unpack the meaning of, what others have experienced. Their systems of articulation may grow so complicated that they come to think of the basic experience not only as unnecessary but even as hindrance; besides, they haven't time for it. They may even nourish delicate dislike for those who share the experience, who return again and again to it—strange creatures, who prefer to so much clarity, to so many elegant ramifications, rough experience. What does a professor have to do with experience?

There are in every religious tradition maxims which warn those who would truly understand to attend to what the experts say— but to watch, also, what they do; and, in the end, to prefer to the clear networks of the learned the inarticulate wisdom of the simple. Religious studies, then, follow an odd code: last are first, first last. A serious student must advance on two fronts at once: in reflection but also in experience, in science but also in wisdom, in complexity and ambiguity but also in simplicity. It is difficult to become a scholar, more difficult to become holy, difficulty squared to become both. The standards by which students in the field of religious studies are bound to be judged make them appear ridiculous. Imagine trying to teach a half-alert classroom the wisdom of Buddha, the meaning of Jesus, the presence of Moses—trying to show, and not only to say, to be and not only to articulate. A man or a woman has to be a little mad to take the job, a little devious in accepting payment for it.

It is easier, of course, if one tries merely to be "objective," to present materials in a more or less neutral, workmanlike, professional way. But a scholar who is not in love with her materials seriously diminishes the frequency and power of her insight into them. And the materials of religious studies are not rocks, atoms, calculators, or even texts but—at the center of records and indices of all sorts—voyages of the human spirit. The man who tries to be merely professional injures, sooner or later, his own dignity. He finds it harder with the years to convince himself that he should conscientiously set aside the vital matters as too personal, too loaded, in order to provide his students with well-honed tools. Surely, his life has not merely so instrumentalist a function.

There lies in an instructor, almost always, a vision to communicate, an experience to transmit, a conversion to trace the course of, a passion to enkindle. Students often listen acutely for the personal story of even the most rigorously professional instructor. It helps to note at whose expense his jokes are made, where his silences occur, how his inflection alters on certain words, where his pace quickens, how vibrations in the room change. In religious studies, such matters are not peripheral. They present a standpoint. And standpoints are the subject matter of religious studies.

The field of religious studies is constantly and inextricably involved in the coincidence of opposites. No principle is more central to the field. The language employed by the simple and by experts in the field is characteristically paradoxical. "God cannot be spoken of," a professor says, speaking of Him. "Faith without works justifies," is adjoined to: "Unless you *do* the will of my Father. . . ." And there are the paradoxes of the Buddhist riddles.

Humans are constantly impelled to speak of what cannot be spoken of. The method employed by those in the field is characteristically dialectical. Affirmations are coincident with negations; they make no sense apart from negations; in a curious way, they *are* negations. "I believe in God," a person says. Then it turns out that he or she talks about God chiefly by way of negations: God cannot be seen, touched, tasted, imagined, or even accurately conceived of. The affirmation that God *is* turns out to be a negation of all the usual ways in which we use the word "is." God is spoken of as if the word were a noun, referring like all other nouns to some object of experience. But negations follow swiftly: God is not a thing, object, person like any other. The form of words is used, then its normal interpretation is denied.

Religious language is regularly and systematically nonliteral and nonlogical because it involves the movement from standpoint to standpoint. In such movement, the context of words changes and the viewpoint from which they are regarded changes; hence, ambiguities creep in and analogies rather than equivalences come into play. Secondly, the word "God" is not wholly understandable within any one human standpoint, and always eludes full definition. Thirdly, the relation of the finite to the infinite constantly intrudes. When language is plain, literal, logical, and under control, it is not—cannot be—religious. We become aware of religious experience as an experience which exceeds any one standpoint, when we find ourselves being converted from one standpoint to another on our unceasing journey.

Thus it sometimes seems to newcomers to the field that "anything goes," and that any sloppy argument whatever, so long as the words "paradoxical" and "dialectical" are thrown in, will be widely accepted. Tidy souls usually declare religious studies "hopeless." If they happen to be in the field themselves, they usually mark off small territories for themselves and try to pay as little attention as possible to the work of those whose methods, they feel, are too messy to be dignified as methods at all. The field, however, requires that one cope with many various stand-points, and with many ambiguities.

Each person's present standpoint is limited and partial. Some people start with a declared faith in God and in his Word as revealed in Jesus Christ, and for them virtually everything that follows is clear; and having, with due anguish, made their leap of freedom, their commitment to the Cross, they scarcely look back at any problematic crumbling at their foundations.[19] Others argue from a "natural theology" that seems to assume that "natural" is defined by the cultural forms of seventeenth-century London, Paris, and Rome, among the ranks of those educated in Latin and Greek.[20] And there are others whose intellectual and imaginative world springs from German preoccupations—from Hegel, Nietz-sche, Dilthey, Weber, Heidegger, and others. The Germans in-vented historicism, dialectic, phenomenology, existentialism, and other determinants of what is called "modern consciousness."[21] The English brought linguistic analysis to a cutting edge.[22] American Midwesterners, meanwhile, seem to have an affinity for the co-creating God described by Whitehead in mildly optimistic, scientific notions.[23]

In a word, the field of religious studies is, at present, character-ized by mutually exclusive allegiances, intellectual contexts, preoccupations, methodologies. What one group respects as good work, another thinks just awful. The differences do not tend to follow denominational lines; they are patterned on the cultural matrices in which reflection is carried out. It is becoming an expectation, however, that men accomplished in the field know how to pass over from their own standpoint to that of others and to move gracefully and fairly in standpoints not their own.

What, then, is meant by a standpoint? A standpoint is a complex of experiences, images, expectations, presuppositions, and opera-tions (especially of inquiring and deciding) by which men act out their own sense of themselves, of others, of nature, of history, and of God.[24] A standpoint may be unthematized or thematized: operating unself-consciously, even unconsciously; or else brought to articulate awareness. Moreover, this "bringing to awareness" has at least six stages. Better, it is a system of coiling strands. I name them as follows: experience, imagination, insight, method, self-criticism, and action. The names are not important; the activities to which they point are present in everyone's life, and each may name them as he pleases.

The stages by which religious experience is brought to awareness are not connected like layers in a cake. They spiral around one another, each fecundating the others. Experience is present at each "stage," and so are imagination, insight, method, self-criticism, and action. The point of distinguishing the coils is to stress how many-sided is human consciousness, and in how many directions it unfolds.

The living matrix among the coils, the one from which the energy of life comes, is *experience*.[25] To be sure, a certain dynamism drives us to seek further experiences, to make them conscious, and to enrich and to direct them.[26] But the mother of everything human is experience—experience more various, more rich, more diffuse than our words, images, or symbols have yet selected for our attention. We swim as it were in a sea of experience too overwhelming to intussuscept. Our equipment is too fragile, too limited, for the discrimination of any but a small fraction of the world in which we live, or even of the world which lives in us. (Experience is indistinguishably "inner" and "outer."[27] The chair on which you are sitting may or may not be part of your consciousness now: the mood you are in may or may not be conscious now.)

We live on only the smallest margins of our possibilities of experience. Constantly, then, we can extend our experience: dream, fantasize, touch, inquire: open ourselves to more of ourselves and our world: notice sights, sounds, feelings that heretofore, although they were at hand, we have not seen, heard, felt. Our immediate horizon teems with vital possibilities, even when we are sluggishly content with safe, orderly, habitual perceptions at its barest edges. Growth consists, in one of its requirements at least, in allowing ourselves to experience more than we have yet experienced. Not every experience constitutes *ipso facto* personal growth. A Nazi Storm Trooper had ever-new experiences of cruelty, blood lust, torture. The Nazi cry for blood and raw experience has not yet dimmed in our ears, and lives still in all of us. The desire "to be where the action is" may spring from an evasion of one's own emptiness, and not from organic growth.

First, then, experience. Sometimes a man simply does what he does, without even being aware of what he is doing. He stands on a cliff over the Pacific and watches the sun glance off the long rolling waves which thunder far below. Let us call this awareness first awareness. He may also, however, become aware of his awareness and gain some distance from himself, as if he were to advert to his situation: "Here I am, standing on a cliff overlooking the Pacific, watching the gleams of light on the blue waves, hearing the tide smash on the rocks, etc." Let us call the latter second awareness.

Without yet reflecting on his experience, a man becomes by second awareness thematically aware of his experience. In a sense he focuses his attention, selecting what he will notice, and impressing upon his memory certain salient features from the otherwise polymorphous and dense "world" of immediate experience. Even in first awareness, of course, a preconscious selectivity is already operating. How often have others called our attention to matters in the "world"—to matters even in our own emotions, say—that we had not adverted to, had, in fact, screened out? Such matters had been in our first awareness, for as they spoke we knew that what they said was true. But sometimes we had not seen at all, not even in first awareness, what they saw. Our imagination, previous insights, the story we are living out—all these shape our experience before we become conscious that our experience is selective. First awareness, then, is already selective. There is no merely neutral experience. But even of the world of which we are first aware, we do not bring more than a tiny fraction to second awareness.

Secondly, besides the awareness constituted by experience, there is also the further awareness constituted by imagination. The patterns of our imagining direct our experiencing (stage one), but also our insights (stage three). Imagining is the chief mediating agent for both experiencing and understanding. It plays the same crucial role for our acting. It is the most "human" operation.[28] It stands between raw experience and intelligence. It is most central in its location and powerful in its effects.

Often a teacher notices that students do not understand a point because their imaginations have arranged their experience so as to direct them toward some other point. Often mutual understanding depends on one's ability to grasp what is happening in the imagination of the other party in the discussion. Insights are highly personal and follow personal laws; they always occur in connection with concrete images. The discerning of a faulty imaginative expectation and the construction of a good one enormously raise the probabilities of insight. A good teacher works to create images that are attractive, surprising, close to lived experience. A sequence of such images will bear the searching intelligence along the stream toward the flash of light.

Conscious attention to the life of the imagination is nine-tenths of pedagogy. The teacher, like the poet and other artists of the imagination, lives by his or her capacity to become aware of, to differentiate, to criticize, and to create imaginative forms. Far too little attention is given in Western science, philosophy, and theology to the imagination.

Thirdly, a standpoint may be brought to a further awareness by intelligent insight. A man who quite clearly to others is experiencing emotional contradictions in his relations with authority figures may not see a unifying pattern in the mass of such experiences throughout his life. Suddenly, say, what he has been doing for years dawns on him.

Further, concrete insights are distinguishable from their conceptual expression. The man we are speaking of may not have a conceptual expression for his insight. He may not have read Freud; more probably, he may have learned the concept long before he had the concrete insight into his own life.

Insight is a highly personal event. It is concrete; it occurs at a time, in a place. It arises out of an imaginative frame and spreads its influence through one's imagination, affections, experiences. It may not prove to be even a broadly correct, let alone a precisely accurate, insight. It may or may not find expression in concepts, words, or actions. It generates intense pleasure—so much pleasure, in fact, that a life of varied and intense experience which does not yield, as well, frequent and penetrating insights is not altogether attractive. People who seldom have insights are described as stupid.

I have taken pains to emphasize that insights are of value in themselves, quite apart from the further rigors of conceptualization. I do this because I know it to be true. Often I have insights which I do not wish to, or need to, put into words. Such are, for example, insights into a course of action open to me, insights into another man's character, insights into what a woman is actually driving at in an argument (who her unspoken enemy is). In principle, even the most subtle insights can, no doubt, eventually be formulated. Blessedly, one need not always do so.

Many forms of art (and philosophy) do not wish to proceed beyond insight to formulation. *Satori* seems to be of that sort. But so also are many poems, cinematic scenes, works of fiction: delight arises from full and accurate reception of the formed images, and is ruined by direct statement. The insight, the illuminating and penetrating peace that comes with resolution, is deliberately left "dark," unabstracted, unstated. The insight remains immersed in the thickness and density of the world of experience and imagination. And it is that wider, subtle contact with the world of experience and imagination, as compared with the thin band of life about which we have clear and distinct ideas, that is so highly prized by a fully developed intelligence. Contrivance and craft have been at work; there is no question at all of *lack* of intelligence. It is only that the artist is content with insight, and cares little for the consequent conceptualization, if any.

But a word also needs to be said about the pleasures which derive from hitting off a happy concept for expressing an insight, and the similar pleasures of finding the appropriate sentence to carry it, of relating that sentence to other living sentences, of completing a set of living sentences with the link which allows one to relate that set to yet other sets. There are enormous pleasures in relating concepts and theories to one another, knowing all the while that such relations mediate (at whatever distance) concrete experience. For theory only *seems* to be irrelevant to life. In fact, the way we experience things—even our own bodies—is mediated by insights we have had and networks of theories which have been, since birth, constituting our language and directing our attention. Theory serves life. Conceptualization serves insight. But notice which is master, which the slave.

No American experiences the paleolithic sensibility. Without theory, in fact, he would not even be aware of other sensibilities. The pleasures of relating concept to concept, sentence to sentence, theory to theory are not for everybody; and for many persons they are positively destructive, alienating them from any capacity for fresh and personal experience. It would be unwise, however, to underestimate their seductiveness, their enormous cultural power, their sheer personal delight. Playing with theories can be like playing games, and while a man might think of other games he would prefer to play, it would be severely Puritan of him to legislate that playing games of that sort is too much fun, too idle and too wasteful to permit to others. The stakes in theoretical games, moreover, are very high; one should not be surprised that connoisseurs play with such intensity.

The conflict between theory and living insight is etched deeply into the soul of the West. In America, in particular, there are recurrent bouts of romanticism and populism in which the plain, untutored, unvarnished intelligence of the ordinary man is exalted. Some Spiro T. Agnew each generation claims to speak for the intelligence of a "silent majority" sick and tired of the bloodless theories of the effete. Sensitivity seminars were in 1970 as popular as revival meetings in 1870. Bodily experience, scorching insight, and shattering conversions have long been precious to Americans. American poets and novelists regularly defend the passions of the heart, the glands, and the imagination from the encroaching rationality of universities, airports, factories, expressways.

In Christian consciousness, moreover, there is the struggle between the letter and the spirit of the law. In education, the advocacy of order, rigor, and precision is opposed to experience, independence, and personal growth at a personal pace. Thus the questions arise: Is education aimed at bodies of systematized knowledge, or at personal insight into one's own identity? Are religious studies a matter of theological systems, or of personal insight? The connection we implicitly make between insight and concept influences deeply what we emphasize in our actual living.

Fourthly, insofar as experience is thematized by insight, and then further thematized in concepts, sentences, and theories arranged systematically, a further stage of awareness makes its demands upon us. Many heed those demands. Consciousness is not only experimental, imaginative, and intelligent but also methodical. To make a standpoint conscious methodically is to give a full and ordered account of its genesis, relations, implications, and moving direction. Those who fear too much clarity and dread the disease of words bitterly resist the methodical exigence. Many disdain it as the prominent, overwhelming error of the West, and they respect the East for its steady renunciation of methodical consciousness. There are many arguments about how this methodical consciousness, if it is to be carried out, *should* be carried out: about what constitutes good, fruitful method and what leads to destructive, alienating method. Few subjects are so hotly debated in religious studies as how to order various standpoints methodically.

Fifthly, however, besides the intelligent thematization of a standpoint through insight and later through method, there is also the thematization through self-criticism. Not all bright insights are sound insights, and not all methodically developed theories turn out to be true, or relevant, or easy to defend. It is not enough merely to announce that you have taken up a standpoint. People will soon start to ask "Why?" In the end, perhaps, pushed to the limit of your ability to justify your position, you will say, "Here I stand. I can do no other." For yourself, that may be the end of inquiry on that point.

The first question for others, however, is whether they should follow your lead. Every choice of a standpoint carries with it, whether you wish it to or not, the implication that such a standpoint is good for a human to adopt; that it is moral; that it is humane. Whether you like it or not, others always feel the moral pressure of that implication. There is, as Sartre makes plain, no *laissez-faire* in human choice. Americans like to think that they can say, "What I'm doing has no effect upon you; I'm choosing for myself alone." But human choice cannot be moral unless it makes a claim on all men. When others examine that claim, they may see that action X obliges you and only you, because no one else is in quite the same circumstances. In that way, they can excuse themselves. But a claim founded on sheer personal applicability is not moral at all. Since people commonly take the considered actions of others to be moral, they feel the weight of the choices made by those who in one way or another are significant to them. Hence, others will immediately take up the task of criticism. Is your standpoint merely idiosyncratic, wholly personal, finally arbitrary? Does it commend itself to others as admirable, pleasing, reasonable, justifiable, helpful, illuminating? A second question will also occur to others, even when you have reached a justification that satisfies you. Why does your justification, they will ask, appear convincing to you? How did you get there? What is there about you that lets you be content with it? A man may silence the critical exigence in his own case; others are not likely to be so protective.

Even in the field of ecumenical and comparative religious studies, it is likely that we have now passed the stage of intelligent consciousness, and are beginning to raise the critical question. It is as though we have subtly become aware of a sort of planetary consciousness that binds us all. We are no longer merely polite strangers. We are all beginning to feel the pressure: "Yes, that is your standpoint. But *should* it be? You would not screen out nearly so much if you moved over here . . . then there . . ."

Sixthly, one of the main tests to be met in critical consciousness occurs in the form of consciousness expressed in deeds. Religion is a way of life. "Taste and see that the Lord is sweet." "By their fruits, you shall know them." The real and important test comes in living. What our experience means to us is shown best by our actions. Seen one way, action comes at the very first stage. We are already acting in the world before we begin to thematize our experience in any of the five stages: action precedes thematization. Seen the other way, what exactly we intend by our other thematizations receives concrete, unmistakable, real force from the actions which follow from them. For what is the point of thematization if it does not lend to fuller, richer life?

The ascent of the mountain is, in part, the acceptance of the diverse and complicated tasks of these six forms of consciousness. These six seem to constitute responsibility at this stage of human consciousness, in this civilization. Perhaps it was easier (but was it?) to be an integrated human being in a simpler time, when fewer differentiations had been made in consciousness. Today the multitude of stories in the world presses upon each of us. We could hardly avoid contact with strange, frightening, exciting standpoints, even if we wanted to. It is part of our destiny, now, that we must make our way from standpoint to standpoint, being "converted" or "radicalized" every so often, seeing our past lives in a new light from each new vantage point, and defining our identity by our pilgrim's progress as we go.

4. EARTHY ECSTASY

"When intellectuals lose contact with the people," Dostoevski said, "they become atheists." The people he was thinking of were the peasants of Russia: earthy, sensual, sturdy, lascivious, shrewd, direct. Alyosha in his moment of conversion in *The Brothers Karamazov* falls face-down on mother earth, the black soil clings to his lips, he presses his ribs against earth's ribs. The Karamazovs "think with their stomachs."

Religious studies derive from roots sunk in the concrete earth: from dance, exultation, song, despair, pain. At the origins of all great religions are sweat, sperm, a woman's cry, soil, grapes, tears, blood. No matter how "spiritual" language about religion may seem, an effort to discern the root, earthy experiences which lend it human authenticity will invariably be repaid. Around the edges of all religious worship have been orgies, feasting, fertility rites, purpled feet pressing grapes, the joys of a sweaty harvest-time. To be sure, the great religions have tried to seize and shape the great psychic energies that spring from earth. When their tie with earth is cut, they die.[29]

For a human is as much a fruit of earth as an apple is of a tree.[30] Without air, water, soil, fire, he could not survive; his destiny is linked with earth's. Biologically, his cells and structures spring from a universal network. What happens at one place resonates elsewhere as on a web. Food, drink, atmosphere, have a great influence upon a man's or a woman's feelings, temperament, judgment. "You are what you eat; you are how you eat" is not fanciful. The rhythms of the organism, its attunement, the burdens it is made to carry, and its vulnerabilities respond to heaviness, to irregularity, to mechanical shoveling.

Many religious traditions appear at first to be based on the total renunciation of matter, the material world, the passions and desires; certain forms of Buddhism, Hinduism, and Christian asceticism, for example. But two considerations should make us pause. First, our own civilization in suburban America is probably the most rationalized and "spiritualized" of any in history. We are more thoroughly sundered from biological rhythms, agricultural rhythms, and even the internal rhythms of our own emotions (for outside stimulants are constantly breaking in) than any people in history. In our lives, mind controls everything possible. Hence, when *we* try to imagine what it would be like to be ascetical, we begin from such an alienated standpoint that the idea of *increasing* the role of reason even further, at the expense of body, is terrifying in the extreme. People very close to the rhythms of their own bodies, passions, and the earth itself can much more sanely make an effort to interrupt those weighty natural rhythms by ascetical practices, and derive a sense of liberation therefrom. Their situation and their needs are the reverse of ours.

Secondly, religious history is characterized by exaggerations and wild oscillations in its pursuit of "higher" or "better" things. Sometimes men and women have truly grown to hate matter, the earth, their own bodies, passions, and desires. But the orthodox impulse in these matters has ordinarily been a search for harmony, tranquillity, and a sense of oneness with all things. As Thomas Aquinas once explained to one of his protegés, the number 5 does not annihilate the numbers 1, 2, 3, and 4, but includes them within it. So the "higher" faculties "include" the "lower." The idea is not to negate the latter, except paradoxically: so that they may live again, in harmonious unity with self and world.

"Body," then, is not simply separable from "mind"; each co-exists in the other. "Man" is not simply separable from "earth"; each co-exists in the other. Man lives in the moist air of earth like a fish in an ocean. He walks not so much *on* the earth (separated from it) as *in* the earth, textured into its rhythms, its vitalities, its laws. He can conceive of himself as *outside* nature, as a stranger or a pilgrim, and he commonly does. But such a conception, especially tempting to some, may easily become a form of alienation, a lie, a comfort in the face of one's own coming death: white bones bleaching in the sand. (It is not by accident that American consciousness evades the theme of death.) Man's ultimate identity may, or may not, be tied to that of earth. Initially, at least, he is one with earth, fruit of the earth, conscious voice of earth.

A tie with earth is important to religion for a second reason. Man's consciousness does reveal to him his uneasiness with nature. A creature able to remember his past and to project a future, able to reflect upon his own destiny and, within limits, to direct it, has a highly problematic relation with earth, ecstasy, bodily solace, and his own natural rhythms. The earth is good, but disease and scarcity and ignorance and malice and sadism make of it also a butcher's bench. At different stages in his development, *Homo sapiens* has tried to forget that the root meaning of *sapiens* is "taste"—biting into a cold apple, a lick of honey, a rinse of bitters, water on the tongue and in between the teeth—and tried to imagine a *sapientia* of mind alone. He is prone to such forgetfulness both at times of ecstasy and escape and at times of calculation and control.

The religious impulse, in particular, tends to veer off either in the direction of the sensual orgies of fertility rites and ecstasy and overpowering concreteness, or in the direction of decency, control, will power, and cold reason. Scylla: without a constant return to its earthy origins, religion soon becomes thin, cerebral, artificial, and evasive. Charybdis: Roman orgies and Nazi bestiality ended in profound despair. To be tied to earth does not entail trying to lose oneself in it.

This dialectic between human consciousness and its earthy, originating base brings to light the third reason why religion needs its ties to earth. Cleanliness not only is not next to godliness; it may in some circumstances be a barrier to God. Decency and order are not necessary marks of the godly man; they may suffocate religion to death. "This place stinks of God!" wrote Leon Bloy of a certain kind of deadly middle-class idolatry.[31] Earthy experience is a source of exultation, of beauty, of tragedy, of despair.

Man's love-hate for his habitat, his struggle-rest, consolation-agony, open him forcibly and continually to reflection upon his destiny. Apart from concrete experience—dirt under his nails, blood upon his clothes, inadequacy of muscles and will, awe before the sunrise over the water, the terror of tornadoes, famines, and plagues—there is always something false and inauthentic in religious reflection. Too much comfort, too much security, falsifies the actual situation of men in the world.

We cling to life—and always have—only by a thread. Our long advance during modern centuries toward mastery of this planet has not ended in the safety of which generations of our ancestors dreamed. Our lives are no more secure than they were in ages past. Standards of personal health and the probabilities of longevity have risen dramatically. But the universal political and military threat that hangs over our entire planet replaces our more local insecurities in ages past. Who plans with confidence today on being alive a decade hence?

It is wrong to imagine that earthy life is sensual, whereas religious life is spiritual. The word "spirit" is best understood from sentences like "What a spirited horse!" Spirit—by which I mean inquiry, attending, intending, straining forward—runs through all the senses, through imagination, through affectivity, through the passions. It does not live only in the rarefied operations of conceptualizing, thinking, resolving. There are panoramas that move us to tears, agonies (like Auschwitz)[32] we cannot absorb with our minds, emotions no words plumb. Experience in a sense precedes and is larger than understanding: it carries burdens of meaning intellectual evolution is not likely to exhaust. To imagine that the best way to organize our understanding of human life is to divide man into body and mind, and to enlist religion on the side of mind is to falsify both the past and the future of religion.

5 .   CONVERSION TO THE SACRED

Religion, I want now to propose, is primarily a conversion to the sense of the sacred. By conversion I mean a focusing of one's way of life: I mean taking up one standpoint, after having occupied another. "The first possible definition of the *sacred*," Mircea Eliade writes, "is that it is *the opposite of the profane.*" The sacred manifests itself, shows itself, to man in a given place, at a given time, and this act of manifestation Eliade calls "hierophany" (Gr., the sacred shows itself). "It could be said," Eliade goes on, "that the history of religions—from the most primitive to the most highly developed—is constituted by a great number of hierophanies, by manifestations of sacred realities."[33]

To be religious, then, is to experience a hierophany. It is to recall a day and an hour—or perhaps a slowly dawning realization during an identifiable stretch of time—when one's sense of reality was altered. It is to be changed, to have one's psychic center of gravity changed. It is to regard the world in a new way. It is to be oriented. It is to be centered. "For the man of all pre-modern societies, the *sacred* is equivalent to a *power,* and, in the last analysis, to *reality.* The sacred is saturated with *being.* Sacred power means reality and at the same time enduringness and efficacity. The polarity sacred-profane is often expressed as an opposition between real and unreal."[34]

The economic order has taken three great shapes in human history: the nomadic, the agricultural, and the industrial. Persons in the first two, Eliade notes, have shared in a similarity in behavior that seems to us infinitely more important than their differences.[35] Both the nomad and the farmer live in a *sacralized cosmos*. Only today have great masses of humans lived in a desacralized or at least largely profane world, in a culture whose institutions are designed to make the whole of life systematically profane.

The ideology behind industrial society speaks of "enlightenment," "autonomy," and "liberation." The sacred is driven out in order that man might be "free." But the practical program of industrial society is to shape man's attention according to a new standpoint, to focus his attention and his energies, and to teach him a new meaning for the word "real." The steps taken in this progressive "secularization" of consciousness are several. Not all are inimical to the sacred, although cumulatively they alter its meaning by creating a new historical context.

One of the key steps is to *relativize* everything. Whereas the manifestations of the sacred "connect" humans to a reality deep in things, in some way at the very center of reality, the man or woman of secular consciousness notes that different people perceive the center differently. Moreover, he or she is inclined to believe that there is no such center. (In practice, most secular men and women seem to act as if the center of history is a line of human progress—progress in human liberation or justice or enlightenment, etc.).

A second key step is to concentrate one's attention upon the practical world of everyday experience, and to call that world the *real* world. The emphasis on practicality is accomplished with sophistication and shrewdness. For ideals, images of a better future, and dynamic intentions are understood to be the driving forces of practical activity. The givens in the human situation are then conceived to be two: man is a dynamic, forward-moving animal; and his progress is made by one practical step after another. Businessmen and university professors, journalists, and military men can share what John Dewey called "a common faith": in a world as wholly profane and thisworldly and practical as one can make it. It is a powerful faith and not without great human poignancy.

Never has this secular faith been so strong in human history as it has been during the generation immediately preceding our own, in the United States and in other industrial societies. For many generations, it had been a minority faith, the faith of underdogs and heroic strugglers. Gradually, the institutions of American society—governments, corporations, universities, schools, armies, the new communications media, and even the churches—began to operate according to that faith, which is, after all, far more directly suited to the aims and functions of bureaucratic institutions than sacral faiths had ever been.

Increasingly, the secular faith began to insinuate itself into the souls of many who still thought of themselves as living in a sacral world and as religious. First the sacral world fell away from consciousness. Then religion was privatized—reduced to a more and more remote corner of the individual psyche. Religion could be less and less spoken of, less and less public. Its locus was "deep" in individual intuitions and feelings. For some, meanwhile, the social relevance of Christianity and Judaism required, more and more, the adoption of secular attitudes, secular methods, a secular sense of reality. In a word, the standpoint of the profane occupied more of the souls of more humans all the time.

And what of our generation? What of the future? There are internal contradictions in the modern secular attitude which will surely grow more severe and more obvious. The standpoint of the profane is immensely powerful. Yet for many, at least, its achievements need not be denied in order to move to a further standpoint, that of a new sense of the sacred. And without movement to some new standpoint, it seems obvious that the contradictions within the profane standpoint will lead to cultural self-destruction.

Paul Tillich pointed out in one of the last lectures before his death that in matters of human freedom there is no guarantee that humanity will not sink deeper into barbarism and destruction as times goes by, rather than move to a level of greater wisdom. "After the first World War in Germany, we believed, just because of the defeat of Germany, that there was a *Kairos,* a great moment, in which something new could be created. In this sense, we were progressive, but we did not believe that it was necessary that [progress] would happen."[36] There is no such metaphysical reality as "inevitable progress." As the hopes of the utopian thinkers of 1920 in Germany encountered the dark, bloody irrationalities of the Hitler era, so human hopes at any time are fragile.

The standard of the profane, the practical, the down-to-earth, imparts an enormously powerful sense of reality to our culture. It is, nevertheless, only one possible standpoint among many. We are not required to dwell forever in the standpoint of the profane which we inherit. Those who are too certain of its progressive direction, and those who despair of its narrowness and pettiness, are well-advised to note that human beings are never irretrievably trapped in the sense of reality given them.

Human experience is many-shaped. There are countless ways of structuring our experience of ourselves, others, the world. No one way imposes itself absolutely upon everybody. Commonly, the experience of living out a human life is the experience of one conversion after another. What one earlier noticed as salient now recedes; matters earlier overlooked gain in importance. Directions of which one was earlier capable but toward which one did not move or of which one was incapable or unaware, now begin to beckon and to absorb one's energies. One feels as if one is a new person. One has, whether unself-consciously or quite reflectively, the feeling of having undertaken a new way of life, of having made a fresh start, of having been reborn.

Human life develops through stages of breakdown, breakthrough, reintegration. One constantly loses one's life, regaining another. Those who grow, in any case, frequently experience such conversions.

Religion is primarily a conversion to the sense of the sacred. How shall one define the sacred? Controversies are many on this point.[37] And it is more than likely that at different stages of human history and in different cultures the relation of the sacred and the profane are understood differently. The crucial points to keep in mind are two. First, the sacred and the profane can be understood only in terms of each other. They are dialectically related, in such a way that a change in the understanding of one always involves a change in the understanding of the other. Secondly, the sacred does not define one class of things, while the profane defines another; the terms do not point to two different worlds, realms, or sets of objects.

Quite the contrary. Nothing in the world is merely profane; nothing is merely sacred. The terms sacred and profane refer, rather, to the light in which things are regarded; they point to human interpretations of the real. I do not mean to say that these words are "merely subjective." "Subjective" and "objective" are also related dialectically to one another. Nothing is merely subjective; nothing merely objective. C. S. Lewis wisely pointed out that when one says a vista from the Alps is sublime, one is not speaking merely of a personal feeling without reference to its appropriateness.[38] To say "sublime" of some vistas—of the efficiency of Auschwitz, for example—would reflect not merely a personal feeling but a peculiarly aberrant one.

The difference between "merely subjective" and "objectivity" is not the difference between feelings and certain mechanical procedures; it is the difference between an untutored and a tutored subjectivity. The judgments of an objective scientist remain quite subjective. They are his own and no one else's. But his subjectivity has been sensitized, trained, and highly developed in the skills required to make a certain type of judgment.

Similarly, a conversion from the standpoint of the profane to the standpoint of the sacred is not a shift from a hard, sensible set of feelings to a soft, romantic set of feelings. It is a shift from a sensibility and intelligence tutored to one set of priorities and operations to a sensibility and intelligence tutored by a new set of disciplines and skills. The world regarded remains the same. Only now one notices aspects one did not notice before, counts them important, pitches one's life in accordance with them. The person working in the standpoint of the profane lives in the same world as the person working in the standpoint of the sacred. But they experience that world (and themselves) differently. They respond differently. They act differently.

What are these differences? Here authors usually begin by comparing the sensibility of a primitive, archaic human, who lived in a sacred world, with the sensibility of a modern human, who lives in a profane world. Since modern human is profane—since it is his choice and destiny to be secular—we are told that modern religious persons, too, should undertake the disciplines of the secular city and celebrate its freedoms. The world of the sacred, we are told, is gone forever.

The reason given is that in the archaic, sacred world, life was experienced as being at certain hierophantic points connected to an absolute, fixed center. Man had not yet assumed responsibility for fashioning his own history. He felt himself to be living in a pattern of cycles, a scheme of eternal recurrence, such that human life, like the seasons and rhythms of nature, was cyclical, static, circular, eternal. Whereas, modern man has seen that he cannot evade his own freedom; he has seen that history is not bound to the rhythms of nature; he has assumed the mastery of his own evolutionary destiny. Modern man, it is thought, is more responsible, more mature, more future-oriented. He has broken the chains of nature, and now bravely faces the uncertain future.

Reason (variously construed, but always demythologizing and desacralizing) is the thought-form of the modern age.

Leave aside the question how many "modern" persons there actually are on this planet at this moment. Leave aside, also, the question whether there is any possibility (whether logical or psychological) of thinking without myth. Leave aside, thirdly, the question whether the impulse of the modern age is, in fact, merely promethean or sisyphean or faustian or eschatological—i.e., a subspecies of archaic myth, but with more powerful instruments for its implementation. Still, the question remains: Is history going anywhere at all?

A discussion of the relation between nature and history will have to wait (below, Epilogue); from our present standpoint too many of the elements required for that discussion are not available. Yet in a preliminary way we can at least allow our repressed doubts about "modern consciousness" to surface. That consciousness, although growing stronger in Asia and elsewhere, is largely European, American, white, and industrial. Its main strength appears to have peaked. Its undoubted achievements brought in their train quite other consequences than visionary generations had dreamed of. Indeed, the self-doubts our culture is living through seem to suggest that a new form of consciousness is being born. It is likely that those who are projecting our future consciousness from its base in the old—and particularly from German thought, which is its center—are inadvertently playing a conservative role. The currently fashionable "theology of hope," for example, seems to represent in theological form precisely the deepest alienations of industrial society: evasive of the present, estranged from the earth, lusting after a better future through chemistry and politics. The "theology of the future" promises a future too grimly like the recent past.[39]

Suppose for a moment that human progress, *human* progress, is much less easy to measure than we had been led to imagine. If the entire planet were made over on the model of Los Angeles, would someone confidently assert that the new human (the Angeleno?) is superior in his humanity to archaic human? Is the civilization of Southern California in 1978 superior in human terms to the civilization of Southern California in 1770? In what respects, and at what costs? Progress may not be as important a product of modern consciousness as alienation, violence, and despair.

A larger appreciation of other cultures on our planet, and the growing implausibility of Western arrogance and bias, suggest that Western assumptions about the direction and movement of history have been far too simple and untutored. If we suppose that the most fully developed "modern man" is not, in fact, mature, free, responsible, genuinely human, but rather conspicuously alienated, manipulated, confused, one-dimensional and impoverished, certain pretensions begin at the very least to wobble. And certain long-repressed instincts seem to cry out at last for a full and open reconsideration.

When one speaks of a conversion to the sacred, however, one does not have to think of a return to the nomadic or agricultural ways of life of the past. The movie *Easy Rider* and the rise of agricultural communes do suggest such a return; but modern technology and mobility have created a new sense of reality unknown to earlier peoples. Some commentators, more optimistic about modern consciousness than Mircea Eliade ever allowed himself to be, seized on his description of "the myth of the eternal return"[40] and took for granted that a culture like ours, committed instead to "the myth of historical advance," was more mature. The dualities "mature-immature," "enlightened-unenlightened," and "progressive-backward" were made to parallel "profane-sacred."

Commentators have come to ask: "What can the sacred *mean* to modern man?"—implying that it can mean very little, if anything. Yet there is a deep hankering in many persons today for a conversion to *something* sacred, to a simpler and more natural and more cosmically harmonious life. What Albert Camus referred to as "the Algerian man"[41] (in opposition to "the man of the North," so intent on taking responsibility for history, and building industries, cities, and armaments) is reflected eloquently by an American volunteer worker. She writes:

In Algeria, in the cool of early morning, people walk as if they found pleasure in the measure of their stride, the feel of earth under their feet, the cool air on their warm cheeks. In Paris it is different—there seems to be no pleasure in walking to do an errand—people walk hastily, almost angrily, as if walking were a nuisance to be tolerated only as long as necessary. There pleasure comes from accomplishing—here, from being.

Perhaps this difference is inevitable because of the concrete and smoke-filled nature of a city. In Paris, New York, Los Angeles, the blacktop and stone seem at home; there is little else. How amazing it would be to peel back the blacktop and find earth! (I sometimes expect the earth, tired of being suffocated by blacktop, to turn and stretch itself, cracking open the streets and buildings of our cities.) The artificial is natural, and the natural seems out of place, contrived, packaged in neat picket fences.

Here the earth presses up at you, overwhelming in beauty and violence. Man's constructions seem not only intrusions, but temporary, comic attempts to hide man's naked impotence from the furious gods of the Sahara.[42]

In a word, many modern men and women intuitively understand that the earth and nature (as opposed to history) are the dwelling place of the sacred.

The sacred can only be understood in and through the profane. Hence, the key lies in probing the radical meaning of the profane.[43] Our civilization dedicated itself to closing off the horizon of the sacred and concentrating our attention upon the profane. For a long time the pioneers of that civilization could blame unenlightenment, lack of freedom, heteronomy, and injustice on the backward forces they struggled against. But now that we are arriving breathless in the modern age toward which our forefathers ran so hard, what do we discover? That alienation, violence, and manipulation have perhaps never been more characteristic of human life; and that self-destruction may be imminent. Nature, which men of history were going to subdue, tame, and master, has turned, reared, and lashed out with vengeance in its maw. The neat, orderly, rational world of practical thinking and scientific order is experienced as a prison, madhouse, hospital, insane asylum, machine, desert, wasteland, military holocaust. Many try to escape.

Around the edges of "modern consciousness" and at the very center of that consciousness enormous unrealities have been discovered, inhospitable and unbearable stretches of emptiness. Those who experience the terror and the absurdity are not, by their indictments of the modern, fleeing from the demands of human freedom. It is rather that they discover in modernity *precisely where it is most modern* so few of the very goods the modern project was supposed to assure: enlightenment, liberation, autonomy, justice. Ironically (human history has not lost its ironic character), the "health" and "maturity" and "coming of age" which were supposed to mark persons of modern consciousness have been converted into descriptions like "sick," "alienated," "manipulated," "doomed." The very persons who, symbolically, were supposed to be the priests of the new era—scientific experts, specialists, rational men—have now been marked, symbolically, as scapegoats. Both the meaning and the validity of the project of "modern consciousness" have become questionable. Becoming a "fully modern man" is no longer the most real, moral, admirable possibility.

Thus, by contrast with the "realism" of the profane standpoint, a new sense of reality is being born. Beyond the one-dimensionality described by Herbert Marcuse,[44] many are beginning to explore other dimensions of human intelligence and society. Beyond the narrow and contrived world of the "sane" and the "well-adjusted" described by Ronald Laing,[45] many are allowing themselves to notice parts of their experience which they have heretofore suppressed or controlled. The sense of reality nourished in other cultures is now accessible, even if in frequently ersatz forms, to those whose consciousness had heretofore been thoroughly Americanized.[46] The profane standpoint is, under many pressures, being shattered.

How can we describe the passing over from a profane standpoint to a sacred standpoint? To answer that question is to state the difference between the profane and the sacred, in terms of a conversion of life.

The heart of the profane standpoint is to call a spade a spade; to break all symbolic connections with "other dimensions." The profane standpoint is organized around practicality. It was a standpoint commonly assumed even in the archaic world, assumed by the majority of people for at least part of their lives, all through the biblical narratives. (Many of the parables of the gospel are addressed to persons preoccupied with their daily business affairs to the exclusion of the sacred.) Archaic cultures are not organized centrally and with highest priority around the profane. But the evidence is overwhelming that the profane standpoint was a frequent occurrence in the ancient and medieval world. The modern European and American culture differs from the cultures of the past in placing practicality at the very center of cultural life. What is not practical is, for us, "merely" symbolic. Our desire to say "merely" when we say "symbolic" indicates an enormous shift in the center of gravity.

The practical man is instrumentalist; for him the world is constituted by ends and means. He "keeps his feet on the ground." He calculates carefully. Effectiveness and efficiency are two of his most important symbolic values. He judges by "results." His analyses are "operational": "How would you put that into actual operation?" Things become more important to him than persons, and he often perceives persons chiefly insofar as they are countable and organizable. The practical man's role in overcoming the scarcity afflicting the human race is important. With the abundance he produces, leisure, reflection, play, and the arts become possible. Here the difference between archaic (or classical) man and modern man becomes acute.

Since archaic man still lived in a sacred world, his practical activities took place in the context of and subservient to larger, symbolic purposes. Work was for play, the servile arts were for the liberation provided by the liberal arts. But in the modern world, the word "real" tends to be given its full content by the practical, the feasible, the workable. The utter concentration on technique provides affluence and abundance by which a larger minority than in the past has resources for leisure, reflection, play, the arts. But simultaneously the utter concentration on practicality deeply incapacitates the psyche. The utterly practical man is rendered impotent for leisure, reflection, play, the arts.

The secular city "liberates" humans in the way the market place, in capitalistic theory, "liberates" supply and demand: the city gathers large numbers of atoms in a situation of *laissez-faire.* In a diminished sense, that is human liberation. Liberal thinkers tend to accept that diminished sense of the word. "A free market place of ideas and values" is the fundamental metaphor in liberal thought. It endures in ethics even when it is rejected in economics. The assumption that a free market place in some *automatic* way leads to genuine liberation seems woefully mistaken when one regards, for example, what happens to individuals in American culture.

There is, then, a gap between the practical world of American (modern) culture and the promises of the profane world. It is, at least, not plain that affluent Americans are, today, more liberated than their ancestors were, more humane, more admirable.[47] It is in the perception of that gap that the conversion to the sacred becomes possible. For once a person discerns that the practical world *qua* practical world is not sufficient for his own liberation, let alone for that of an entire culture, the meaning he gives the word "real" changes its meaning. Where before that was real which worked, which was countable, solid, manipulatable, predictable, controllable, now "real" extends to grace, style, impracticality, impulse, fantasy, delight, ends in themselves, doing nothing at all. The future diminishes in importance; the present grows. Things diminish; ego and libido grow and, just possibly, persons become more important.

But how can we distinguish among various kinds of rebellion against the practical? Is that not the usual dodge of the lazy, the incompetent, the losers, the noncompetitive? The rebellion against the profane can be regressive: infantile indulgence of ego and libido replace discipline and self-directedness.

The rebellion against the profane can be romantic: all standards, all criteria, all possibility of failure disappear. Sweet nonjudgmental paradise!

The rebellion against the profane can be evasive: one covets all one's neighbor's goods and cleverly changes the rules for hustling them, under cover of some "sacred" impulse. (The con man is the mother of invention.)

But even these fraudulent standpoints are important, if only to show that the system does not exhaust reality.

The conversion to the standpoint of the sacred occurs when one becomes aware of feelings, instincts, questions, sensitivities, too long repressed; when the neat, orderly, manageable world of conventional practicality no longer contains one's spirit; when words like "realistic," "feasible," and "pragmatic" no longer intimidate and make one blind; when one suddenly becomes aware of one's capacity to shape one's own identity, to respond to things and to people as to *thou,* with reverence and full attention rather than with instrumentalist design; when one moves out of the standpoint from which everything is a means into a standpoint in which persons, play, art, silence, and other similar activities become ends in themselves. Above all, one's sense of what is real becomes expanded. One seems, to oneself at least, so much more acutely aware of things and people through a sort of participation—as if one were already living in them, and they in oneself. The sacred is, as Eliade said, a *power,* a *reality,* a common flow of *being* to which one feels "connected," in which one senses one's own participation. "The polarity sacred-profane is often expressed as an opposition between *real* and *unreal."* [48] One's sense of what is real has been altered.

Holding a twig in one's hands, or a flower, one finds oneself absorbed in its singularity, its own inexhaustibility, its *haecceitas,* [49] its own utter distinctness from oneself: it, not one's own ego, feelings, needs, is allowed to be the center of attention. Suddenly the world seems overridingly mysterious. Dimensions beyond dimensions are revealed in it. Nothing is too simple, too ordinary, too routine, to escape one's wonderment. Even the repetitions and rhythms of nature catch one's astonishment and attract one's imitation.

It is, today, as though after a long, dark trek through modern, alienating consciousness, the world of the archaic and the primitive, the sacred world, were being restored. Not exactly as it was, because for those who have taken that bitter pilgrimage home can never be the same. Nevertheless, in some powerful and compelling way it does seem possible to imagine a conversion to the sacred which does not mean a linear rejection, but rather a sublation, of the profane. A spade is a spade is a spade. But it is also a black man, a penis, a plunge into mother earth, a reminder of graveyards, an instrument of sharing in divine power, an artistic tool by which man completes and enhances creation . . .

Who takes spade in hand grips a sacrament. Eliade again:

It is impossible to overemphasize the paradox represented by every hierophany, even the most elementary. By manifesting the sacred, any object becomes *something else,* yet it continues to remain *itself,* for it continues to participate in its surrounding cosmic milieu. A *sacred* stone remains a *stone:* apparently (or, more precisely, from the profane point of view), nothing distinguishes it from all other stones. But for those to whom a stone reveals itself as sacred, its immediate reality is transmuted into a supernatural reality. In other words, for those who have a religious experience all nature is capable of revealing itself as cosmic sacrality. The cosmos in its entirety can become a hierophany.[50]

Several generations of total commitment to the profane, in which organized religion seemed more and more peripheral, has set in motion a reversal. It is not, I think, merely a pendulum swing, although in these days of fads it may well be so for the larger number. But for those who do not pitch their lives by fads the cultural opportunity is surely present to imagine themselves assuming the standpoint of the sacred, and thus to think of themselves as having undergone a basic conversion which it is not erroneous to call religious, removed though it well may be from the orbit of "organized religion."

TWO

Autobiography and Story

Who am I? On Monday, I try to set down on paper the seven or eight experiences in my life which most sharply define who I am. On Tuesday, I reread my notes, tear them up, try again. On Wednesday, I tell my story anew and this time I've got it. On Thursday, I am embarrassed: what a one-sided impression I've given, and besides, fantasy is hard to separate from fact.

Or I try to tell someone, at length. Or I lie awake, reminiscing: painful scenes come back, sweet ones. How like an actor. The roles shift often.

Observing my own conversational patterns on any given day, I note that I assume at least seven voices (seven: ancient number for the unlimited). I am strong, weak; helpless, infallible; dictator, slave; gentle one, angel of doom; Bogart, Mitty. With various others, in various situations, in various roles: how many different selves.

Knowledge of self is more like ignorance than like knowledge. The more deeply I go, the less clear my self-knowledge becomes, the more ambiguities and perplexities and unresolved contradictions I discover.

Who am I? One or many?

1.   RELIGION AS AUTOBIOGRAPHY

A purely pragmatic civilization assigns me a social security number. Key decisions about my future are made by men who shuffle in their hands a set of papers on which, at various times, the standard measures of my performance have been recorded. They read brief recommendations about the way I appeared to virtual strangers at various times. I am known from outside, given a character, assigned a place and a role. Those others think they *know* me. More or less "objectively."

And often, when I try to be "objective" about myself I know myself rather in the way that they know me. I see myself through other people's eyes. But that objective portrait "out there" can be shattered so easily by one outrageous act in an otherwise droning life. "I never would have thought he was capable of . . ." The images one has lived out until now are subject to change. Until provoked, perhaps, by a time of great danger and enormous social change, mysteries hidden deeply in the self await their liberation. What we have been we do not have to remain.

On the other hand, most personal growth is organic, continuous, gradual. Humans grow, like oaks, in silence and almost imperceptibly. We invent our identities and fashion our characters through hundreds of thousands of tiny gestures, intonations, acts. People often look alike, seem all the same, appear as if of equal substance; but then tragedy, calamity, or necessity strikes and thin surfaces are sheered away. We see, then, who stands on a base of thousands of repeated acts, fashioned hard, firm, unyielding, and who stands on the crumbling fungus of appearances. Langdon Gilkey's marvelous book, *Shantung Compound,*[1] shows how many Christians who had preached eloquently were stripped by the pressures of a Japanese concentration camp to their petty souls. When the test comes, as it inevitably comes for all, the chaff is beaten away, the cheap metals are melted off, and only hard grains of wheat, only the gold, still stand.

Religion, some think, is believing in doctrines, belonging to an organization, saving one's soul through an attitude (trust in God) or works. But there are countless ways of living out the same doctrines, many different ways of "belonging," an endless number of ways of misperceiving one's own soul. That is why it seems better to imagine religion as the telling of a story with one's life. Willy-nilly, each person's life does tell a story. Often the stories are pointless, meander, seem to have no single thread or set of threads. "Purity of heart is to will one thing" (Kierkegaard).[2] Few persons tell one single story. Few lives are wholly integrated. In lives as in works of art there are few masterpieces. Most lives are somewhat stale, flat, dispersed, undirected.

Still, even dispersal is a story and an astute novelist might untangle its many threads. To trace the history of acts of will, the history of choices made (even those made not by choosing but by drifting), is to trace a voyage, a pilgrimage, a search in a labyrinth, perhaps an endless struggle like that of Sisyphus. No man or woman does everything at once, chooses infinitely, acts with infinite scope; men and women are finite. Their freedom is a selection among possibilities. Acting, they define a story.

In this weak sense, all men and women are religious. The completed lives of each trace out a story, whose implications reveal what they took the world in which they lived to be, who they thought they were, what in their actions they actually cared about. Action is a declaration of faith: one cannot act without implicitly imagining the shape of the world, the significance of one's own role, the place at which struggle is effectively joined. It is not true that faith, creed, convictions come first and then action. It is rather true that we are already acting long before we are clear about our ultimate convictions. More important still: our actions, reflected on, reveal what it is we really care about, more accurately than our words or aspirations about what we would like to care about. We do not know what our deepest views and root concerns may be until we see them bloom into action.

Action is the starting place of inquiry. Action reveals being. Action is our most reliable mode of philosophizing. In action we declare our cosmology, our politics, our convictions, our identity. Who am I? I am what I do.

The word "religious" is used, then, in two quite different senses. In its most neutral sense it simply means that a human life is a declaration of identity, significance, role, place: all action is the living out of a story in a cosmos. In this sense, whether they are aware of it or not, all men and women live out a commitment, a faith, a selection. In its second, more normative sense, religion is the awareness of the story dimension of life: it is an awe, reverence, wonder at the risk and terror of human freedom. It is an awakening from a merely routine, pragmatic round of actions and a sense of being responsible for one's own identity and for one's own involvement with the identities of others.

The two fundamental religious questions are: Who am I? and Who are we, we human beings under these stars? The person who treats his life as taken-for-granted, and unreflectively defines it wholly in terms of its instrumental functions (eating, sleeping, making friends and influencing people, storing up goods), is virtually nonreligious; his story lacks awareness of the choices he is in fact making. It is the sense of choice, of selection, of commitment, of contingent existence that gives rise to the primal religious sense.

There is, of course, a third and stronger sense for the word "religious." According to this sense, not only does a man or a woman in fact live out a story; not only is a man or a woman aware of the alternatives among which he or she is choosing; but also, a man or a woman adds a *religious interpretation* to what each and others are doing. Each interprets the operations each is performing (of wonder, inquiry, commitment, longing) as signs that each is in the presence of—in Dante's words—"the Love that moves the Sun and all the Stars." That is, they take humans in their striving and freedom as a clue to the central significance of the universe, interpreting it in the image of the human person. They address the moving power and presence of existence as "Thou." They see the world not in the metaphor of objectivity, mechanism, science, but in the metaphor of persons. Although the unseen, untouched, to which they address their "Thou" is, they know, unnamable (we cannot know him/it as we know other things we name), they may be willing to place the letters GOD where in normal speech they would speak of a person.

This third meaning of religion is often taken to be the basic, traditional, orthodox, and normative meaning. But it seems wiser to take the first meaning as our own basic term. *In fact,* humans live out a commitment, select their own identity. In religious studies, one ought to study all such possibilities, including the unreflective, self-satisfied, pragmatic one. There are people whose metaphysics are, in effect, the comfortable feeling they have just after a heavy lunch; they see no need to raise ontological questions. They live and they die; and they think persons who torment themselves about ultimate questions both waste their time and overlook the pleasantness of the present. To such people, Jesus and the prophets addressed some of their most moving discourses. Among such people, the Buddhist "way" begins. From one point of view, such persons live in a prereligious state; from another, they too are freely declaring their own identity.

In any case, each person can become aware of the story each is telling with his or her own life. Without such self-awareness, religious studies are pointless: like persons deliberately starving themselves at a banquet table. To enter upon religious studies perceptively is to make one's own story conscious to oneself.

Such questions as the following help to uncover one's own story: What are the experiences of my life which, when I look back upon them, most tell me who I am? This emphasis upon *experiences* is important. Often our experiences have been far richer than the images or concepts by which we earlier dealt with them. Their original fullness, charged with new, conflicting experiences, often lies buried in memory, awaiting our exploration. The search for self takes place in large part through memory.

What has been my history in the use of the word "God"? Our notions of self and of God are correlatives; and a surprisingly fruitful way to uncover some things about one's own identity is to explore one's resistances and attractions to the ways one has encountered the uses of the word "God."

To tell a story with one's life is simply to act. One may be oblivious to one's own story or quite aware of it. One may be, as it were, the author or the reader: creating it, shaping it, or, on the other hand, looking back afterward on what has been happening. Since we are far from wholly being masters of ourselves and our destiny, it is always true that the significance of the story we are trying to tell in large part escapes us. It may not be quite as we imagine it. The image of the story in our consciousness may not be very like what we are actually living out. The impact of our story on others, or its meaning in the context in which we live it, may not be as we imagine it. "There's a divinity that shapes our ends, Rough-hew them how we will" (*Hamlet,* V. 2).

What David Riesman has called "inner-directed" people tend to be quite stubborn and self-directing in the story they are trying to live out. "Other-directed" people tend to let the story be shaped by the audience.[3] It is quite American "to hang loose," "to play it by ear," "to wait and see what develops," "to take it easy," "to play it cool." In a highly organized society, where roles and stories are quite clearly tracked out, individuals in self-defense try to work out their lives in the interstices. It is risky to have too strong-minded a story of one's own; irresistible forces collide with immovable objects. The result is an extraordinary amount of drift, lack of self-direction, waiting for things to happen. Americans do not so much tell stories with their lives as expect to be amazed by the unsolicited things that happen to them. A mobile society fills the vacuum where self-direction used to be.

2. CULTURAL STORIES AND PERSONAL STORIES

What is a story? A story is a narrative that links sequences. A story is a structure for time. A story links actions over time. The more integrated a life, the more all things in it work toward a single (perhaps comprehensive) direction. The richer a life, the more subplots the story encompasses. Interesting people are full of contradictions. Strong drives of various sorts compete in them. They are motivated simultaneously by ambition and gentleness, hostility and humble charity, weakness and strength. To bring integration out of wildly disparate tendencies is the mark of a great soul: a harmony, as Nietzsche pictured it, of passion and intelligence.

How does one acquire a story? The culture in which one is born already has an image of time, of the self, of heroism, of ambition, of fulfillment.[4] It burns its heroes and archetypes deeply into one's psyche. The tendencies and fears of one's parents, the figures one hears described in church, the living force of teachers and uncles and grandparents and neighbors, the example of companions along the way, the tales read in books or visualized in legend, cinema, the arts: all such influences impress one's imagination with possible courses of action, possible styles of life. One economic class visualizes certain possibilities and certain styles, another visualizes another. The Catholic way is not identical with the Methodist, Lutheran, or Presbyterian way. The Jewish sensibility and imagination project a unique way of life. The Buddhist does not imagine the basic story of the noble man in the same terms—or in the same context—as the Christian. The American style differs from the Italian style. In a word, cultural stories as well as personal stories are in question.

A lower-middle-class male in the United States, for example, whose father is a construction worker, mailman, gas station attendant, owner of a small business—a man who probably did not go to college and is a Veteran of Foreign Wars—was probably brought up to live out some variant of the following story. Life is hard, and its few rewards go to those who achieve public respectability, who work hard, and who are willing to sacrifice themselves for the community—to work to put themselves through school or to help support their family, to give up two to four years of their youth to demanding military service and perhaps the risk of losing their life, and to have nightmares about a future of failure and lack of status and security. It is, perhaps, to labor under a name that is not Anglo-Saxon but "foreign," and to feel the suspicion and distrust of those who speak more smoothly and who seem to know what to do on any social occasion. It is to be less than certain of oneself when dealing in ideas, historical parallels, information about other cultures. It is to imagine culture, education, and morality as a matter of absorption, docility, and conformity rather than as a matter of alienation and dissent. It is to suppose that radical social change is not possible in this life, and that God is the God of good order, the God of stability, the God of peace. Life is lived mainly for eternity, not for evanescent, passing political changes. By and large, authorities know best. One is endlessly cynical about the persons who fill public office. But the office deserves respect, as if it were from God himself. The story of the good man is the story of affirmation, docility, cooperation with authority and customs, good will, and optimism—not the story of dissent, disobedience, change.

The story in which this same man shares, as an American, is by and large the story of confidence in American goodness, shock and dismay and disbelief when confronted with institutional inequities or official iniquity. Americans do not assume that American institutions, like all human institutions, are corrupt, inadequate, and less than humane: commonly, they are shocked

by the discovery of the truth. Americans view the world as if
America is at the center of world history and on the very cutting
edge of human progress and human hope; they regard virtually
all foreigners with a mixture of pity, compassion, and distrust. In
foreign lands, Americans huddle together. Few books written
about other lands by Americans illuminate the cultures of those
lands from within, as Tocqueville's *Democracy in America* illumi-
nates America in American terms;[5] American books are more
often guides for fellow Americans through the strangeness of
foreignness. Innocence, Americo-centrism, moral hubris, a missionary sense of destiny, trust in the power of sheer good will, and
instant techniques—such qualities characterize Americans, con-
servatives and liberals and radicals alike.

The American story, until Vietnam at any rate, did not include
the expectation of a serious national defeat, both military and
cultural. "I will not be the first president to lose a war," both
Presidents Johnson and Nixon have said. The prospect of a
thorough defeat, of thousands of lives lost in vain, of enormous
destruction wrought upon the people of Vietnam for very little
gain, is extraordinarily hard for the American psyche to contem-
plate. "Americans never lose" has long been an integral part of
the American story.

That Americans are an essentially good people is also part of
a leading American story. "I know America," President Nixon
said often. "And the heart of America is good." Americans always
mean well. That officially, under orders, through due process of
law, America could do violent and outrageous evil is virtually
impossible for many Americans to imagine. Many cannot believe
that My Lai happened, that the average decent boys involved
could be at fault, that the episode was a normal, everyday expression of calculated policy. For generations, the American Indians
were portrayed as "savages" even while white men appropriated
their lands, slaughtered their men, herded their women and children into death camps, virtually committed genocide. The out-

rages of 350 years of slavery committed upon the dignity and self-esteem of black people still cannot be looked in the eye. For Americans are well-meaning, innocent, godly folk.[6]

The university environment generates its own stories. The best-educated man is precise, clear, hardheaded, analytical, articulate, objective. He is an expert. He is a missionary of enlightenment, a problem-solver, a crisp and authoritative counter of the countable. Numbers are the key to reality: he accepts the mysticism of the quantitative. ("How many indifferent men are equal to one man of courage and determination?" the Vietnamese guerrilla asks. "What makes Americans believe they understand Vietnamese reality because they have counted everything? No number is commensurate with one man of determination.") The American sense of reality, as it is defined in the university, strikes many persons of other cultures, and some in our own, as most unreal.

In a word, the woman who wishes to understand what stories she is living out does well to ask herself what it means to be brought up as an American, of a given social class, ethnic background, religious or secular tradition. All such cultural forces generate their own way of structuring human life. All have their own set of stories which they invite their young to live out, some stories for men only, some for women.

In a pluralistic culture, in which many stories are simultaneously and powerfully presented to the young, a certain confusion, malaise, and loss of confidence often result. No one story commands allegiance. Action, therefore, lacking a story to give it significance, seems pointless. Why bother to do anything at all? What is worth trying to become? The young often begin to sleep a lot.

Not to have any story to live out is to experience nothingness: the primal formlessness of human life below the threshold of narrative structuring. Why become anything at all? Does anything make any difference? Why not simply die? . . . Or drift: which is a death-in-life.

3. STANDPOINT TO STANDPOINT

In later chapters, we shall explore the power of cultural and social stories. At present we must advance in the clearer, simpler context of the personal story.

A story does not merely connect action to action. It also recounts a struggle. It is *agon* (Gr., contest, struggle)—the root of "agony"—that stirs the deepest primitive emotions of our souls. Life, when it is life, is struggle; when struggle is taken away, life goes flat; boredom, shame, uneasiness emerge. The key struggle of life is that of psychic transformation: of breakthroughs in the way one perceives events, imagines oneself, understands others, grasps the world, acts. *KNOW THYSELF!* Greek wisdom enjoined. "The philosopher [lover of wisdom] is one who has been converted," Clement of Alexandria said. A story, then, not only links actions; more profoundly, it links transformations. The line which a story follows is not straight, logical, step-by-step. It varies from life to life. Most often it zigzags, as if seeking out the spot for a breakthrough. Occasionally, then, there is a leap ahead, a profound shift in perception and purpose, "a new life." In the last few years in the United States, many have experienced "radicalization" as such a shift. They can remember the day, the hour.

A story—to put it in another way—is a linking of standpoints. A standpoint is not a theory. It is the subjective context in which a theory is held. It is a sense of who. *Who* specifies the direction in which the theory looks, establishes the way of perceiving required for it, supplies the imaginative context and the uneasiness out of which the theory grew, shapes the judgments and actions which follow. *Who* is to a theory what blood and air are to a human being. A standpoint is the *who* at a given point in time. A story links these points in time.

Frequently, in trying to specify what a man was thinking of and why, in trying to establish the direction and force of his thought, we note many "turning points" in his development. We distinguish different periods. We speak of "the young Marx," "the later Wittgenstein," "Luther at Wittenburg." The *content* of what men hold is inextricably bound up to *who* they were (their sources, their judgments at that time, their purposes, their direction).

A standpoint in humanistic thinking is different from a standpoint in scientific thinking. Even in scientific thinking, to be sure, creative thought and invention and judgment are eminently personal. *This* man has the clues, the hunches, the originality of image and insight that constitute the breakthrough. But the heuristic ideal of scientific thinking is to formulate the insight in such a way that the particularities of the *who* are irrelevant.[7] It is crucial to scientific thinking to formulate the experimental evidence in such a way that the experimenter is replaceable. It is even important to formulate the experiment in terms that make the particularities of time and space irrelevant: *anyone* of requisite skill should be able to repeat the experiment by re-creating the requisite conditions at any point in time or space.

In humanistic thinking, the *who* is not excluded to the extent desirable in science. The heuristic ideal is quite different. In humanistic thinking, *Who am I?* and *Who are we?* are the underlying, indispensable questions. The point of humanistic inquiry is *who*. The heuristic ideal, therefore, always includes the standpoint of the thinker. In science, the person inquiring is replaceable, without loss to the inquiry. In the humanities, the person inquiring is of the highest interest, and it is, in a sense, the theory he holds that is, if not replaceable, at least in many circumstances of secondary importance. Thus, we often hold that the theory held by an influential man was distorted, one-sided, or even wrong, but that the changed perspective he introduced, the breakthrough, the altered viewpoint or world view, is of decisive importance. The transformation of consciousness arising from his achievement of a new standpoint may shed important light on all previously held theories.

A man might not be a very good theorymaker and still be extremely important in the history of human inquiry. He might, for example, achieve a new standpoint but be deficient in abstracting accurately the general truths to be drawn from that standpoint; or he might be deficient not so much in the abstraction as in the precise formulation of his insights. Polemical or other motives may have imbalanced or distorted his formulations. Still, the creation of new possibilities for consciousness through the attainment of an original, fruitful standpoint may be sufficient grounds for commending a man's or a woman's genius mightily.

For the truth is that human experience cannot be interpreted except from a standpoint, except as seen in a certain light, except as assessed in view of certain purposes, except as grasped in the context of experiences and insights and judgments accumulated to that point. The human being in search of his identity cannot stand outside the arena of human life, and he is not infinite in his perspective: does not incorporate in himself all actual, let alone all possible, perspectives for understanding.[8] In his finiteness, he operates from one standpoint at a time. To grasp the import of what he says, therefore, one must grasp clearly the standpoint from which he says it. To rip a humanistic theory untimely from its human standpoint is, almost always, to deprive it of its concrete rootage, its historical significance, its bearing and its purpose. In humanistic studies, standpoint is as critical a focus as theory is. *Who* is as critical as *how to* or *what*.

A standpoint, more concretely, is a complex of all those things that compose an inquiring *who*. It is a complex of past experience, a range of sensibility, accumulated images and imaginative patterns, interests, bodies of insights already appropriated, purposes, structured and unstructured passions, criteria of evidence and relevance, the repertoire of already affirmed concrete judgments, values, goals, decisions.

In order to come to discern what one's own standpoint is, one ought to examine one's own favorite metaphors, verbs, adjectives. In the contemporary university, for example, there is a decided preference for theories that are "hard," "rigorous," "clear," "quantifiable."[9] Such preferences exert great pressures on what may be considered real. The standpoint of one major modern sensibility and consciousness is quite constrained. Its interest lies in prediction and control. Its passion is for power over nature and society. In order to understand why modern men of such a type value some theories and operations as they do, one must assimilate their standpoint. It is an ascetical, demanding standpoint: many habits of analysis, many skills, many constraints upon other interests, must be inculcated, usually over the period of a great many years of discipline.

One needs to devise techniques which draw out into the open the contours of one's own sensibility and imaginative habits. The Jewish sensibility (Bellow, Roth) is not like the Protestant sensibility (Updike, O'Hara). Among Protestants, the sensibility of diverse figures like Robert MacNamara, Lyndon Johnson, and Adlai Stevenson, while typical of various traditions, is quite diverse. (Among theologians, one could contrast the metaphors and "feel" of Harvey Cox, Paul van Buren, James Gustafson.) Among Catholics, Joseph McCarthy, John Kennedy, and Eugene McCarthy represent three main traditions of American Catholic sensibility. One soon finds that central words like "love," "faith," and "action" conjure up quite different images for people in various traditions. "Reconciliation," "stewardship," and "prophecy" are chiefly Protestant words. The impact of the almost daily feasts of the martyrs and of the daily sacrifice of the mass upon the Catholic sensibility have been testified to by Mary McCarthy and Mario Savio: pragmatism seems like thin soil to build a life upon.

Underlying all propositions, however theoretical and abstract, are frameworks of experience, imagination, and remembered or projected action. To become as conscious of the contours of one's own experience, imagination, and story as one is of one's theories, then, is immensely fruitful. Too often, the Western tradition since the Enlightenment concentrates on "clear and distinct ideas," and neglects to clarify the matrix of experience and imagination in which those ideas are rooted, and through which they contact the concrete world of human experience. Experience, imagination, and remembered and projected action (story) are, in several respects, prior to ideas, notions, and theoretical propositions.

What is it that intelligence aims to understand if not human experience? In whose service is it if not in the service of human action? The imagination organizes the matrix of patterns and structures and relationships in which insights occur. Many people of good intelligence lack imagination, and hence insight. Dumb data, randomly arranged, yield no insight until the imagination captures the intelligence and tempts its attention toward unities and relations which the imagination shapes.

Thus, pedagogically, good teachers aim directly at the experience, imagination, stories of their students. Only in that matrix can understandings occur. The teacher tries to surprise students, explode their too limited patterns of expectation, raise the counterexamples that direct their attention in new ways. Good education is a constant series of new births: new ways of experiencing, perceiving, imagining, proceeding. When breakthroughs happen frequently, education is a joy.

There are a great many insights, in any case, which simply cannot occur until the underlying experiential and imaginative base has been prepared. Reading Shakespeare at forty is not like reading him at twenty. (It is surprising how much Shakespeare has learned in the intervening years.) As Aristotle pointed out, young people find ethics (by which he meant discernment in singular concrete situations) very difficult to understand. They are too idealistic, see things too abstractly, lack the dense experience that is required. Wisdom, the ability to go to the heart of the matter in concrete situations, is acquired slowly: it is a discipline of experience, imagination and story, not of naked intelligence. Often in America, unfortunately, one's intelligence develops more swiftly than one's experience, imagination, and story.

To grow in wisdom, then, is to have undergone many transformations. It is to have known joy often. For joy is the taste of reality. And each transformation of one's horizon is for the sake of a profounder, more comprehensive penetration into the mystery of one's own existence, into the reality of the world in which we live. We are never directly in touch with reality. We proceed, little by little, into an ever more tutored, more accurate grasp of what it is to be a human being under these stars.

Implicit in the notion of standpoint, then, is a drive toward growth. We would stay forever within one standpoint except for our restless quest for sharper, broader, deeper understanding. There is in us a thirst for life. It is not merely a quantitative, self-aggrandizing thirst. It is, on the contrary, a terrifying, risk-filled, humbling desire to explore. Advances in wisdom are, as Socrates already saw, advances in ignorance: we discover more accurately how little we know about ourselves, how complex and delicate we are, yet able to endure the night. Nietzsche did not put it quite exactly. We are quite capable of the will to power but it is the will to live that is deeper still: the thirst to live.

The drive in us to move from standpoint to standpoint is sometimes called "intentionality" or, as I have called it in *The Experience of Nothingness,* "the drive to question." It is a drive that has two rhythms. At times it impels us to push beyond our present horizon, to snap the safe membranes of the present, to venture into the dark toward a new standpoint. At other times, when we have just achieved a fresh standpoint, it leads us to explore around us from our new vantage point, to absorb slowly all our new discoveries, to follow out all its implications, to consolidate our grip, and to assimilate the new position thoroughly. At times we fill up a horizon newly achieved; at others, we break through into a new darkness. Differentiation and integration.

The drive implicit in the notion of standpoints gives rise to the metaphor of ascending the mountain. From each new height, a new viewpoint: more comprehensive, from a different angle, of a fresh clarity. At times one new standpoint on the mountain seems continuous with others, at other times whole patterns seem rearranged; a sort of quantum-leap of breathtaking beauty has occurred. (As in the Alps a climber suddenly comes upon a crevice and stands before a silent, seldom seen range of peaks, a hidden valley: *"Fantastisch!"* he whispers.) Climbing requires effort: tiny efforts, steady efforts. It requires patience, shrewdness, discernment—but especially patience. And above all what St. Teresa of Avila[10] cherished, *determinaçion:* will, resolve, endurance, even when blisters on one's heel are rubbed raw. The ascent of the mountain requires both largeness of soul and exquisite willingness to take one endless step after another.

But effort is not everything. Life is also grace, gift, serendipity. Often we are *moved* from standpoint to standpoint, swept up, taken by surprise. Someone says something, her words gash sparks in our soul, life is never the same. We struggle with a long-term personal problem, someone else says something that tangentially sets off an insight, our perspective changes. We are puzzled about what to do and an unexpected event makes up our minds for us. We did not want to do something, but do it because for some other reason it seems we should—and what we did not at first want, would never have chosen, turns out to be the best thing that happens to us in that decade. We don't recognize our own motives for taking up a line of work, but the years gradually reveal to us that we were led by obscure instincts in making each unreflective choice, whose correctness we never could have guessed. So many of the best, deepest, and most important turns in our lives were not exactly of our own choosing, certainly did not spring from careful analysis, but came as gifts: the flight of the dove.

4. "STORY," ELABORATED

A "story" ties a person's actions together in a sequence. It unites past and future. It supplies patterns, themes, motifs by which a person recognizes (or someone else recognizes) the unity of his or her life. Some lives are more integrated than others. Some are more full of conflict—a battle between warring stories. There are often, in many lives, long stretches of disunity, meaninglessness, and boredom which seem to have no story; wanderings in a desert; the accumulating of weeks, months, or years like so much debris; drift.

A man does not "invent" his own story out of whole cloth. In part, he "discovers" it. Long before he can choose for himself or seize direction over it, his life has been launched within certain limits of possibility and probability. He has no ear for music, he can't carry a tune; his health is poor; his imagination is typically morbid, etc. There is no use pretending to a story he could not act out with grace or authenticity.

A man can try to act out a story that, for him, is false, inappropriate, destructive. Commonly, in fact, people try to be what they cannot be, pretend to be other than they are, overlook their own best strengths in imitation of someone else's story.

Thus we can use the category "story" both in a merely descriptive way, and also in a critical way. Descriptively, every man or woman who ever lived has lived out a story. The story may be diffuse, broken, contradictory, made up of countless subplots with countless loose ends, be almost wholly devoid of integration and singleness, etc. There are picaresque stories, stories merely of more or less aimless, disconnected wanderings. Counterpoint and dissonance occur in lives as in music. Even "absurd," "meaningless," and "underground" lives can be understood by contrast with their opposites.

Critically, however, the category "story" is useful for asking oneself: "Have I discovered, and am I inventing, the story most appropriate to my possibilities? Am I being true to myself?" It is difficult to discern just which story it is that I am acting out. Subconscious stories may have an influence upon my perception. My actual actions and my presentation of myself to others may not be telling the story I consciously believe I am acting out. My friends, or enemies, may discern more accurately than I what I am up to, and how my story will end. Our capacity for self-deception has no known limits.

In fact, descriptively, I may be acting out one story. Normatively, critically, I ought to be acting out another (according to my own or someone else's norms, depending on who makes the normative judgment, and according to which standards).

What are the criteria for which story I *ought* to be acting out? Proximately, these criteria may be stated as if they were ethical principles. Ultimately, these criteria are, in fact, a "second-level" story.

The proximate criteria of one man—let us call him Erasmus—are the following: (a) My story ought to be proper to me and no one else; there ought to be elements of uniqueness in it. (b) My story ought to be appropriate to the times: partly in harmony with and partly in dissonance with the general cultural story to which it contributes ("in" the world but not "of" it). (c) My story ought to be appropriate to my own possibilities. It ought to maximize the liberation of my potential—mine, not that of some other. (d) My story ought to be appropriate to the stories of those to whom I am bound by family, friendship, community—partly in harmony with and partly in tension with theirs ("unless a man leave father and mother for my name's sake, he is not worthy of me . . .").

But second-level criteria are required to determine why *these* proximate criteria and not others should be employed as norms. And second-level criteria themselves have the form of a story. A man who consciously or subconsciously imagines himself to be acting out a certain way of life chooses one set of proximate criteria, a man who imagines himself to be acting out a different way of life chooses another set.

How, then, does one criticize one's "second-level" story? First of all one must become aware of it. How does that occur? By a breakthrough in one's self-perception, by which one moves to a new standpoint—by a "conversion." So long as we are standing within a standpoint, we do not see the force of the story of which that standpoint is a part. When events or critical perception reveal to us what our standpoint had until that given moment been, they have moved us beyond it, in search of a newer and fuller standpoint.

There is no place to stand, apart from a standpoint.
We are always living out a story.
There is no way to live a storyless, or a standpointless life.

But we can make progress in discerning what our stories *are*, and in moving from one standpoint to another.

The proximate criteria for the story which "Erasmus" is living out, in the example above, are the judgments of a person caught up within one Christian-humanist story. That is his second-level story. But why on earth should a person live out *that* story? And does he, in imaginative grasp and in actual living, understand that story profoundly or superficially?

A second-level story is subject to further penetration. One can easily observe that some people really have a profound grasp on what they are living out in their lives, and others only a half-hearted one. (I don't necessarily mean *introspective* when I say *profound*. Some people, with very little self-reflection or self-consciousness, are quite clear about who they are and quite determined about where they are going.)

A second-level story is also subject to revision, rejection, or transformation. One may be converted to a wholly different view of one's own life and possibilities: as if beginning a "new" life. Or one may "awaken" and pursue seriously what one has heretofore treated casually. Or one may discover that the story one was trying to live out is self-destructive, or empty, or fraudulent; but one does not yet have a new one to take its place. Or one may find that one has no particular story at all—not even storylessness and drift—and becomes increasingly listless and inactive. Some persons *expect* life to have no point, and wait for things to "happen" to them. Storylessness, in that sense, is a kind of story very powerful in a technical, mechanical, and high-speed culture. So much "happens" that one can comfortably be passive and enjoy watching the excitement, or lack thereof.

The category "story" cannot be reduced to a set of principles or criteria. The reason is that man is a dramatic animal. His actions are larger, more comprehensive, and more complex than his capacities for analysis. A statement of principles is an abstraction from the rich tissue of human action. No one of us knows himself very well. We know neither all the motivations and sources of our actions, nor all the qualities of their performance, nor their end. Far less can we detail an adequate list of general principles for all human behavior. Ethical writers have always known this; but philosophers have long tried to attempt the route of analysis anyway. In attempting their analysis, they chiefly analyze *general principles*. An analysis of *stories* is far more productive.

One of the functions of the category "story" is to draw our attention to a *type* of analytic capacity that has so far lain largely dormant in our philosophical tradition.[11] The use of the category "story" is not intended to weaken our employment of intelligence, but on the contrary, to extend it into places we don't usually take it. Its point is to *enlarge* our capacity to understand and to talk about our actions and our values.

The dominant model in the philosophic tradition for discussions of actions and values is the model of argument. An argument has axioms, principles, premises, and conclusions. Philosophers and laymen too easily come to believe that argument is the paradigm for reason. They then conclude that if *actions* are to be reasonable, they must be patterned in some fashion after arguments. Hence, it is assumed that actions "flow from" something (opinions, convictions, motives, principles) in the way that conclusions "flow from" premises, principles, and axioms.

Action is not, however, a species of argument. Argument is a species of action. Logical inquiry and scientific inquiry are actions —it is for that reason that the word "justification" is applicable to them. They represent one subset of ethical problems. We speak truly of a "scientific conscience" and of scrupulous adherence to the rules of argument.

Action—and ethics—, however, cover a much broader range of human affairs than logic or science.[12] Those who try to reduce ethics to the normative confines of a model appropriate for logical and scientific argument place human action on a procrustean bed, and lop off most of its intelligence, subtlety, richness, and depth. The man of action does not want his mind cut to the size of the man of argument. The latter has a limited set of tasks to perform. The former has a much larger set. Logic and scientific argument, for example, do not tell a graduate student that he ought to marry Jane; but he (and his friends) will certainly judge whether it is intelligent for him to do so. Logic and empirical evidence do not tell a politician to choose theme x over theme y in the last three weeks of an election campaign; but one choice may well be judged, even in advance, a more intelligent choice than the other.

There are other functions of the category "story." To grasp consciously the story one is trying to live out at this stage of one's life, is to cast an illuminating light over one's whole past. How did one come to this story? What instincts, hunches, and inhibitions were operating before the pattern became conscious? What chance events interrupted, generated, or reinforced the basic story? What subplots and loose ends have there been?

Similarly, a grasp of one's own basic story offers some guidelines for the future. One becomes quicker to discern, in new and surprising situations, which suddenly assumed roles are "out of character." One gets a sense of being more "together" with oneself, more "connected," more able to be "present" to others. One is more—to use Gabriel Marcel's word—*disponible:* others can see more clearly who and what one is, and make their peace. Again, one is more likely to be on the lookout for the cues that call for movement to a deeper standpoint, because the present one is becoming outgrown.

In general, the category "story" is more flexible than the category "principles." The reason for this is that, at least unconsciously, a principle (like "Always be honest") is understood by the one who holds it in the light of his own previous experience. What he means by being honest will ordinarily be different at age seventeen from what it was at seven, and different again at twenty-seven, thirty-seven, and so on. The danger is that the one same unchanging formula will take his attention away from concrete experiential differences, and lull him into believing in a stability, unchangeableness, and generality which he does not in fact practice.

It is true that we can impose a story upon events, and that we can understand a story as if it were something to copy, imitate, or follow like a predetermined script. To treat a story in this way, however, is to adopt it as if it were an abstract principle, to be followed by rote. Whereas a principle is honored in every observance, a story merely copied is a cliché. To avoid being hackneyed, a story must be fresh, unique, singular. Above all, it must spring from inner sources of creativity and perception. A story treated like a principle can be boring, rigid, and inflexible. But a story treated like a story is full of invention, surprise, and originality.

Take, for example, the partial story "graduate student at Chicago." There is a certain *noblesse oblige.* Hardheadedness, carefulness, precision, articulation are expected. As part of the story of one's life, one might accept the more grim, demanding, and merely analytic arguments as an unpleasant but necessary *rite du passage.* One might, on the other hand, accept them as a model for one's entire life story. Never will there be (one might resolve) a scholar more clear, more precise, more orderly, more discriminating than I. Tough, hard, able to "unpack" six or seven meanings in even the simplest sentences. So committed does one become to "objectivity," "dispassionate analysis," and "precision," that one does not regard such a commitment as a "story." They are reason itself. One doesn't have time for fiction.

Then, suddenly, the fact that for the intellectual life "the Chicago syndrome" is only one story among many may strike home. The "story" may suddenly not seem obvious and necessary, but in need of an argument. Next, one may notice that certain kinds of argument, in certain forms, strike one as "impelling," and other kinds of arguments seem dangerously "soft." Part of the story of one's psyche then comes into question. What sort of life is it that is gratified only by "hard" arguments? Is that one gratification among many? Merely a professional specialization? Or the dominant passion of one's life? Granted one's own preference for the story of the hard-nosed scholar, does one admit that there are other useful stories for scholars to live out? Or only one "real" story, the rest being for weaker spirits?

Not infrequently, a student has given himself so thoroughly to one story that he has not considered other possibilities. The fact that he is free to change his story, without changing the principle "Be an excellent scholar!" strikes him as a sudden liberation. His story changes. The principle (as is the wont of principles) remains inflexible.

Another example. A young man learns the principle, "Be chaste." Riding on the bus one day, age twelve, he looks back. The wind just then lifts a girl's skirt; he averts his eyes. On other occasions he avoids impure thoughts and sights. And he abhors pornography. Later in life, he decides that fidelity and loyalty between man and wife is a precious and unparalleled joy. He also recognizes that nothing is so beautiful as a woman's body, and no harm comes to him though giving rein to all his sexual and other fantasies. He delights in exploring what heretofore he had forbidden himself, including pornography. Since pornography is artificial, he finds it well done sometimes, more often not. When not well done, it is boring, repulsive, or both. But when well done, it is as civilizing an art as the use of wine in cooking—inessential but delightful, a source of pleasure and amusement. His principle ("Be chaste") has not changed: his story has.

A famous debate rages in ethics, between those who defend an ethic of "principles" and those who defend an ethic of "the situation." The latter say that principles are too legalistic and inflexible, and that we should decide what we ought to do by a kind of intuitive response to each concrete situation as it arises. The former say that each "intuitive response" must be guided by principles previously formed and become like second nature. James Gustafson rightly argues that this debate is "misplaced."[13] Each argument is strong where the other is weak; each complements the other.

One of the ingredients missing in the theories from which the debate arises is the category of story. A person does not live primarily by principles but by stories. And he or she comes to each situation as if it were a new episode in a story. One's personal story carries with it one's internalized experience, reflection, and sensitivity developed over the years. One comes to a situation, not newborn, but already in mid-course. One's tone of voice, mannerisms, intuitions, and sensitivities reveal the "role" one is implicitly playing out.[14] And that role may or may not be appropriate to one's own basic story or to the situation.

You may, for example, be trying to be terribly calm in the midst of a crisis. But your enforced calmness may stem from fear of expressing strong emotions; you play the role of "the imperturbable," not because you are imperturbable, but because you aren't. Someone present may see through your ruse and challenge: "Doesn't anything ever move you? Are you a stone?" What once would have been received as a compliment now comes as a shocking insight. You had *thought* you were being calm, sensitive, reasonable. But you weren't hearing the anguish of others, or your own repressed turmoil, at all. You discover that the role you were trying to play (the story you were living out) had distorted both your adherence to principle ("Stay calm") and your responsiveness to concrete situations.

For awhile, you try the new role, called "oh you spontaneous kid!" You let your emotions rise to the surface immediately. You become a bore to yourself and a pain to others. You finally settle on the story of letting your emotions become conscious to yourself, without feeling compelled to make others cope with them. You don't worry about a "role." You try to keep your consciousness open to your feelings, uncharacteristic, unscreened, unshaped (so far as you can let them be so), and open to the needs of others. Such a story is fresh with each event. Yet it *is* a story, with its own internal consistency and clear contours. When you lapse from it, you can recognize the lapses, face to face with yourself or others.

A story is more concrete than a principle; like a principle, however, it connects present situations with a past and a future. A story is larger than a situation; like a situation, however, it bears upon every detail of tone, manner, style, perception, intensity, aim, and commitment. As a category in ethical discussion "story" mediates between experience and intelligence more adequately than "principle" or "situation."

Finally, the category "story" is not only personal. Institutions instruct persons in roles they should play, in manner, style, seriousness, initiative, etc. Language itself tutors one's perceptions and emotions. So also do cultural history, economic system, class or status, profession or occupation, age, race, sex, religion, and the like. Each of these determinants inhibits the unfolding of some stories and encourages that of others. Besides one's own personal story, therefore, there is the further question of how one's story bears on those of the institutions and groups to which one belongs. The story articulated as the "ugly American," Graham Greene's "quiet American," and Richard Nixon's "silent American" influence profoundly our own consciousness of what it means for us to be Americans. Does one define oneself *with* or *against,* or independently of, such larger stories?

The category "story," then, helps one to understand why other people misunderstand one's own favorite words, or at least react differently to words or actions than one expects. Often they share the same general principles (liberty, justice, equality, honesty, etc.) and the same goals (peace on earth, domestic tranquility, racial justice, etc.). But the concrete bearing of those principles and goals is different in their story from their bearing in one's own story. The struggle each person is living out is so different from the struggle another person imagines himself to be living out that all such principles and aims have a different meaning in each different story in which they occur.

If we listen for one another's stories, there is more of a chance that we will understand our differences than if we listen for one another's principles. A principle has concrete significance according to the story within which it falls. Stories are not *instances* of principles. They are the concrete context within which principles acquire sense. Confronted with a principle, therefore, we rightly say: "Give me a concrete example." Such an example is one event in a sequence constituting a story.

Events as science understands them are either instances of general laws, or random. (They are random if they deviate nonsystematically from some norm.) Human actions, as ethics understands them, however, are neither instances of general laws nor merely random. Insofar as they are instances of a general law, they lack uniqueness and show the human agent acting routinely, at less than moral awareness. Insofar as they are merely random, they do not represent the direction and unity of his life; they warn the critic to be alert, but they do not compel judgment.

What makes actions ethical is awareness, choice, decision; these are always singular. Moreover, they distinguish human action from all other processes. They are the essence of story.

Thus, the key difference between a scientific and a humanistic point of view is established. In human affairs, one expects a uniqueness in human action that is not reducible to a general law. Whatever can be generalized is not the chief concern of ethical inquiry. That in human actions which can be linked in generalizations, universals, or laws is not what is of the highest ethical interest; nor is it what makes actions ethical.

Actions are linked through a story. All the events of a life constitute a story. Many singular, unique stories can each be an original variation on one basic theme. Most novels are variations on "the triangle," for example. It is the variation, however, which commands the interest. In science one notices the singular in order to derive a new general law. In ethics, one looks past the general to fasten upon the singular. The general term in science is "law." In ethics, it is story.

To say, for example, that each year twenty million Americans fall in love is to overlook the enormous ambiguity in the general phrase "fall in love." No two loves are alike. What is unique in each is what is of greatest interest both in ethics and in story.

Ever since Kant, ethicists have been concerned about what is "generalizable" in ethics, on the ground that the validity of a law of reason rests upon its being a general law. A merely self-referential act ("I do X just because I want to") seems to be the opposite of ethical. The mistake is to use "generalization"—a term taken from scientific discourse—as a model for ethical discourse. An act is moral, first, insofar as it is singular: proper to this person in this situation. It is moral, secondly, if and only if the story of which it is a part is moral, and if it adequately fulfills that story. One can criticize the story a person chooses to live out (i.e., "Nazi Storm Trooper") on many grounds. The Nazi who prided himself on living out the Nazi story to perfection was, in a limited sense of the word, a "good" Nazi. But in the moral sense of the word, the story he chose to live out was murderous, barbarous, and destructive. What he did was wrong because his story, judged against other human stories, was wrong.

The logic goes like this:

The Nazi story was wrong because it was murderous.

A murderous story is wrong.

Why? Because the Christian (or Liberal) story rejects murder.

Why? Because murder makes "living a story" impossible for the one murdered.

The right "to have a story" cannot be infringed.

The Christian (Liberal) story is a story of the right to choose a story of one's own.

On Christian (Liberal) grounds, the Nazi story is wrong.

On Nazi grounds, the Nazi story is particularist: only Nazis have rights.

It is appropriate to ask whether a story (or a sense of reality) is *true*. A response cannot be made in terms of a direct glimpse of *real* reality, by comparison with which various views are measured. We test our sense of reality and stories in a way analogous to the way in which we test our scientific theories. The criteria we use, here as in science, have an open texture; they cannot be totally stated, in a closed system. The first observation to make is that people *do* change their sense of reality and stories; they sometimes feel uncomfortable with them; they sometimes feel a conscientious satisfaction in noting how their sense of reality and stories are borne out by their experience of life; and they sometimes willfully cling to them even when they know, or merely suspect, that they may be inadequate. That is to say, in our working practice we do discriminate between "unreal" senses of reality and valid ones, between suitable (true) and unsuitable (false) stories to live out. ("Why try to be what you aren't?") Self-deception is frequent. But we are quite practiced in detecting it, especially in others.

We sometimes judge a sense of reality to be inadequate by quietly slipping away from it, sometimes by shattering it. Our actions can be increasingly pragmatic and practical even when our instincts and imaginations still construe the world in the sense of reality we nourished in an Orthodox Jewish household; gradually, our center of gravity has become secular. Or a vision of police bloodying the heads of one's classmates shatters one's sense of being innocent, safe, protected, living under law. Or, much as one loves many experiences of being Catholic, a break with authority clumsily and stupidly exercised comes with steady inexorability: the whole reality that one had been before slowly slips away. It is not, usually, that one has learned new facts or new theories; it is one's whole way of looking at things that shifts.

Psychoanalysis has by now accumulated masses of date about shifts in persons' sense of reality and story. Such data, Rollo May writes,[15] "are revealed only when the human being can break down the customary pretenses, hypocrisies, and defenses behind which we all hide in 'normal' social discourse." But it is *not* "only in the critical situation of emotional and spiritual suffering— which is the situation that leads them to seek therapeutic help—" that people will endure the pain and anxiety of probing their own sense of reality. Sometimes, it appears, people grow by steady and "normal" stages, including dramatic and sweeping conversions in standpoint. They steadily come to terms with the dynamics of their own unconscious and the demands of the world in which they act.

We change our sense of reality and/or our story when (a) they are out of harmony with the dynamics of our unconscious, which become more and more insistent; (b) they are out of harmony with our efforts to change the world, to get along with others, or to be at peace with ourselves; (c) they are superceded by new ones that offer more illumination or satisfaction; (d) they are unable to account for contradictions introduced by new experience, or tensions inherent in their own structure; (e) they give rise to repeated failures in predicting consequences or interpreting the behavior of others. (This list is not exclusive.)

It is difficult to alter the sense of reality or story of others. For the commitment to a sense of reality and a story is much more deeply buried in the person than a commitment to a theory or to a set of facts. Many arguments about important human matters— love, politics, religion—go astray because they are conducted as if facts and theories were at issue. Whereas what is at issue, while equally subject to intelligence and criticism, is far more supple, far more protected, far more powerful. Fear generates defensiveness; hence, fear must be disarmed. Counterstories and counter-perceptions must be designed, to suggest to the other a new way of looking at things. But if one party insists on remaining within his present standpoint, the two senses of reality can scarcely meet; each will be tempted to return to his own accustomed world undisturbed. ("Whew! All those crazy people out there.")

The most interesting arguments in the world concern senses of reality and story. For these are the arguments in which what is most intelligent, most critical, and most basic to the person is at stake: his own intelligent subjectivity. To dismiss such arguments as "merely" subjective is to be alienated even from one's own subjectivity, by pretending to select "objectivity" as one's own sense of reality, one's own essential story. But objectivity is nothing but subjectivity tutored in a selected way.

5. WHAT CANNOT BE SAID

The more one tries to penetrate the depths of one's own identity, the more reverential one becomes. On the surface irascible, impatient, inconsistent: in silence and solitude moved to an inner unity and quiet. Deeper still, the ambiguities, the terrors of insanity, conflicting passions. Deeper still again, the still darkness of the night and the pure dark desire: the drive to live, the longing to become, the fierce will to be—and laocoönian dread, suicidal fears, nameless obsessions. The soul is contested, *agon* is the law of life.

Why am I doing what I am doing? The reasons tumbling to one's lips are not the answer. Why, indeed? How deep is deep? The more one learns of the self, the greater one's ignorance. One becomes cynical of too much speech. The man or woman who has wrestled with personal snakelike inner demons is suspicious of the clear-eyed.

As one respects silence about the self, so also one respects silence about the mystery of man-in-the-world. The apple tree *apples,* the peach tree *peaches,* cows *calve,* the universe *peoples.* Man is in-the-world, one-with-the-world, fruit of the earth. He *is* sky, sun, mountains, oceans, trees. Of all of them he properly says "we." And, on the other hand, a stranger, fearfully self-conscious, aware of his fragility and transience. He is, perhaps, the instrument through whom the universe, as we know it, comes to incandescent holocaust. It will, perhaps, end incinerated, like a great radiant ash. He is awed by his own power and his unreliability of soul.

That consciousness should have such power over the earth frequently suggests to humans that the greatest power of all is conscious. A human easily takes himself as a clue to all that is. He finds an inner stillness when he addresses everything that is as "thou." Easily enough, he imagines this "thou" either as, quite properly, everything—a kind of pantheism, a world-vivifying spirit in all things—or as such a pantheistic spirit present in all things and yet in some unimaginable way more than they—immanent within them, yes (in every blade of grass, every grain of sand, in the droplets down the side of a cold glass of beer), but also transcendent. In the latter case (Bishop Robinson calls it "panentheism"[16]) he is unwilling to think of this "thou" merely as the *sum* of all things, but in some way *more* than they. His mind rides comfortably up to the point of imagining all things in a sort of unity, knitted through and through with the tracks of insight and intelligibility which with diligent effort he can slowly trace; he is impelled also to strain to catch sight of something *more.* But there is only silence. And so the most reverent name of all for such a "thou" is silence.

We are impelled, Augustine once wrote, to speak; yet that whereof we are obliged to speak we find ineffable.

As men and women find a mystery in their own identity, so also they find a mystery in the identity of the world, and how they are matched with it. Is the tissue of existence disconnected, absurd? Is insanity more in tune with it than sanity?

Those who are pragmatically inclined, of course, those who take life as it comes and concentrate their attention upon what works for them, what keeps life more characterized by pleasure than by pain, resist ontological questions. They avoid existentialist anguish. They discipline their sense of order, like a master heeling a wayward pet. Yet in their quest for a rational, pleasant, ordered life, they affirm by their actions their own sense of reality: most often, in America, a benign social darwinism. By the accumulated actions of growing numbers of reasonable persons, faithful to scientific intelligence and a reasonable politics, they seem to believe, the world steadily becomes a better place in which to live. By cutting off religious wonder at the root, they prune the tree of attention to day-to-day concerns.

Will history be kind to them? Is the universe such a place as they implicitly imagine? Are their heads buried in consumers' goods like ostriches in sand, before the deluge?

Ontological choices are implicit in every way of life. Every action has in it an implicit story of the world. The nonreligious, too, have an implicit view of the world. They, too, live out a story. They, too, select from among countless possibilities what they will count as real, firm, reliable. They, too, make a wager. Persons can do no other than decide, by action if not through reflection, who they are. Each interprets human existence as best each can. Each risks missing the heart of the matter.

Those who are religious interpret the world, and human existence, as in some way personal, in some way a conversation between men and a "thou." How to conceive of that "thou" more exactly has been the subject of centuries of sustained inquiry. The many traditions regard the question differently. But for virtually every religious tradition the very deepest parts of the inquiry trail off in silence. Arrows of ritual, worship, dance, discourse are sent off into the dark. They fall shot of pinning down precisely the one at whom they aim.

The *who* at which religious intelligence aims cannot be said. There is no name for GOD as there is for other objects in the world. For, unlike those other objects, the *who* at whom purported names are aimed does not wholly fall within the comprehension of human experience or human intellect.

Hence, the silence at the heart of worship, in the stillness of the heart.

> Teach us, Lady, to be still.
>
> —T. S. Eliot, *Ash Wednesday*

6. THE AESTHETIC, THE MORAL, THE RELIGIOUS

It would be wrong, however, to suppose that there are no standards for discriminating true religion from false, genuine prophets from false prophets, authenticity from fraudulence. In all religions there are traditions for nourishing "the discernment of spirits." There are grades of penetration, praise for the truly faithful, contempt for the hypocrite, the shallow, the lover of two masters. There is an elitism of the spirit. Populism and egalitarianism are seductive currents; but it simply is not true of the growth of the human person that all make equal use of their liberty. First, all persons are created equal. They have the same rights: to dignity, to freedom, to operations of discernment, choice, decision. Secondly, nothing is more to be expected than that persons should use their freedom differently. Persons respond differently to the human situation. In a third sense, many persons are deprived in fact of what they possess in right.

In this variety lies both man's glory as a race and an evolutionary pathway strewn with tragedy, malice, inequity, and corruption. *Corruptio optimi pessima:* corruption enters into the hearts of those consecrated to stand holy in the sanctuaries, symbolic of the "thou" at the center of life.

The discernment of spirts is not, like so many modern measures, quantitative. It cannot be applied by any interchangeable technician. The discernment of spirits is learned through living in a certain way. Those who ascend the mountain, who are gifted by the flight of the dove, recognize their peers. Speaking to one another, observing delicate but unmistakable signs, they recognize how far each has proceeded in the *agon.*

Many persons merely drift or are driven by ambition toward immediate rewards, or flee from the relentless demands of honesty, courage, freedom, community. The sociopolitical order itself, arising from the accumulated choices of humans, favors alienation and inauthenticity. "There are not," Pascal said, "three honest men in a century." There are still fewer liberated men, liberated women. What, then, should we expect but unequal trajectories of growth? Some, gifted by circumstances, go far; others squander their resources. Some, struggling against enormous odds, wrest stunning human beauty from their *agon.* The human person wrestles where he is, with his own peculiar struggle. There is no common measure. In their personal growth, in their liberation, there are vivid and incontestable differences between person and person. But one person with another is incommensurable.

Still, there are some general signs by which to measure how deeply a person has gone. Aristotle distinguished between the man of pleasure, the man of calculation, and the man of wisdom. Augustine describes in one of his early dialogues seven of the levels of development distinguished by the platonists. Medieval writers distinguished the "fourteen steps" on the "ladder of humility [reality]." In Buddhist sects, the Zen Master leads students as far as he can, and when they exceed his capacities—as either he or they may be the first to judge—they leave him, or he sends them away. Along "the way," persons vie with one another, not for competition's sake but as aids in stimulating one another beyond their present development.

Kierkegaard's distinction between the aesthetic, the moral, and the religious may point toward some of the discriminations experience calls for; but we must reshape these categories in a contemporary, American way. In brief, the person who judges matters aesthetically judges according to his feelings and sensibility; the man who judges morally judges according to principle, to reason, to duty; the man who judges religiously judges according to a holistic view of his own identity and his situation.

If a person says, "I did X because it felt right to me, I felt better about it right away," his eye is focused on his own sensibility. When it is in harmony with what he is doing, he feels a certain sweetness. When it is maladjusted, he feels tension. The aesthetic conscience includes what Philip Rieff calls "the therapeutic consciousness."[17] The aim of the aesthetic conscience is to create of the feelings a work of harmony, balance, pleasure. In its higher ranges, the aesthetic conscience pursues beauty at any cost, independently of honesty, of courage, freedom, community, and other human values. It prefers form, sweetness, ecstasy. It involves, often, the pursuit of "beautiful moments"—all of life is subordinated to arranging a series of at least small ecstasies. (Gr.: Ek-stasis, "standing outside of," as outside one's own skin: it easily becomes escape). In its lower forms, the aesthetic conscience is the pursuit of novelty, sensation, adjustment.

The heart of aestheticism is the image that the human organism functions like a delicate machine, whose equilibrium must constantly be attuned. The self attunes itself, its moods, its judgments, to certain inner guides it has learned to trust. "Feeling right" is its criterion for being humane. The aesthetic alternative has a great attraction for those brought up in a highly moral and disciplined way which has excluded it. In *The Greening of America*,[18] Charles Reich recommends it as "Consciousness III"—the most painless and consumer-oriented revolutionary manifesto on record.

The moral conscience has a somewhat more chastened, even dour, estimation of human sensibility and human desire. Masochism, sadism, and illusions of all sorts are so common that the moral person does not wish to entrust himself to his feelings. At his worst, he regards emotions and impulses as corrupt; at his best, he willingly listens to their signals but never allows them to be the final determinant of his actions. The moral person has trained his head to take command over his body and his feelings. He has long practiced self-control and disciplined his spontaneities.

There are, however, several different ways in which he can "use his head." He can imagine morality to be a sort of cool calculation of his own best interests and/or the best interests of others. He can imagine morality to be fidelity to rational principles, rationally arrived at. He can imagine morality to be fidelity, in Kant's sense, to a good will: a categorical imperative of sheer duty, appealing neither to beneficial consequences nor to sweet desire.

Ordinarily, the person of moral conscience is susceptible to argument; at least, he *claims* to be doing not merely what he feels like doing but what reason obliges him to do. He may tend to have an arrogance and missionary fanaticism of his own. Believing as he usually does in the generalizability of his own judgments, he tends to give his choices a universal weight, even if politically he does not insist on forcing other people to be as enlightened as he is. Some Americans, for example, believe that American values of freedom and justice are universal—and are at least tempted to oblige others to live accordingly.

The vast majority of people who claim to be religious, it should be pointed out, have not developed past the aesthetic or the moral conscience. Are there not many who shed tears when the organ hits certain notes? It is precisely on the highest and most solemn feast days that the perception of Christians, and even of the preacher and at the climatic point in his sermon, descends most frequently to the aesthetic consciousness.[19] For there where perception ought to be at its highest, the devout hear, instead, how beautiful things are and how touched they should be. The preacher, the music, the occasion contrive to move them into direct contact with some universal harmony—to pull aside the veils and let them look with direct recognition upon a concordance of order and sweetness.

Life, however, is not like that. Direct recognition is a lie. For Christianity, there is the crucifixion; for Buddhists, the law of suffering; for Jews, he who is yet to come. Direct recognition falsifies the deepest perceptions of the religious consciousness. The aesthetic temper loves harmony so sweetly—God's in his heaven, all's right with the world—that it allows itself to imagine that its feelings of direct recognition are religious perceptions. The aesthetic conscience pretends to be the religious conscience, when it has in fact merely made the latter over into its own image.

Similarly, the moral conscience apes the religious conscience by making enlightenment and righteousness do service for grace. Those persons are religious, it holds, who do their duty, who are faithful to reason, who are honorable. Surely, nothing is plainer in the New Testament than its denial that Christianity can be understood by the merely moral person. And, surely, the point of many Buddhist *Koans* is similar: it is not by activist, individual self-will that one attains *satori*.

The aesthetic conscience occurs most frequently, the moral conscience somewhat less frequently, the religious conscience—even among those who call themselves "religious"—most rarely of all.

What, then, is the religious conscience, rare as its exemplification in practice may be? The truth is that only those who share the standpoint of such a consciousness can recognize it and plumb its depths. Ineluctably, those who measure it by the aesthetic or the moral consciousness reduce it to their own level. An external description, however, may be given; there are signs to watch for. Of course, those signs can be learned, mastered, and used inauthentically. Discerning the spirit demands a full and authentic growth in oneself. We easily judge those who follow behind us; we waver concerning those more advanced than we—if we can bring ourselves to admit that there are such. Which is itself a fundamental wisdom.

Men and women of religious conscience understand that experience, including impulse and emotions, is richer than our capacity to verbalize or analyze it; so they have studied and assimilated the workings of the aesthetic conscience. They also recognize that all experiences, emotions, impulses are structured in certain somewhat self-serving patterns. Consequently, they cherish the intellectual honesty and self-analysis by which one can become conscious of one's heretofore unconscious patterns of feeling, passion, desire, and the like. They recognize that the feelings— even the more refined ones—are inevitably drawn toward a class or tribal exclusivity, and that intelligence has within it some possibility of opening human beings to universal standards of freedom, justice, equality, and brotherhood. They have absorbed the lessons of the moral consciousness. But still they do not quite trust themselves, either their feelings or their moral consciousness.

Even in what is best in them they have often enough been shamed into seeing racism, self-righteousness, defensiveness, a destructive rage hidden under enlightened sentiments. a proleptic egocentrism masked as humanism. The religious consciousness is the consciousness of fallibility, but of more than the possibility: the fact of self-betrayal, the betrayal of friends, the fall. The Jewish Testament tells the story of Adam and Eve; the Christian Testament makes the dialectic of fall and rising up again central to its understanding; Buddhism delights in exposing the pretensions of the subject who strives too hard to be perfect.

The religious conscience begins, then, with a recognition that the self is not at the center of the universe, not the focus of high seriousness, of self-importance, of earth-shaking guilt. It begins with a kind of self-acceptance: the acceptance of oneself as one is, self-betraying and often untrustworthy, flawed and not able steadily to accept oneself. (A reduplicative paradox: to accept the fact that one only imperfectly loves, accepts oneself.) Spare me, Yeats wrote, a woman who does not love herself. There is, then, a peace in the religious consciousness, whose origin is limpid honesty and the ability not to be afraid. The man or woman of religious consciousness pretends to be no other than he or she is. Such lack of pretentiousness is rare.

It goes without saying that "religious" here does not mean "goes to church," "belongs to a religious organization," or even "believes in God." It refers to a level of development in self-perception: of peace, of simplicity (i.e., sophistication), of self-acceptance, of humor. The ancient word, now badly twisted, derived from the metaphor *humus* (L., earth), was "humility." Its root meaning was that of earthiness, reality, lack of pretense, artlessness. Even the word "simplicity" meant, not näiveté or simple-mindedness, but *sine plexu* (L., without fold): wholly integrated, one, willing one thing. It connoted, not fanaticism, but an instinctive and direct sense for nuance.

What, then, is the religious conscience? It is a level of human awareness in which the subject does not imagine himself to be the central pivot even of his own universe. His actions are directed neither to the satisfaction of his own desires or needs, nor to the fulfillment of his own goals, principles, or sense of duty. They spring, rather, from an effort to see himself in context, as one fallible self among others in a world of surprise and contingency. It is an attitude of respect, even reverence, for ordinary life, for the small and often trivial details that reveal what other persons are trying to say or that suggest how to read a complex situation. It is, therefore, an other-centered and (so to speak) reality-centered view of the world. One assumes that one's own standpoint is not quite accurate. Thus, one tries to be alert to signals from others and from situations which suggest where one's own inadequacies occur. One regards *others* as of precious value, because they live out values different from one's own, correct one's own deficiencies, complete one's own incompleteness. One longs to attune oneself to real situations as they are, in their complexity, as if in the concrete world of everyday God himself were making his presence felt. One wishes to miss none of the nuances of the delicate shadings of his handiwork.

"Be it done to me according to thy word!" the Virgin Mary prayed, in a most perfect prayer. "Not my will, but thine," Jesus prayed. The Buddhist longing to be one with all the universe in the very concreteness of his surroundings is similar: the creative force of life shines through every detail of events and situations. The religious conscience is an attempt to be *responsive:* to take one's eyes off oneself, to attend to others and to the concrete world with reverent discernment. What is the "it" which the Virgin accepts? What is the X demanded by the will which Jesus embraces? The religious man struggles to discern, from the signals of daily life, what is intended for him in each event. He responds to life as if it were a conversation. Life is not, for him, "one damned thing after another." It is a voyage along which he is being led. The signals he receives are neither magical nor mystical, and contain no more than life contains for anybody else. But in those events which promote (or hinder) honesty, courage, freedom, compassion, community, and other values nourished in his religious community, he discerns the working out (or the obstruction) of God's creative will. To have a religious conscience is to cherish concrete other persons (neighbors, not "mankind") and concrete, ordinary reality—to love this world and to respond to its needs creatively—not out of self-indulgence, and not out of missionary zeal, but because to create is to be like life itself. To have a religious conscience is to wish to imitate whatever one can best discern as being most like God.

7. AMONG THE MANY RISES AND DECLINES OF REASON

The meanings attached to the word "Reason" vary enormously, even in Western culture. For those Americans whose normal thought-world is more or less contemporary, the two chief models for understanding "Reason" are science and its technical application. Prediction and control are the dominant interests. To be reasonable is to be analytical, clear, detached, and—it appears—manipulative. Treat the world as a giant mechanism, and take parts of it apart to discover what makes them tick and to subordinate them to one's own desires.

"Desire" is the least scrutinized concept in modern civilization. Most often, it is taken to be an equivalent of "need"—the human is regarded as a mechanism of inputs, outputs, functions, necessities. Although we have made reason a servant of power, what methods have we devised for deciding what we desire, what we need, what we ought to desire? Have our desires no limits, no contours, no constraints, no directions? Granted that we are free to do as we desire, what in fact do we desire and what, if anything, ought we to desire?

The question, "What ought we to desire?" comes down to what identity we wish to give ourselves. Who are we? We make ourselves who we are; we invent ourselves. What is it, then, that we desire to desire? What is the model that we are imitating? What goals have we set ourselves? Industrial society is in search of a humane story to live out. For generations we have been accumulating power, wealth, and the rationalized, disciplined structures of bureaucratic life that are wealth-producing. But the person does not live by production alone. What, now, shall we do with ourselves?

Many persons today interpret their own identity outside the organization, the symbols, and the language of the major religions. It does not follow that such persons develop any less fully in that form of wisdom and liberation Dostoevski called "humble charity" and we are calling religious consciousness. The serious atheist and the serious believer today often *do* the same things, live by the same values, live out virtually identical stories. Where their stories differ one cannot predict in advance: Albert Camus may penetrate further into the human riches of Christianity than a given Christian, even a serious Christian; and a believer in God may know more about the darkness of the spirit, the absurd, and solitariness than a serious atheist.

What is most in question today is the meaning given to the symbol "Reason." The connotations of the word seem to have been won over by everything that suggests the hard, the clear, the precise, the rigorous, the quantitative, the analytical, the operational. "Reason" is what generates prediction, power, and control, under cover of the story of "progress."

The temptation, then, is to flee from Reason and, correspondingly, we see arising everywhere again, not least among theologians, the cults of Dionysus: festivity, celebration, orgy, passion, emotion, touch, letting go. In a culture too rigorously disciplined to Apollonian constraints, there may be health in sudden communion with the "darker side" of our being. But to identify religious consciousness either with Dionysus or with Apollo is surely to have failed to share such consciousness.

I am not my body, I am not my passions, I am not my mind: I am I. What we need today, most earnestly, is a way of imagining intelligence that is not objectifying, manipulative, alienating; a way of feeling within oneself the coursing of one's blood, the aliveness of one's nerves, the power of one's passions, the labyrinthine intricacies of one's perceptions—and still of acting intelligently. We need models of passionate intelligence, intelligent passion.

But the precise duality we are engaged in healing is not that between body, passions, and mind, but that between subjectivity and objectivity. The self is not an observer merely. The self is an agent. Every part of the self is involved in the self's agency. A theory of intelligence worked out thoroughly in the context of action is our most fundamental and primary need. It is entirely likely that such a theory must be lived first, in action, before it can become a theory. Life precedes theory. It is also entirely likely that such a theory must spring from social, political, and economic consciousness, since the social order in which individuals live arranges the realities through which they interpret who they are. Religious thinkers may well pioneer in working out a model of intelligent subjectivity, the desperate and long-term need of our planetary culture, just because religion itself stands at the crossroads of the objective and the subjective, intelligence and the passions.

It is, in fact, precisely in the light of that need that our present emphasis has been on autobiography and story. The self exists and is acting out a set of stories long before it learns to analyze, to construct, or to criticize theories. And every theory with which a man or a woman deals depends upon an imaginative structuring of history and a limited historical standpoint from which to shed whatever light it can. Whether a person counts a theory as true, or relevant, or useful depends upon his or her own autobiography; only through autobiography do theories touch ground. Autobiography, to be sure, is not everything about theory: and autobiography itself is an interpretation making use at every point of a body of theories. But in a culture that counts the objective, impersonal side of theory-building far too weightily, critical intelligence must inevitably note how crucial to our lives, not least in the creation and in the use of theories, is story-making.

To construct an interpretation of human life is to weave a complicated, nuanced, carefully discriminating story. For a human life manifests growth; growth is not merely organic and direct progression but transformation; and transformation is described by the moves from standpoint to standpoint, through long and intimate struggling, that constitute both human liberation and human story.

Only when one can talk at some length about the human subject and his struggle toward personal and communal liberation has one entered the arena in which discourse about religion makes any sense at all, the arena in which religious consciousness is born. For if the world in which we live is more like a mechanism than like a conversation, if it is impersonal, discrete, and all its parts alien to one another, then religious consciousness is not realistic at all, its joy is illusory, and its peace an opiate like any other. To assume the standpoint of religious consciousness is to undergo a transformation in which it is proper and significant to address ocean, clouds, birds, meadows, death itself, as "thou"; for in them one is present who cannot be named but only loved and adored. Or, at the very least, respected by silence.

THREE

Cultures

Not long before his death, Paul Tillich said that if he had time to do the three volumes of his *Systematic Theology* again, he would begin them on a new basis: that of the concrete experience of the world religions.[1] Recently nothing has had as deep an effect upon religious studies as the interpenetration of the world cultures. We can no longer live isolated in one culture only. We are coming to understand how having begun life in one culture affects one's sense of reality, one's world, one's communities, one's identity.

So far in our inquiry we have primarily explored the standpoint of the individual. But that standpoint does not do justice to what we discover to be true about ourselves. Our identity is cultural as well as personal. Our autobiography is a story which, in exceedingly large measure, a whole society imparts to us. Even an act as personal as suicide, Emile Durkheim showed, has a social base and form.[2] Our identity is both social gift and personal achievement: dove and mountain. We need to construct a standpoint that is cultural.

1. PARADOXES OF THE FINITE

The paradox of human life may be stated in two propositions. First, from a scientific point of view, biologically and in its social structures, the human race is one. Secondly, there is vast cultural variation in the concrete forms of life, beliefs, values, images, affections. Can we, then, speak of unity in diversity? Is there one human "story"? And if empirically there is not, ought we to work toward one? Are we entering what Teilhard de Chardin called the "noösphere,"[3] that shared planetary consciousness in which each of us has begun at last to live in all, and all in each?

The root of all human consciousness lies in primal formlessness. It is symbolized in myths of initial chaos. . . . "And the earth was without form, and void" (Gen. 1). When a given social structure, a given cultural sense of reality, begins to disintegrate, we experience the initial formlessness. At such moments, we feel lost, anomic, directionless, at sea. Action, having no solid starting point and no goal, seems pointless. We experience "nothingness."

Why are we human beings so tormented? On the one hand, we are not constricted to what our bodies need, desire, sense. "For, beyond the indispensable minimum with which nature is willing to content herself when she functions instinctively, reflective thought, being more vigorous in man than in animals, leads man to imagine better conditions which then appear as desirable goals and incite his activity."[4] In man "it was the awakening of the mind which began to upset the equilibrium in which the animal lay sleeping." There are drives in us in which other animals do not seem nearly so developed. And these drives of ours, in imagination, passion and understanding, are boundless and insatiable.

On the other hand, our perceptual, imaginative, and cognitive abilities are not able to act infinitely. We cannot comprehend and satisfy all their possibilities in one simultaneous act. We cannot

(1) receive at once all the stimuli bombarding us in any given moment, nor (2) structure them imaginatively in all possible patterns at once, nor (3) simultaneously grasp the many unities, identities, wholes which those patterns yield to the inquisitive intelligence. At each of these stages, we make a selection.

Further, in order (4) to make judgments about *which* data are relevant, *which* imaginative patterns are fruitful, *which* understandings are correct, we ordinarily must take a series of steps, arraying and assessing evidence in the light of limiting criteria—whose selection must also be (5) justified. And (6) to act we select one among possible courses of action. Finite creatures, we define ourselves by finite selections of *this,* not *that,* at every stage of our psychic life.

On the one hand, unlimited; on the other, constrained to select. Human beings meet an inescapable paradox in the very structure of human existence.

The social selection of one form of life out of many possible forms is what is meant by culture. Over and beyond chemical, biological, and environmental determinations, human beings have invented many variations in the patterns of their consciousness. They select from among possible experiences, images, understandings, judgments, justifications, actions. These selections are taught to the young (who today as in the Stone Age are born *tabula rasa*) by their parents and the institutions of society. It is not only the superego of the child that is social and cultural in its origin (that "normal, spiritual side of human nature," Freud calls it, which we have taken into ourselves from our parents). The ego and the id—the entire personality, as Freud's own definitions show—develop according to variations in the structure of social systems.[5]

Under the term "culture," then, humble objects are intended, like the shape of utensils, fashions in cooking, automobile designs, as well as profound and subtle determinants of consciousness like patterns of speech, images of the cosmos and of time, child-rearing practices, methods of inquiry, and social organization. Anthropologists have wrestled with many conflicting ways to define the baffling richness of culture. At the end of a stimulating criticism of alternatives, Clyde Kluckhohn appends a formulation most behavioral scientists might accept:

Culture consists of patterns, explicit and implicit, of and for behavior acquired and transmitted by symbols, constituting the distinctive achievement of human groups, including their embodiments in artifacts: the essential core of culture consists of traditional (i.e., historically derived and selected) ideas and especially their attached values; culture systems may, on the one hand, be considered as products of action, on the other as conditioning influences upon further action.[6]

In other words, the sense of reality communicated to us by our own culture—what we call real, true, good, beautiful—is a selection among the possibilities open to the human race.

Many Americans never doubt that "the American way"—or even "the Iowa way"—is the best, the truest, the only really advanced and humane way. Many relatively unsophisticated Americans simply lack experience of any alternative. But even many of the well-traveled and the well-educated judge other cultures by standards of "enlightenment" that are American rather than universal, by a "realism" that is parochially American, by a "radical politics" that is pathetically Americo-centric.

Others, however, have peered into an abyss of relativity. The "sense of reality" by which others live strikes them as a plausible alternative to what they themselves find to be real, meaningful, significant. They wonder whether their own sense of reality is not "out of touch" with something more real—whether their emptiness, alienation, or aloneness is fake. In a word, their own sense of reality is "relativized." They have no Archimedean point by which to assess which of many competing relative standpoints is a more "true" or even "appropriate" standpoint to assume. The formlessness they feel is what is meant by "nothingness." For many, nothingness is not as it was for Nietzsche a "joyful wisdom," the fruition of a lifetime of reflection. It is a fact of their youthful consciousness, from which the adventure of life begins. *Granted* that I experience nothingness, what do I do about it?

Perhaps nothing at all. Perhaps one evades it, avoids it, turns on the radio, joins a movement, looks for someone to hug. Some commit, or dream about, suicide.

Nothing forces one to do anything at all. But if one allows oneself to share the experience of nothingness for longer than one second, it is because one has chosen not to turn one's attention away. We are, in Sartre's phrase, condemned to freedom. Not to choose to turn one's attention away is still to choose. To relish the experience, touching it again and again as a tongue touches a decayed molar, is also a choice.

Moreover, what makes the experience of nothingness possible at all is our willingness to probe beneath the surface of what we have hitherto accepted as real.

Without honesty, courage, and a willingness to explore, we would close ourselves within the limited horizons of our own tribe. Thus there is, underlying the perception of relativity and providing the indispensable condition of its emergence, a drive in us to question, to explore, to expand the horizons originally given us. This drive is often referred to as the basic intentionality of human existence. It is an *in-tendens,* a tending onward, a dynamism propelling human beings to enlarge their experience and their wonder. The variety of human cultures manifests the creativity and fecundity of this drive.

Thus we come to the basic principle of the cultural standpoint: *Human intentionality operates in all men and women everywhere; but it becomes articulated in all the concrete variety of human cultures.* The same dynamism of intentionality; but different selections of what and how to experience, imagine, understand, judge, justify, act.

There is a corollary. *Individuals differ in the extent to which they live in the depths of their cultural way of life; or, conversely, how close to its surfaces they live.* The institutions of their culture can so thoroughly provide the pathways of their consciousness that individuals are content merely to accept as real what their culture says is real, experience what their culture directs them to experience, etc. Or individuals can question the structures of their culture in order to recapitulate in personal consciousness the traces followed by their culture's deepest genius. One might call this the difference between conditioning and appropriation.

To deepen oneself in one's own culture, moreover, is not merely to learn well its rationale and apologetical justification; a merely clever individual could do that. To deepen oneself is, by meditation and by action, to make one's own the illumination and the decisive selections achieved by that culture in its formative periods. Rituals and arduous exercises are commonly designed by durable cultures, in order to provide for each new generation an experience of this living recapitulation of the past. Some youths merely "endure" these rites; others seize their living power and nourish it in every action of every day.

A second corollary follows. *Human cultures in their depths are remarkably analogous to one another.* People who live on the surfaces of their culture's way of life are easily disconcerted by an encounter with another culture; they retreat into the purported superiority of their native way of life. Those (relatively few) who live at the depths of their own culture usually recognize much more readily the depths beneath other cultures. They remember the struggles they underwent in order to penetrate into the depths of their own culture. Thus they seek out in that other culture persons who live at its depths, who can guide them, too, to its living sources.

It is a striking fact, moreover, that men who live at the depths quite often easily recognize their counterparts in other cultures. There is between them a kinship which reaches across cultural boundaries. Since their attention focuses on the underlying intentionality—a path of perception, judgment, decision—they see past the concrete dissimilarities on the surface.

Erik Erickson, in fact, has discerned at the base of all the world's cultures an imperative that may be stated differently but whose point is remarkably consistent: "Be compassionate!" "Do unto others as you would be done by!"[7] It has been the experience of many in ecumenical and intercultural discussions that the profounder and more authentic exemplars of the particular ways of life seem somehow closer to *one another* than each is to less authentic members of his own culture.

We come to a third corollary. *At their depths human cultures tend to converge.* I do not mean by this that there is one human nature, an essential core, lying beneath the surface of cultural dissimilarity. Just as in the second corollary I used the word "analogous," here I have in mind the metaphor "family resemblances." I do not know of any findings by anthropologists which would suggest that there is a set of values, beliefs, practices which forms a basic human essence, upon which the diverse cultures are merely variations. The third corollary merely notes that the *process* of appropriating one's own culture in its depths links one in a set of operations performed by those undergoing the process of appropriating their own different culture. The *contents* (values, beliefs, practices) of the operations may be quite divergent. But the act of going through these same generic operations fashions in human beings a base from which to recognize, not exactly their similarities, but at least their resemblances to persons in other cultures.

Take, for example, the operations generically required by such imperatives as these: *Be attentive. Be intelligent. Be critical. Be loyal. Decide. Endure.* The style in which these imperatives are voiced and lived differs from culture to culture. The social structure which furnishes their context; the sorts of situations which would make them appropriate; the rewards and sanctions accompanying them; the self-consciousness of their performance; the significance attached to them; the estimation of what counts as fulfilling them

—all these things differ. Still, those who have lived according to them in their own culture will come to recognize those who do so in another culture. Without such operations, no culture long survives. They are the modes through which intentionality manifests itself.

If we may apply these general principles to religion as one element of culture, the closing words of Paul Tillich in *Christianity and the Encounter of World Religions* may be accepted as corroborative. The way, he writes, to break through the particularity of one's own religion

... is not to relinquish one's religious tradition for the sake of a universal concept which would be nothing but a concept. The way is to penetrate into the depth of one's own religion, in devotion, thought and action. In the depth of every living religion there is a point at which the religion itself loses its importance, and that to which it points breaks through its particularity, elevating it to spiritual freedom and with it to a vision of the spiritual presence in other expressions of the ultimate meaning of man's existence.[8]

2. SENSE OF REALITY

On May 4, 1970, National Guardsmen in Kent, Ohio, shot and killed four students of Kent State University. Eighty per cent of the American people, according to polls, approved of the action at Kent. Around the nation, many white students experienced rude shock; "Four of us were killed; this is war," their posters read. One black policeman, resigning from the force of a major city, said he decided that if white people would shoot their own children there was no hope for blacks. It is clear that different groups in America had a different view of what was happening in the nation in 1970. They differed not so much in the raw data they had to work with. They differed not so much in general goals, or even in questions of specific strategy. For if these were all that was at stake, argument would have been easier between them. Instead, many could scarcely speak to one another. They lived "in different worlds." Their sense of reality was almost wholly divergent. Were the four at Kent "shot" or "murdered"? The choice of words reflects a different sense of reality and, consequently, a different expectation and perception of "the facts," all the elements of which may be equally known to all.

In the Western university tradition since the Enlightenment, the approved sense of reality has been established mainly by a generalized conception of scientific theory, coupled (especially in American universities) with a commitment to, and a belief in, a steady forward march of progress. The generalized conception of scientific method entails (1) a precise description of relevant data; (2) a clearly analyzed and testable hypothesis; (3) evidence to confirm the hypothesis. Those things are considered real which are founded upon the successful employment of this method.

Schools commonly test young people in their ability to store information, to analyze it into generalizations, and to adduce reasons for the adequacy of their generalizations. The human attitudes selected from among all human attitudes as guides to what is real are: respect for "hard" quantifiable data, analytic precision, and care in matching hypotheses with data. American schools select these attitudes for reenforcement. They neglect many other important human attitudes: personal experience, imagination, a criticism of the goals and values and purposes which form the context of every judgment and supply its criteria of relevance and evidence. How many examinations in one's school career test the depth and richness of one's personal experience, the range and flexibility of one's imagination, one's skill in criticizing values and goals?

When we use the word "myth," we usually use it of the selections which *other* cultures make in deciding what is real. The records of the American usage of the word "myth" reported in our dictionaries contrast myth with what *we* mean by "reality": the facts, confirmed hypotheses.[9] It seldom occurs to us to notice that our sense of reality is merely our selection of one way to interpret human experience. Scientific method was invented for purposes of prediction and control; its aim is power. Our own sense of reality, then, reveals a primary commitment to the acquisition of power, through the heightening of skills which lead to prediction and control, and through the inhibiting of skills which stand in the way of "progress."

Still, there is nothing in the world of experience labeled "data" or "reality." We must select those things we want to notice. Our own culture, by and large, selects those things that are countable, analyzable, and most easily accessible to prediction and control. We are, as every culture is, entitled to call "real" what we so select. But we are as obliged as other cultures to note that our "reality" is but one selection from the rich texture of human experience—even of our own experience. In our most advanced sciences, like physics, these points are well known.[10] What the scientist knows is not "reality" pure and simple, but the answers he gets back to the questions he elects to raise. He gets back, to a disturbing extent, a reflection of his own interests, procedures, and imagined models. Our science is no more sensitive, flexible, delicate than our prior commitments to clarity, quantification, and similar preferences allow it to be.

Since our personal sense of reality is tutored by the culture in which we live, we are obliged to notice the ways in which education directs our attention to those "facts" suitable for scientific procedures. Experiences of ours—personal, mystical, intuitive, instinctive, groping—which are not "hard" or "objective," our teachers insinuate, are beneath our notice, unreliable, dangerous. "Oh, but you're making a value judgment!" is sometimes considered a put-down.

To be educated for a technological role in a technological society is to learn to be detached from one's own subjectivity. Rollo May uses the term "schizoid" to mean *"out of touch; avoiding close relationships; the inability* to feel," and he writes: "The schizoid man is the natural product of the technological man." Our progress has brought us a world in which "actual personal communication is exceedingly difficult and rare."[11]

It is reasonable to ask whether the sense of reality inculcated even in our best universities is a distorted selection from human experience: distorted in the sense of damagingly and unnecessarily narrow; self-defeating; alienating; destructive both of our environment and of ourselves. We have been living, after all, on the cresting wave of liberal revolutions since the Enlightenment. Perhaps it is time for a transformation of consciousness at least as profound as the Renaissance, the Reformation, and the Enlightenment were: a revision in what we in the West count as real.

Such a transformation, if it is not to be merely reactionary but is to subsume all that was good in what has gone before, would have to include a new theory of reason or, better, of how we decide what is real. The categories "horizon," "standpoint," "autobiography," "sense of reality," "story," "symbol," and the like are steps toward such a reconstruction of our experience. They do not cancel out what has gone before; without the Western past, they would be inconceivable. They attempt to extend the achievements of the past into new territory: that of intelligent subjectivity. No doubt it is the special nature of religious studies that has made such invention necessary. But the pressure of experiences we can no longer contain within the old methods would in any case have required it.

The next category to make part of our new working apparatus, then, is the notion "sense of reality." One's sense of reality is one's instinctive selection of (and trust in) those aspects of one's experience that one takes to be "real," as opposed to those one ignores as insignificant or illusory. The technique for making one's own sense of reality fully conscious is to note especially well what one's *actions* are. Do you believe that what is really real in education is the quest for truth? Then why your concern for grades and for the esteem of your colleagues?

A second technique is to observe one's use of the words "real," "relevant," "meaningful," "significant." What was your most "real" experience during the past year?

A third technique is to note the patterns of selection in one's attention: How much of the world near at hand do you neglect, in order to "concentrate"—and on what? Do you hear the fly buzzing at the window? Do you hear the humming of electricity? You cannot hear *everything*. What do you select?

A fourth technique is to ask yourself *why* what seems real to you should be counted real. Suppose you have been misconstruing your own best instincts, have been doing what you don't for a moment truly value, would never choose?

A fifth technique is to notice, and to map out as sympathetically as you can, the quite different sense of reality of others. Why is it that your Uncle Andy, looking at the world, sees Communism as a great menacing evil, while you have to think twice even to notice Communism, and even after you hear his arguments still don't see matters his way? Why is it that one man responds to God's presence in everything, while another man present at the same location sees no signs of God at all? Why is it that Egyptians and Israelis, Viet Cong and Americans, seem to be reporting— and not only reporting, but seeing—different realities in the struggle between them?

To respond to the last questions in the simple phrase, "It's all a matter of personal bias. Objectively . . ." is to miss the point. The point is that most employments of intelligence in human experience, including the employment of science, depend upon the needs, purposes, visions, goals, and priorities of human subjects.[12]

"Objectivity" has two common senses. The first sense suggests that a person shall take account of his own passions, interests, desires, and biases in order not to be swept away by them. In this sense, "objectivity" is an admirable desire to respond to others fairly, on the merits of the case, and to respond to events fairly, on the basis of the evidence. But "objectivity" sometimes has a second, stronger sense. It represents the ideal man as an *observer*, dispassionate, uninvolved, as self-disciplined as a delicately perceptive machine. It connotes a sort of inhumanity or, possibly, super humanity. It tends to value those aspects of experience that are most easily detached from personal reference and subjective nuance. (The Vietnamese distinguish "objective" from "subjective" as *Khách quam,* the view of the guest, from *chu' quan,* the view of the host.)

In this second sense, "objectivity" is often a useful attitude to assume. It affords significant analytic power and disinterested critical acumen. At the same time, its preference for the impersonal, the quantifiable, or even the clearly articulable limits its success in some important human matters. It imposes a rigorous selectivity on what may be noticed, thought, or weighed as evidence. It tends to screen out vibrations, hunches, affinities, sympathies or antipathies, that are in practical affairs the bearer of significant insight and evidence.

Moreover, both of these senses of "objectivity" can be practiced only by human subjects who have trained themselves to the appropriate rigors. For this reason, objectivity in its first sense should be taken as prior to objectivity in the second sense. It is more open and less rigorously selective; it is less affected by the well-defined bias that characterizes the second sort of objectivity. The woman who is objective in the first sense, for example, will be alert to the bias to which she is prey if she practices too rigorous an objectivity in the second sense. In most situations in which action is called for, vital information is conveyed to us by "body language," "the language of the stomach," instincts long tutored and sharpened to a fine edge, and other sensitivities not easily reduced to the sort of evidence which would pass muster before the bar of objectivity in the second sense. Persons who practice a high degree of objectivity in the second sense are often highly deficient in their openness to more subtle forms of evidence.

For such reasons, "objectivity" is a poor word to suggest as a model for what to count as the quality of spirit a person should most emulate. It is more instructive, I believe, to speak directly of "subjectivity"—not *any* kind of subjectivity, however, but only one that is "intelligent." In order to perceive oneself, or others, or events well—rather as they are than as, given our own interests, we would like them to be—it does not suffice to trust any and every perception that we have. We learn by experience how wrong we can be—how our selectivity tends to follow the contours of our own personal needs, history, and aims.

An *intelligent* subjectivity is one that is tutored by such experiences; that longs to catch as early as possible the signals of its own errors, in order to correct them; that sends out all the attention its acquired skills (of empathy, of observation, of precise detail, of nuance, of comprehensiveness) can marshal. For its aim is to "attune" its own subjectivity, in its fullness, as thoroughly as possible to the matters with which it is engaged. It enters situations not with a maximum of detachment, but with a maximum of attachment. It does so, not in order to "lose itself" by becoming too involved for the maintenance of critical distance, but in order to understand its object as fairly, generously, and—so to say —"from within" as it can.

In cultural matters, for example, the kind of objectivity appropriate to the physicist or chemist is not nearly so fruitful as the disciplined, tutored subjectivity of a man or woman whose emotions, instincts, and imagination are free to feel their way into connections and contradictions they might not otherwise notice. Consider the feeling an Irish peasant has about "the faith" (as distinct, say, from a peasant in Mexico), or the meaning of Jesus to a black teenager struggling for her civil rights in a poverty-stricken corner of Tennessee, or the instincts that guide a surgeon as she makes a decision about a patient's probable fate. So far as external, easily quantifiable data go, most of what is crucial in such matters may escape detection. And yet a highly skilled and experienced observer might be able to extend herself to an astonishing degree into "the interiority" of a culture not her own, and report upon its character with enormous insight. De Tocqueville on the United States; Paul Mus on Vietnam; the Presbyterian Robert McAfee Brown on Catholic matters; a missionary's report on "Bantu Philosophy"—these are examples from among many of intelligent subjectivity at work.

How does one "tutor" one's subjectivity so as to be able to enter into standpoints not one's own? The first requirement is to gain as strong a hold as one can on the contours of one's own sense of reality. Without recognizing the limits of one's own perceptions of the real, the true, the good, and the beautiful, one will tend to impose one's own perceptions—unavoidably—upon the perceptions of others. *Their* reality will appear to you in the colors and lineaments of your reality. In order to allow their divergent sense of reality to appear, one must be able to suspend the authority of one's own sense of reality; and one can hardly do that if one does not know where that authority ends.

Cultures, even more than individual persons, are at odds with one another. Federal troops on Confederate soil are an affront not merely because they are an opposing army, but also because their culture is so different: their manners, their values, their sense of what is significant and true. U. S. troops in Vietnam brought with them perceptions, procedures, disciplines, and biases the likes of which villagers in Vietnam had never encountered. Even apart from acts of warfare, both sides experienced "culture shock." An American adviser and his Vietnamese advisee, even if they became good friends and came to love each other, as was sometimes the case, often could not even begin to comprehend what the other took to be most real or significant or cause for joy or uneasiness.

A Vietnamese does not commonly think of honesty in terms of

principles or rules, but rather in terms of a difficult and delicate attunement to subtle relations of power, the drift of events, personal feeling, and family or village welfare. Behavior which an American considers dishonest, a Vietnamese may believe the highest form of humanistic perception. What the American calls honest, a Vietnamese may believe willful, self-deceptive, and destructive. Direct speech is to one a sign of manliness and candor; to the other, a sign of lack of culture, delicacy, and subtlety.

Thus, the meaning of Zen cannot be simply translated into American idiom. Quite apart from the discipline implied in Zen, there is the added difficulty of the huge gap between Eastern and Western cultures. Sense of reality, story, and symbols are different. The consciousness of individuals and groups is different.

A sense of reality reveals itself chiefly in action. How does a culture see its destiny? Does a man become a man by dominating nature or by becoming attuned to it? Is time circular or linear? Does one attend to the future or to the ancients? Which is more real and more to be reverenced, one's individuality or one's fidelity to communal ancestors? When an American enters a crowded room, at a cocktail party or college mixer, he imagines his task as a problem of *community:* how can he go from his inner self out across the no-man's land and make contact with another separate self? For members of other cultures, the problem is the reverse: how can those who are tangibly and emotionally "brothers" and "cousins" differentiate themselves as *individuals* at all? Why would they want to?

In the United States, several different cultural stories are available. The story of enlightenment is one: a story of constantly more acute individuality, based on an ever more thorough employment of one's own reason and choices. The story of imitating Jesus Christ is sometimes perceived as congruent to the story of enlightenment. For some Christians, the "good" Christian "matures" through an even greater exercise of individual moral responsibility.

For others, the Christian story is perceived as a story of growing *community:* a community of concern and responsibility. The story of individual enlightenment is rejected as too atomistic and alienating, and too neglectful of the indisputable bonds of dependence among men.

A counter story against this Christian story of community is that community represents a "failure of nerve." The *true* Western story, one avers, is the story of the lonely heretic going his solitary, arduous way—a Prometheus defying the gods; Sisyphus scorning his absurd fate.

A cultural story plays several functions. First of all, it provides a model by which to live one's life: a measure of good performance and bad. Beneath every metaphysical or scientific system of thought there is the underlying logic and structure of a way of life to be lived. "Story" is a category prior to "first principles," "imperatives," "axioms," "duties," "rules," or "ethical systems." Before analyzing the ethical thought of a philosopher or theologian or ethical teacher, it is fundamental to discern the story a man must live out in order to find such thinking plausible and, perhaps, compelling. If one has a fundamental resistance to the basic story, one will find no end of objections to various steps in the systematic thought. (Even if one accepts the story, one may find the articulated system wanting.) Story is prior to systems.

Secondly, a cultural story is an illumination. It "lights up" or "highlights" certain aspects of a people's experience. If Karl Jaspers is correct in suggesting that Socrates was the first man in Western history to think of himself as an individual, able to assert confidently that his community was wrong, it remains true that Socrates went rather peacefully into exile and even to his death. So strong upon him was his sense that the community is prior to the individual that he scarcely challenged the right of the city to exile him for his views; so faithful was he to himself that he did not falsify his views in order to conform them to that of the city. A poignant historical moment! And quite different from the agony of Jesus when he, four centuries later, faced his own imminent death. For Jesus, aware of the love of a good Father, felt the sharp contradiction between such a personalized world and an absurd death. Socrates, accepting an impersonal cosmos, accepted death as a natural event, to which reconciliation is the only wisdom. The Greek reconciliation to natural cycles; the Christian struggle to make persons and history break through the bonds of nature, flash here into the lives of those who live under the spell of such stories.

A cultural story is subject to fundamental changes of axis and direction. As long as a culture is living, its basic story is a living form, not a script laid down in advance. Under intense pressures or new experiences, the whole direction and significance of what a culture has been doing until that point appears "in a new light." The war in Vietnam, for example, has led many Americans to reinterpret the whole of American history. Belief in America's basic innocence and goodness ("a new world," "the new Adam"), snapped like thread. The significance of John F. Kennedy's Inaugural Address in 1961 has already been altered; its stirring and bold phrases now read, after Vietnam, like unwise and unguarded boasts.

Reading their own story with fresh eyes, many Americans now see the slaughter of the Indians, centuries of slavery, and a persistent racism in an excruciatingly painful light. Whether the American story can absorb this new and unflattering light, or must reassert its earlier romantic innocence, constitutes a major crisis for the American spirit.

Thirdly, a cultural story is an organization of data, inasmuch as it provides an overall view of a people's past actions and future hopes. It lifts events out of the past and makes them significant by linking them to our present identity. In earlier American folklore, the Indians were savages who treated innocent whites barbarously. But if the whites herded the Indians into virtual genocide, then the story of genocide may become for some the significant thread linking other movements in American history: the fate of the blacks; "the only good dink is a dead dink." The story a people believes its culture is living out boosts or cripples their morale. The young, in particular, enter upon adult life either with confidence that the professions they are about to enter are noble and humane, or else with dismay because the future seems to require their complicity in evil or their acceptance of meaninglessness.

Fourthly, a cultural story operates as a selector of goals. A people confident of the main lines of its traditional story, or entrusting itself to some fresh adventure and new direction, chooses one set of goals with alacrity and rejects another as irrelevant or retrogressive or damaging. When the story itself is in doubt, however, the choice of even fairly proximate goals can be a grave torment. Whether through some general malaise and apathy, or through bitter, almost internecine disputes, there may be much thrashing about in the dark, a sort of wandering through a desert. The cultural confusion serves to disorient the individuals within the culture, too. The personal stories they are trying to live out are deeply affected by the crisis of confidence in the cultural story of which they are a part. What constitutes a good, noble, brave man? With which parties should a good man cast the energies of his life? "These are the times that try men's souls" is a maxim more truly spoken, not in a time of clear and defined danger, but in a time of confusion and darkness. The cultural story does not supply its customary light; men must reach into their souls and invent a fresh cultural direction.

Story is a richer concept than goal. Goals do not, by themselves, constitute a story. A story belongs in the kingdom of ends; it expresses solely and only the life of persons and human communities. Goals confer identities only in the kingdom of means: X is a means to goal Y and gets its significance from Y. But persons are not merely instruments of, or pursuers of, goals. A people may decide at a certain point in its life that the goals it has been pursuing are too narrow and inhibiting, and don't really fit the basic story it has been trying to live out. The goal of "victory in Vietnam" may be in conflict with one version of the American story. It is in harmony with the story "America never loses a war."

The United States is perhaps the only nation in the world dedicated to living out a story which is the living out of a proposition—"testing," as Lincoln put it at Gettysburg, "whether that nation, or any nation so conceived and so dedicated, can long endure." The story involved in attempting to realize in an entire body politic the proposition that all men are created equal, entitled equally to liberty and justice, has necessitated a frequent uprooting of established social goals and frequent new beginnings. To this extent, the American *story* has been more humane than actual American arrangements.

On the other hand, another strand of the American story is a commitment to "progress," i.e., to establishing scientific and technological advance at the very center of American consciousness. Such a story leads to the selection of only those goals which are clearly linked to the prediction and control of means: a wholly rational and efficient organization of ever larger areas of life. Under such a story, the very concept "story" declines in value and significance: persons themselves are reduced to means.

By contrast, Gandhi said that means give significance to goals, and are not just a technique; means are a way of life. They are at once both the means and the goal. Technology is merely a means, but nonviolence is a means that is also a goal. Nonviolence is a story to be lived. The fundamental Gandhian story is that progress occurs in men and nowhere else: if and only if a man voyages deeper into "truth-force."[13]

When the essential metaphor for life is "way" or "voyage," the concept "story" is at work. (When men speak of a trampling, relentless progress from goal to goal they speak of "the march" of progress or of time; as if to suggest: "stay out of the way!") The concept "goal" often figures in stories as the focal point of the journey: heaven, the promised land, utopia. But quite often the goal spoken of as the object of a voyage turns out to be not external to man, but within him. It is a *metaphor* for a change in his own way of life. The goal of the voyage is to become a different kind of person. The story, then, is a passage from standpoint to standpoint, conversion to conversion.

A cultural story, fifthly, is a guide in concrete situations. Action is not merely a matter of measuring means and ends, and of estimating consequences. It is also a matter of quality, of manner, of supple attention, of awareness, of grace. Some people are more "present" in each of their actions than others. Some act efficiently and effectively, but with very little self-involvement. For these latter, action comes closest to the category "behavior": it is pretty much what it is observed to be, from outside. Action of this sort is, it appears, an escape from the presence of oneself and the presence of others; it is kept as close to the surfaces as possible. If the cultural story is that of living as appropriately as one can in a machine culture, highly mobile and rational as that is, the individual in every concrete situation need only try to remain cool, detached, and expeditious. In such cases, courtesy, for example, is not to be confused with presence or communication; it is merely grease on the cold wheels. The airline hostess is paid to smile in order to keep the impersonality of the mechanism from terrifying humans to death.

The way we act in concrete situations—attention to detail, to consequences, to consideration for others, to what acting is making of ourselves—reveals the story governing our behavior, as well as how good we are at it. Conversely, the story selects the degree of attention we choose to give to the texture of the situation in which we act. The Buddhist monk and the American student act in qualitatively different ways. But each may further judge himself a not sufficiently good exemplar of the story he purports to live.

Briefly put, the category story brings out the human structure of behavior: it is what makes mere behavior human. "God made man," Elie Wiesel writes," because he loves stories." Did he make diverse cultures, then, in order to share in many stories?

3. FROM CULTURE TO CULT

Cult is the center of culture. Cult dramatizes the mysterious sources of a culture's vitality. A cult reenacts a culture's sense of reality, story, and symbol.

The Catholic culture of medieval Europe, for example, cherished community more than it cherished the individual. Correspondingly, its God was communal: a Trinity. Knowing well its own aggressiveness, cruelty, and ferocity, it cherished a childlike veneration of a gentle virgin, the maiden Mary. Both masculine and feminine symbols were powerful: knights tried to be as gentle as the Virgin.[14] The sense of the absurd was celebrated in haunting frescoes, in fantasies of the diabolic, and in the sacrifice of the mass.

Every smallest concrete existent—a rock, a flower—was also a mysterious sign of God's presence everywhere in daily life. "Reality" was not coterminous with what the senses could detect or what the intelligence could reduce to articulation. Legend and song celebrated stories a man or a woman could live out. The lives of holy men and women—new kinds of story, in each new time, each new place—instructed all in new possibilities to seek out in their own lives. Darkest evil, cruelty, lust, and cunning were not denied; Machiavelli worked at the papal court and described what he saw. Political power was not evaded; men did not have scruples about "dirtying their hands" in politics. "Power" was a sound and substantial word; one did not fear it or disguise the fact that one had it.

Three convictions of the Middle Ages generated enormous cultural power for the future. According to the medieval sense of reality, not a swallow fell in a field nor a hair from a man's head without God's knowing it. In other words, every single random and obscure event was understandable from one point of reference: everything in all its limitless detail was known to God.[15] Consequently, if men tried to understand anything—no matter how trivial or seemingly unimportant—they could be sure that it *was* intelligible. If they couldn't penetrate the secret yet, perhaps a greater effort would succeed. For *God* knew. And therefore, even if not yet intelligible to humans, still every event in the universe was intelligible. Newton was to reflect upon the fall of an apple; Freud was to notice the rationale behind slips of the tongue and absent-minded choices.

Secondly, according to the medieval sense of reality, every single human person—male or female, slave or free—was beloved of God. Christ spilled his precious blood for each. "In Christ's blood!" men swore daily. In an era when the average age of mortality was in the early forties, when three of five children might die in childbirth or the first year of life, when plague might take one-half or one-third of the lives of an entire region, it seemed clear that this earth was not paradise. Yet the Lord who made the heavens loved each man, each woman, each child. Reflecting on that, many shed tears: when, for example, they re-created the birth of "The Lord Jesus" in a stable. God became an infant, cold and poor and vulnerable, for love of us! In his bitterness against Christianity, Nietzsche was later to record his gratitude for its two contributions to his "overman": Christianity taught Western men and women to love honesty ("God is Truth"), even if ultimately honesty was to overturn Christianity itself; and Christianity taught Western men and women to love and to value themselves—it saved them from self-hatred.[16]

Thirdly, Christianity instructed men (as did Judaism, perhaps more ardently) to believe that history has a direction and is not circular, that the future will be different from the present. "Our father, who art in heaven . . . thy kingdom come . . . *on earth* as it is in heaven." Christians are responsible for taking history into their own hands, and slowly building up therein a kingdom of justice, truth, freedom, and love. In the medieval period, to say that "there is nothing new under the sun" seemed plausible enough; the prospects for seriously altering the technical, economic, or social structure of human life did not seem good. Yet almost everywhere—and not only in the widespread millenarian sects[17] that preached the "coming of the Third Age, of the Holy Spirit"—there was a sense that a person fulfills his true story by contributing his talents, whatever they might be, to beautifying and sweetening the bitter life of men and women on earth: whether by contributions to agriculture, to government, to armed service, to the crafts, to the arts, or to the direct, transcendent service of God in a religious community symbolic of heaven: monastery or convent or priesthood. An unabashed worldliness, a daring otherworldliness—the medieval psyche was more comfortable than the middle-class psyche of later centuries with extreme images of life.

Whereas for the Greeks life was repetition, for medieval Christians life was a looking forward to a new kingdom. Life was a story moving forward: The creation, the fall, the birth and death and resurrection of Jesus, the indwelling of the Spirit spreading around the earth, the Second Coming of the Lord. Man was not chained down to the cycles of nature[18]—human history had broken free, had broken into story. As the sacrifice of the mass showed, the story is bloody. Its symbol is the sign of the absurd: plane contradictory to plane: the cross. Light came into darkness and the darkness snuffed it out. If light was reborn—if Jesus rose again—the good news was detected not by the naked eye but by faith. The bitterness of life must be drunk to the dregs. "My God, my God, why hast thou forsaken me?" The Christian, like the unbeliever, labors in a dark night.[19]

In such a sense of reality, such a story, such a set of symbols, economic, social, and political relationships were also expressed. The rise of capitalism, science and technology, and world exploration would disrupt them. Individuals rather than the community became focal points of action. The power of individuals to take control of political, economic, and social history grew stronger. The ties of family and clan were matched in power by ties of money, class, and ownership. Knowledge came to mean not some sort of unity with being but rather, as Francis Bacon succinctly put it: power, the power to predict and to control. The Christian faith came to be embodied not by one historical people, the Catholic people, but by many, Anglicans, Lutherans, Evangelicals, and others. These many were for centuries at war and hostile one to another, opposing sense of reality to sense of reality, story to story, symbol to symbol.

If one may speak all too simply: the Western story fragmented. The Catholic symbol (rather like the Confucianist) was authority and community; the Protestant symbol was the individual and a more pure or spiritual Christianity; the Humanist symbol was the power of man and his liberty; the scientific symbol was power. "Progress" became the key word. The Dynamo, as Henry Adams put it, replaced the Virgin; Reason replaced mystery and sensuality; action replaced passivity; the masculine replaced the feminine. The most powerful cultural maelstrom in the history of our planet was unleashed, spinning off through Marx and Engels to Russia, China, and Africa its convictions about man's responsibility for history and its confidence in the intelligibility of the whole.

To study religion in the twentieth century, then, is to study not only church organizations and the doctrines of professional ecclesiastics; nor is it to study the religious person in his formal religious practices. It is to try to fathom the many senses of reality, the many stories, the many symbols that give sense and plausibility to human actions. It is to reflect on sequences of human actions, in order to discern what view of the world, self, and others might be required to make those actions attractive to their agents. Why do they act as they do act? What is it they perceive, fear, desire, dread, delight in?

At the center of culture is cult. Humans show their cult not by what they do in prayer but by what they do in action. "By their fruits shall ye know them." "Attend not to what they say, but to what they do."

A psychologist, sociologist, or anthropologist may also study those phenomena which are of greatest interest to scholars in religious studies. But the perspective of the scientist is ordinarily that of the observer. She tends to rely heavily on data suitable for analysis and, if possible, for quantification. The scholar in religious studies has exactly the same reliance. But she also has one additional task. When she has understood everything that can be understood by way of scientific method, she still is interested in "feeling her way into" the sense of reality, the stories, and the symbols of those whose way of life she is studying. She wishes to pass over from her scientific standpoint, and from her personal standpoint, to the standpoint of those others—to do so as fully as she can.

For religious studies have as their main focus precisely the phenomena of standpoint, sense of reality, story, and symbol. These phenomena cannot be thoroughly understood merely by observing them "from outside." One must also be able to enter into them, provisionally of course and with self-critical sympathy. Even a scientist depends upon her ability to do this. But she does so in the service of objectivity; whereas those in religious studies do so in the service of intelligent subjectivity. The scientist desires a sound theory; the student of religious studies desires a sound theory, but also an attuned sense of reality, participation in the story being studied, and an empathetic appreciation of the power of the given symbols.

Why does she desire these difficult achievements? Not only because they vastly enrich her life. (One could imagine an excellent scholar in the field exercising all the relevant skills but not really allowing her findings to enrich her own life—more than mere empathy and acuity are required for that.) But also because

the study of standpoint, sense of reality, story, and symbol necessarily conducts the investigator beyond the realm of theory and
into the exercise of the very activities she is studying in others.
Her own standpoint, sense of reality, story, and symbols are
matched against those of others. To refuse to pass over from hers
to theirs is to cease practicing her profession. Religious studies are
such a "passing over." The point of religious studies is not just
the acquiring of information, not just the achievement of a clear
analysis, but also a growth in one's capacity for sympathy and
connaturality. One wants to know what it is like to share in other
standpoints than one's own.

Thus, a sharp eye for the cults basic to a way of life is indispensable. In a modern secular society, the cults are not of course
services of worship. They are, instead, communal acts of rich
emotional significance and presupposition. The cocktail party is
a modern celebration. Articulation, talk, and an "objective" sharing of ideas are celebrations of a way of life whose significance
exceeds the mere sharing of information that occurs in them.
They confirm the rationality of man, the faith in human communion through reason of a certain type. The reading of many books
and participation in the argument of a seminar (or discussion
group or conference) are symbolic acts as well as practical acts.
They signify participation in "the life of the mind."

They symbolize a certain achievement, discipline, and selection
among life's possibilities. They highlight a "stimulating" way of
life, a kind of personal pilgrim's progress toward greater and
greater knowledge. They symbolize the quality of individuals in
the pursuit of "truth." The modern seminar, moreover, lacks the
mystical sense of "dialogue" of the Greek seminar, which as Plato
describes it was based on a kind of "music" and "inspiration" and
"communion." What modern man wants from a seminar is new
information, clarity of organization, and a defined course of action.

To be sure, there are several kinds of "modern" man. A

majority do not take part in the pursuit of rationality. They share a "neighbor culture." The opinions and feelings of their neighborhoods tend to define their sense of reality, story, and symbols. Suburban living—its neat lawns, controlled asphalt streets, and neighborly barbecue pits—provides their central cult. The "controlled violence" of football observed may provide the most profound emotional release.

Among the educated, meanwhile, a new longing for "sensitivity," "encounter," and "group dynamics" provides a new center of gravity for the definition of a sense of reality, a new kind of story to live out, a new set of symbols. A huge, quiet, sensitive crowd at Woodstock fills the soul with a sense of fulfillment. Nude bathing, the innocence of the mixing of the sexes, a quiet joy in human presence—a little dirty, rough, uncontrolled, outside the grounds of the neat suburban hedges and the isolation of nuclear families—a "new culture" is born around a new cult.

Cult is the center of culture. When do people feel awe? When does a hush steal over them? Where do they feel most satisfied, as if at last living up to the archetype of what they think a human being is and ought to be? And how do they celebrate their satisfaction? These are among the questions religious studies try to pursue.

FOUR

Societies and Institutions

It has become fashionable to despair of institutions. Freud himself lent power and credence to anti-institutional sentiment. His standpoint was not only tragic but pessimistic. He held in *Civilization and Its Discontents* that institutions are necessary, but at the cost of repressing vital instinctive drives in their members.[1] Some followers of Freud, meanwhile, have taken the utopian view that the goal of human striving is the creation of a "nonrepressive" society. Affluence will make it possible for the state and its attendant bureaucracies to "wither away." Individuals will be free to indulge impulses and fantasies which in times of scarcity they had to repress in the name of hard work, discipline, and sacrifice.[2] It is as if an innocent Garden of Eden waits up ahead, as if institutions were necessary only in a more primitive, more straitened, more corrupt era of human history.

Against such views—against both Freud's pessimism and the utopian optimism of others—I would like to propose that man is a political animal; and that institutions are both his natural habitat and the chief instruments of his growth in liberty. To develop such an argument, we need to take up a standpoint less heady and less "superstructural"[3] than the cultural standpoint. We need, as it were, to touch earth.

1. INSTITUTIONS ARE MAN'S NATURAL HABITAT

An image of a society in which institutions fail to function was furnished by Vietnam in, say, 1967. Imagine that you were there at that time. The most salient characteristic of such a society is lack of trust. Neighboring families may be siding with the enemy; even members of one's own family may be secret agents. To whom can one speak freely? A citizen can be shot down even by his associates and in any crowd. Often the national government seems to exist in name only, except that taxes are collected and sons drafted. The nation has no one universally used language. There are almost no truly national political organizations except that of the National Liberation Front and the Army of the Republic of South Vietnam. The Buddhist church is a national institution, deeply formative of the Vietnamese character; yet it is politically not able to bring order or unity. The local village institutions, on which the sense of reality, the stories, and the symbols of Vietnam were based for centuries,[4] have been seriously disrupted. On whom can ordinary people rely? Halfway between a local, agricultural economy and a modern state system, the Vietnamese are whipsawed by shifts in role, livelihood, hope, despair. It is not only the physical, but also the institutional, destruction that one feels in Vietnam.

Institutions are structures of meaning and differentiation. They assign roles, in recognition of the diversity of persons, tasks, and needs. When we hear the word "institution," we tend to think of organizations and authorities. It is helpful, then, to recall that language is the first and basic institution.[5] It assigns speaker, spoken to, spoken about, and provides the forms along which different meanings can be communicated in different circumstances.

The human ability to experience, to imagine, and to think is both enriched by, and limited by, language. Without a fund of words and linguistic forms, our attention could scarcely be brought to certain aspects of experience; an impoverished linguistic frame almost certainly means a smaller range of perception and thought.[6] On the other hand, language can have the effect of channeling our experience, stereotyping and conventionalizing it, so that we develop a pattern of repression and forgetfulness regarding our own primal experience.[7] The child lives in a rich, undifferentiated sea of experiences, which as he is "educated" becomes more and more conventionalized and is directed into "approved" verbal channels.[8] He sooner or later gives up trying to express his highly personal experience.

Thus even so basic and fluid an institution as language is profoundly ambivalent. Many of the things we feel and care about are not easy to put into words; and without words our feelings and concerns would be far less discriminating, far less tutored, than they are.

Trust is a precondition of human institutions. By "trust" I point toward facts that Hume[9] referred to as "fellow-feeling" and Max Scheler as "sympathy."[10] Without trust, human intercourse is not conceivable. "A demoralized people," Walter Lippmann wrote in the depths of the depression in 1932, "is one in which the individual has become isolated and is the prey of his own suspicions. He trusts nobody and nothing, not even himself. He believes nothing, except the worst of everybody and everything. He sees only confusion in himself and conspiracies in other men."[11]

Erik Erikson has formulated the notion as "basic trust,"[12] and Reinhold Niebuhr in *Man's Nature and His Communities*[13] referred to it as "common grace." Basic trust is the reaching out of man toward man across the seeming separation between them; it is a risk, a willingness to sustain rejection, a creative gesture toward the other. It unites two (or more) so that where there were many there is now, in some respects at least, one. Such trust, it seems, is even more primitive than isolation; for centuries the feeling of community was dominant among humans, before the individual became sufficiently differentiated to distinguish himself from the group.[14]

Only in the modern West, under the impact of the Renaissance, the Reformation, and the Enlightenment, has the individual gained the ascendance in human awareness—probably in too ideological and exaggerated a way. For even the movements designated "Renaissance," "Reformation," and "Enlightenment"—all of which celebrate man's individuality—were social movements and social achievements. As John Dewey has brilliantly pointed out,[15] the individual in the modern West lives on a fund of social knowledge and social liberties. He does so, despite the fact that Western ideology constantly emphasizes his individuality and hardly ever draws attention to his social dependence. The auto mechanic is not any more intelligent than his primitive ancestors. But given the fund of social knowledge to which he is heir he takes apart, re-creates, and invents engines that would seem to his ancestors astonishing magic.

Trust, however, is an ambivalent value. A large part of our maturing involves learning to what an extent we cannot trust others, and learning to discriminate whom to trust and when. We also discover, to our regret, that we cannot always trust ourselves. We are obliged to cope with our own betrayals—betrayals of those we love, betrayals of ourselves.

Institutions of yet another kind spring as naturally from our activities as words from our mouths, drawings from our hands. We organize our communities to seek goods we could not acquire by ourselves, or at least not so readily, and not on so regular and reliable a basis. It is good to have cornmeal or bacon for breakfast today. It is better to have a system for providing them every day. It is good to have, today, a carefully tutored sense of reality, stories, and symbols, apt not only for my physical survival but also for my sense of dignity, significance, and meaning. These goods are made available in my culture in a way suited to the major events and crises of my life, and in the moments when I am most ready to grow in understanding and commitment. Thus economic and political, religious and cultural institutions meet long-term and recurrent human needs.[16]

The human being is not only an individual but a member of a historical race. Some of his goals are not achieveable in his own lifetime—acquiring and clearing land sufficient for the livelihood of his children, perhaps; the invention of an art like sculpturing or painting; advances in science, wisdom, and moral insight. His efforts are extended over generations. What one person does not live long enough to do, institutions are established to carry on. There would be no memory without institutions, no cumulative invention, no history, no sustained direction. There would be no technology, no affluence, no power against the elements, no habits of thought, art, and perception acquired through centuries of exploration. Without habits and routines, there would be no freedom.[17] The "state of nature," fortunately, included man's ability to speak, to trust, to organize, and to extend his efforts over time by way of institutions.

Humans live in institutions as their natural habitat; hence, their capacity to endure. They are able to shape their institutions to their needs and aspirations; therein, their capacity to grow. Most important of all: it is in and through their institutions that humans acquire their sense of reality, stories, symbols. It is in and through their institutions that they acquire roles and tasks, learn their identity, test their capacities, differentiate themselves as individuals from others and ultimately from the group, learn to differentiate aspects of themselves, learn to recognize in themselves a plurality of "selves," discover new possibilities for exploration and growth. Persons learn all their skills—economic, political, moral, intellectual, personal—through the scope of activities provided by institutions.

Freud's image, that first there is the unrepressed individual of whom civilization demands (as the price for his security) an enormous cost in repressed instinct, is complemented by another. Instincts do not come to expression *except* through cultural forms. Diffused and formless, they find no satisfaction, have no special intensity, focus, or elegance, are reinforced by no patterns of meaning, significance, or power. It is not true that the state of formlessness is a state of delight; it is, on the contrary, a state of anguish, passivity, and frustration. Civilization in supplying form channels instinct as a deep cut does marshy water. Even in beating against the banks, the waters of instinct run deeper and faster. Nonrepressiveness is not freedom, and it does not guarantee vitality. The metaphor "repressive," in fact, is misleading. To concentrate on Z rather than on Y is, in a sense, to block out or to repress Y. But one might equally say that from a state of formlessness Z is given existence by my attention. It "stands out" (L., *ex-sistere*) into being. Y is not repressed; it remains in the formlessness of its original state.

A person, of course, is not infinite and cannot heed all his instincts and drives simultaneously. If he chooses to heed A, he foregoes B. Many of the most difficult choices in human life require a choice against one good, in the name of another. Man's discontent, then, is due not only to the fact that in order to gain the respect and affection of his fellows he must control his vagrant impulses of lust, savagery, and other direct, primal satisfactions. It is also due to the fact that he is not the simultaneous Pure Act —infinitely exercising every energy at once—which Aquinas imagined God to be. Man must choose. It is not only civilization, moreover, which imposes this choice on him. Even were he solitary, still he could not satisfy all his instincts in one single act.

It is gratuitous, then, to imagine that civilization and its institutions are foreign, repressive agencies descending upon the free and unspoiled individual. That is but one mythical picture, among many from which persons may choose. Surely it seems much more plausible that civilization and its institutions are enabling agencies, representing far more possibilities for experience, imagination, intelligence, and action than any one individual can assimilate.[18] But, like individuals, institutions are not infinite; they represent a limited selection of possibilities. Hence, they are subject to periodic crises, to transformation, to reformation and revolution, to decline and death.

In some ways, institutions are more sacred than individuals: they represent the enduring good of the many. Sacrifice of self for the good of the institution has since the beginning been a feature of human behavior. In other ways, the individual is more sacred than the institution: the law is made for humans, not humans for the law. The institution is a means, an instrument. Persons are ends.

2. FREEDOM AND COERCION

When enlightened persons in the West think about freedom and coercion they commonly line up freedom with the individual and coercion with society. Individuals and society are seen as competing for the same quantum of control; if the share of the society grows, that of the individual shrinks.

There are serious intellectual and pragmatic questions involved in the relation of freedom to coercion. But from a faulty bias many pseudo problems arise. Several propositions may bring some confusions, at least, to light.

First, freedom is a social as well as a personal achievement. Personal freedom is not a moral ideal in all known historical cultures, nor even of all persons in American culture. Only for certain social groups does freedom receive the attention, definition, and practicability that constitute it as a *goal* by which to direct one's efforts. The children of construction workers in New York, for example, are taught to obey the "old man" in a way that children of wealthy families seldom are. Only through the means of a certain kind of family upbringing and educational development can freedom become a way of life. Only in the context of certain types of institutional arrangements can freedom actually be exercised. Such exercise is different in a jail, the army, a university, a commune, a large corporation, a family business, a dictatorship.

As an ideal, as a social and personal goal, in its genesis, and in its actual exercise, freedom is dependent on a social order, even on a social evolution.

Finally, for a precise and workable definition, freedom is dependent upon the achievement of institutions, languages, and methods of inquiry and analysis. What we mean by "freedom" depends on a body of social experience, a network of social insights, a set of social images, a tradition of technical definitions, an evolutionary set of judgments about matters of fact. Moreover, the way we criticize one another's conduct for manifesting freedom or unfreedom is also socially attained.

It is not true, then, that society is simply an enemy of freedom. It is also an agent, nourisher, and perfecter of freedom.

Secondly, society is not a monolith but a highly differentiated set of variously interlocking systems. Besides the state bureaus and officials, there are cultural agencies and social groups of varying scope and power. Families differ from one another in the theory and practice of freedom; individuals within families also differ.[19] Ethnic groups exercise more or less strength in shaping theories and practices of freedom. The poor and the rich often have different theories and practices; a group's relation to the "instruments of production" and the like bring about different theories and practices. Various intellectual traditions, embodied in different sorts of schools, nourish different theories and practices. Voluntary agencies in cultural, political, economic, and social matters incarnate different theories and practices of freedom. Various corporations (business, education, ecclesiastical) operate on different sets of theories and practices. Religious traditions differ. Personal psyches are at different stages of development, develop along different lines, and experience diverse social relations in diverse ways.

Thirdly, the interactions of social groups and individuals occur in many modes, not all of them properly called "coercive" or "repressive," even when they exceed the control of the individuals in the group. Ordinarily, participation in any group entails the acceptance of certain constraints; groups, in fact, cannot exist without selecting some definition of purpose, order, and direction among virtually infinite possibilities. To conclude that groups, then, are necessarily repressive is to assume that selection is counter to freedom. But no action of any sort can occur without a selection among possibilities. A free act is no less such a selection than a coerced act. Social action, even of a most free type or of a type most highly supportive of freedom, cannot occur except by a selection that is, in effect, a choice against other possibilities.

What makes a social act free? What makes a social act coercive? The human being is a highly complex animal, both biologically and symbolically, and his actions spring from many sources. Each of these sources is affected by the social groups in which he lives. Social groups affect:

genetic heredity;
diet;
medical care;
environmental protection;
instruments of production;
repertoire of roles and tasks; assignment of same;
imaginative, symbolic inheritance, richness, diversity, changeability;
linguistic forms and operations; possibilities or transformations of same;
accumulated and preserved insights and formulations of same;
routine practices of survival; personal and familial deportment, etc.
laws, practices, customs, expectations of social interchange;
sense of reality, adjudication of disputes, judgments upon the meaning and validity of experience;

patterns of acceptable decision-making and group dynamics;
sanctions (raised eyebrows to death penalties) for group values.

Human actions, whether free or coerced, occur within the
context of all these sorts of social inheritance. There seems to be
no spot in his make-up in which the individual is ever clearly
distinguishable from his social group. His groups live in him
thoroughly; he as accurately says of himself (and his actions)
"we" as "I."

On the other hand, no one group wholly possesses him, wholly
exhausts his possibilities. The effects of many groups upon him
are in conflict with the effects of many others. The calculus of his
actions seems, then, to have an irreplaceable uniqueness; no other
single person, even if that same person shares all the same groups
as he does, appears to perceive or to act or to develop in precisely
the same way as he. It seems legitimate for a person to say "I"
in contradistinction to each group of which he is a member, to
each other individual in such groups, and to the class composed
of all his groups and all their members. Uniquely, he is the
originating source of some perceptions, actions, personal development. (His uniqueness may be highly developed or hardly at
all; he may prefer to drift or to lose himself among others.)

It is tempting, at this point, to imagine that freedom is composed of (a) conscious acts of (b) the self-originated perception
of (c) a unique human person. The metaphor "Enlightenment"
expresses such an image. Freedom is the tiny light of the individual emerging out of social darkness. The image glorifies originality as opposed to conformity, individuality as opposed to
community, self-direction as opposed to communal harmony. The
free person is solitary, and stands *over against* community. He
becomes free by ever more intense and penetrating acts of self-
consciousness, ever more resistance to social groups, ever more
distance between himself and society. He wrestles against society

for a larger personal space. Every infringement on his psyche is a form of repression or coercion. The free man is "the Marlboro man."

It is just this view of man as a monad struggling to break out of the group, living freely only apart from the group (the cowboy[20] outside the law, the cities, fellowship), that is both powerfully attractive in our culture and yet indefensible. *Freedom is social.* A theory dealing with freedom and coercion must spring from a social perspective, not merely from the perspective of the individual.

Thus, for example, under present conditions there is for most American children no escape from television. On the average, they watch television more than six hours a day. It is difficult to imagine that there is some private psychic space outside the reach of television—some inner sanctum of individuality. One expects, rather, that information, affects, patterns of action and movement, symbols of what counts as reasonable discourse, and emotional release come to them as television in fact presents them. These givens become the most accessible patterns for their own initial development. Surely, one must conclude that children are stimulated far more than they would be without the motion, sounds, and emotions in which television involves them.

In one respect, their options are enlarged. Television brings them a certain openness vis-à-vis the values, acts, and emotions that form the psychic environment created by their parents and neighborhoods. They are not subject *only* to their parents, as children were before. In another respect, it is rather depressing to think of all children (a) watching the same programs; (b) learning human responses from the simplifications induced by the boxed-in dimensions of television, rather than from a richer life with their parents and other human beings; (c) learning an inferior, cheap, or degrading set of values from carelessly put-together, merely gimmicky, "fast-paced," repetitive themes.

Insofar as television is accessible to all homes, it creates a possible enlargement of freedom and a possible diminishment of freedom. That is to say, it may as a social instrument either invite children to achieve those developments in self-confidence, enabling skills, clear perception, and boldness of heart that lead a human being to a greater range of action; or it may stereotype children into fixed and prepared patterns—destroying self-esteem, teaching few skills, demanding little perception, stunting boldness of heart. Television may stimulate or it may pacify. That it *affects* freedom is perfectly clear.

Again, what is the comparative effect of "permissiveness" and "authoritarianism" upon the development of children? What sense of reality follows from the one, and from the other? Perhaps there are intelligent varieties of each. Thus, authority of tone and clear commands may, for some children, be keys to their eventual liberation. It is possible that children do not learn well when they sense uncertainty, or self-doubt, or lack of direction, or *laissez-faire*. It is possible that the skills required for liberation, being social in origin, definition, and transmission, may be learned through intelligent discipline from adults.

To state the general principle once more: Every form of freedom is social. The fact that an emotion, perception, or action is in part due to its social origin does not make it *less* free but is, in fact, a condition both of its very existence and of its freedom. For without the prior achievements of society, we would neither recognize freedom nor desire it nor know how to achieve it. The problem of freedom and coercion, therefore, is *not* the problem of holding societies at bay and protecting the privacy of the individual. It is the problem of deciding *which* social actions contribute to freedom and which block freedom at its sources or in its development.

Does social innovation X (e.g., genetic engineering) promote the development of human freedom? Every social structure sets in motion countervailing forces and has unforeseen effects. Hence, what social protections are needed to counterbalance social innovations, in order that the freedom of persons and groups may develop further? Was the inhabitant of New York City more or less free in 1878 than the commuters and laborers of 1978? In what respects? Every social innovation modifies the social environment in which individuals must work out their destiny.

Social innovations, merely because they are innovations, have no special claim to represent an advance in the possibilities of freedom. Every social innovation has a certain coercive force to it, if only because members of the society must come to terms with it, and often because failure to accept innovations invites penalties. Do persons accept the sanctions involved in social innovations only if the development of freedom made possible outweighs the coercion imposed? Or do men fear freedom?

Freedom and coercion are not antagonistic but mutually interdependent. Without social constraints, there is no freedom. Without freedom, social constraints are forerunners of petrification and social death.

3. ARE INSTITUTIONS OBSOLETE?

When institutions work well we do not notice them. Their function is to enlarge our liberty by quietly making available its prerequisites. When an organization "hums smoothly," its members are free to attend to the purposes that drew them together. Even when institutions challenge our self-interest, we often accept them as given features of reality. What is the point of blaming the English language for the difficulties one has spelling many of its words? Who blames scientific organizations or schools because becoming a physicist demands long hours in the lab? It is no fault of friendship if selfishness, cattiness, or betrayal ends it. We do blame institutions, however, when they no longer serve the ends they were established for; when they don't produce the benefits they are needed for; when they are no longer needed but continue making demands of us; when they stand in the way of real and more important needs; etc. We become aware that we are living under institutions when they break down, become dysfunctional, experience obsolescence.

It is not by accident that when many hear the word "institution" today they think "obsolete" and "dehumanizing." Many key institutions (government, law, medicine, religion, education, publishing, broadcasting, sports, etc.) serve values we no longer rate so highly; serve our values badly; or demand too high a cost for too few benefits. Institutions are intended to be among the things "taken for granted." A social "crisis" is occasioned by the discovery that what has heretofore been taken for granted must be brought under scrutiny and transformed. Existing institutions are failing and the quiet organic birth of new ones is now proceeding.

It is difficult merely to "invent" new institutions. The fundamental institutions of a way of life are intimately connected to the consciousness of their members, which they shape and by which, in turn, they are shaped. To institute a new curriculum in a university, you cannot simply pass new legislation, reorganize procedures, assign new course titles, etc. If the teachers continue with the same attitudes they had before, or if the students maintain the same attitudes they had before, new curricula will soon be the old curricula in new packages. The life of consciousness, tutored by institutions, develops laws of its own, which institutions (new or established) alter only slowly if at all. The life of consciousness is based upon the long, social, and personal acquisition of habits, skills, purposes, the experience of success and reversal, adaptation to new demands, and the like. One can easily "engineer" opinions and fleeting attitudes; but it is hard to move people who lack certain skills, and who maintain whole sets of insights, resistances, and purposes of their own.

Two temptations are powerful among Western theoreticians on these matters. One is to think of the intractability of human affairs as evidence of the "irrationality" of traditions. People should be more pragmatic, flexible, reasonable—and less attached to the habits, skills, and experiences of their past. A corollary of this view is that people are fundamentally individuals, self-directed and open to "reason," needing only to be "awakened from their dogmatic slumbers." To hold on to views or affections that are "merely" traditional is not nearly so admirable as to "question" everything and to be "open-minded."

The second temptation is to regard the individual as totally conditioned by economic and other institutions. No matter what the individual perceives, thinks, or chooses, its source lay not in her but in her "conditioning."[22] These two temptations—that the individual is reasonable and free, that institutions wholly determine her actions—have not yet been resolved in Western social thought.[23]

In the interim, two complementary principles may be recalled. First, the identity of a person cannot be defined without reference to the institutions under which he lives. All such institutions influence his experiences, perceptions, understandings, actions. Secondly, the person is not exhaustively defined by a list of the institutions under which he lives. A person is somehow more than the sum of social pressures. Although a person cannot escape living in institutions as his natural habitat, he gives more or less of himself to them, derives more or less strength from them, plays one off against another, to some extent chooses under which ones he will live. As Sartre puts it: *Valéry is a petit-bourgeois; but not every petit-bourgeois is Valéry.*[24] An adequate theory must be thoroughly concrete. And in the end concreteness means singularity: the uniqueness of the person. Many human beings do not, perhaps, attain to much singularity. Men and women of genius do. The rest of us no doubt resemble one another far more than we—with our ideology about how unique each is—would like to recognize.

And yet, somehow, the life of each utters in history a word voiced by no other.

4. THE NEW HETERONOMY

In the past, when theologians spoke of the meaning of prayer, they tended to speak of what prayer meant to theologians. Techniques for finding out what prayer meant to the great mass of people out in the pews (not to say in the society at large) were hardly developed. The modern empirical sciences have given students of religious studies a new possibility: they can examine the phenomena of religion not according to what they *should be,* or according to scripture, doctrine, and tradition, but according to what they *are,* descriptively. What do people *actually* believe? What, in fact, is their behavior like? How do they actually understand the traditional words their lips express?

In their great formative figures—Weber, Durkheim, Freud—the social sciences tended to "explain away" religion, by reducing it to something else.[25] Religious needs were not primal and original, but "really" expressions of some more fundamental impulse: the need for security, for a father, for community, etc. To this day, great and violent angers sometimes flash forth between students of religious studies and students of the social sciences.[26] The methods of the scientific observer are, for many persons,[27] more than methods merely. They are a way of life. They constitute a sense of reality. They function as the ultimate symbols for a defense of human reason, and even for a defense of human society against totalitarianisms of many sorts. The institutions of science —universities, research institutes, academies, professional societies, and the like—are thought to embody a method that is more pure, more noble, more precious than anything else to be found in human life. For some, science is sacred, for it is the organ of reason itself. And reason through the canons of science discerns what is real and what is not. For some, science is the access to reality.

What would happen, we may wonder, if science filled the place in a culture which some other religion had filled before? What would happen if the center of a culture were science? If science provided the sense of reality, story ("progress through chemistry"), and symbols ("enlightenment") of a society? To raise such questions frees our minds in one respect. It allows us to see that while cult may be the center of culture, the cult in question need not derive from one of the historical world religions.

Talcott Parsons, the great American sociologist, has argued throughout a lifetime of reflection that "society is a religiously based moral order."[28] To put this phrase in our own vocabulary: A selected sense of reality, set of stories, and set of symbols—i.e., a culture—find expression in social institutions. These social institutions generate roles, sanctions, and expectations. The institutions work if and only if the persons involved have some degree of trust in one another and in the institutions—otherwise, only brute force would keep them together. If each person is a wolf toward every other,[29] not society but chaos ensues; all energies are absorbed by mutual war. Thus, it is not force that keeps a society together, or keeps institutions functioning, but a "moral order"; i.e., shared values, in which all freely concur, to whose exercise each person commits himself.[30] Citizens can rely upon one another. Such reliance frees each from the tasks of self-defense. The phrase "moral order" suggests that the most powerful ingredient in a society is not money, nor power, nor influence, but the values whose acceptance makes money, power, and influence operational. War, revolution, and other forms of turmoil render the possessors of money, power, and influence vulnerable. The "hard facts" on which they tend to think their security is based depend for their solidity upon the symbols which give them "legitimacy."

The symbols which constitute the "moral order" are "religiously based" in the sense that when persons act, their actions "tell a story." That is, action always has implicit within it the agent's sense of who he is, where he is, what his situation is, how his action affects that situation, what direction his action is carrying him in, etc. In a word, action implies a view of the world. The fundamental fact about action is the imagined story that gives it shape. A person who is acting out the story of "the advance of science" discriminates accordingly what to do and what not to do, the manner of his acting, its satisfactions and disappointments, and its consequences. To participate in such a story, is what is meant by being religious. A culture that is wholly "secularized," i.e., based not at all upon belief in God, nor upon the stories of Christianity or Judaism, is, in our neutral sense, a suitable object for religious studies.

But Parsons adds a further refinement to his notion of society. *"Society is a religiously based moral order characterized by congruence between the cultural, structural, and personality levels of the social system."*[31] The sense of reality, stories, and symbols which constitute the culture are "reflected" in the social institutions of the society. And they are also "reflected" in the personalities of the participants. But a serious question has arisen about this "congruence"[32] in American society today. The American social system is, in one sense, very loosely held together; in another sense, it is incredibly intertwined and compacted.

Individuals in American society appear to be astonishingly free to *choose* the sense of reality, stories, and symbols they are living out, more or less independently of the culture's "official" sense of reality, stories, and symbols. They choose more or less independently of the family, church, job, political party, or other institutions to which they belong; and even more or less independently of the sense of reality, stories, and symbols they held last year, or in some other situation, or in some other segment of their lives. It is true, of course, that both the traditions of Judaism and Christianity and those of the Enlightenment announce in advance that American culture, American social institutions, and the American image of personal freedom *should* promote such radical individualization. It is not *against* the fundamental American sense of reality, stories, and symbols that individuals should become their *own* centers of reality.[33]

But the theory of "congruence" is placed under special stress.[34] For it appears that what *my* sense of reality, stories, and symbols are may *not* be "reflected" in those of any single institution in which I live, or in those of the culture as a whole. Individuals belong to many institutions, and tend to give all their allegiance to no one of them. Thus the sense of reality, stories, and symbols that inform my actions have no one social, institutional, or cultural base.[35] So "loose" is the tie between culture, institutions, groups, and personality that one might just as well speak of "incongruence" as "congruence."

On the other hand, now that my sense of reality, stories, and symbols find their basis more directly in my own autonomy rather than in some social or institutional center, what leverage do I have to criticize or to direct the moral shape of institutions? Sense of reality, stories, and symbols tend to become *private* rather than social or public. The "system"—government, industry, technology, university, and even my own family—seems to roll on independently of my sense of reality, stories, and symbols. And by what right, even if I so desired, could I insist that it be altered to suit *my* values?

Thus there is a new, odd form of "alienation" spreading throughout modern society. Insofar as the ideal of personal autonomy is realized, the social system itself seems to elude the capacity of individual persons (or even associations of persons) to make the system "congruent" with their own sense of reality, stories, symbols. The more autonomy they pursue, the less their hold upon their culture, their society, and its institutions. The more their culture, their society, and their institutions are brought into "congruence" with their own sense of reality, stories, symbols, the less freedom seems to be allowed to those whose sense of reality, stories, and symbols diverge from their own.

Thus individuals—if not openly, at least potentially—are at war with individuals, groups with groups. And probably everyone, without exception, feels that "the system" is out of his control—out of anyone's control. The pursuit of autonomy has brought us under a new heteronomy: we live under a law not our own. (Gr., *hetero* [other] + *nomos* [law]).[36]

Nevertheless, the system under which we live does embody a sense of reality, stories, and symbols *of its own*. For one thing, nearly all the institutions under which we live try to leave a "private space" within which individuals can formulate a sense of reality, stories, and symbols for themselves. Even the churches make as few serious and profound demands on the inner life of their members as they can. Many Americans change their church affiliations rather effortlessly. The relative peace and harmony of American life is bought at the price of disengaging the individual's sense of reality, stories, and symbols from any serious impact upon his institutions. When one enters a corporation, government position, university, school, church, association, job, one checks one's personal visions at the door.[37]

Almost never are Americans called upon to challenge one another on the serious value divisions between them—sometimes even in the family itself a great "gap" is silently allowed to take shape. There is a "conspiracy of silence" about those symbolic issues that divide Americans. In politics, on television, in the university, in public debate—almost everywhere internalized warning systems instruct Americans when they are treading near to "explosive" or "touchy" matters. A person's sense of reality is "his own private business." But if one person cannot engage another on *that* turf, how can either be genuinely "present" to the other? American society seems bent upon what Philip Slater calls "the pursuit of loneliness."[38] Even the Beatles cried out: "All the Lonely People!"

We could imagine a highly developed economic system in America, together with its greatly differentiated social possibilities, which, nevertheless, did not treat a person's sense of reality, stories, symbols as each person's own "private concern." People might be taught to feel restless until they felt they were truly in the "presence" of the other; i.e., until they began to participate in the sense of reality, stories, and symbols of the other. More attention might be paid to the physical scale of neighborhoods, schools, parishes, and other institutions, so that participants in them might more frequently than now explore one another's sense of reality, stories, and symbols.[39] Moreover, it could be accepted as an imperative that isolated autonomy is not the goal of a fully developed human life, but is, in fact, an aberration. Persons grow by learning from, criticizing, cherishing, and stimulating one another. A fully developed person has been given many perceptions, insights, judgments, and aspirations by other individuals, other communities; he is as much a "we" as an "I." Were we to emphasize the communal aspects of our experience —they are present throughout our experience, but are often screened out by our individualistic bias—we might be more careful than we have been to make our social institutions reflect our communal sense of reality, stories, and symbols.

To put the matter more harshly, however, we might notice that present American institutions *do* embody a sense of reality, stories, and symbols. These are, radically, the symbol of the "free market place"[40]—an impersonal mechanism designed to allow a maximum of private space to individuals. That symbol dominates American economics, "value free" universities, pluralistic political arrangements, and even that part of church life which appeals to the private heart and the private mind of each individual. The story Americans are encouraged to live out is that of "economic growth" (for the sake of growth), ethical *laissez-faire* ("Do whatever you wish—I don't care—so long as you don't injure others"), and private freedom from coercion or disturbance by others. American society is built upon a flight from others. Americans try to have as little to do with others as possible.[41] Mechanical procedures (ticket windows, subways, girls at cash registers, passengers on planes who do not speak to one another, automobiles that search for deserted beaches and quiet mountain retreats, etc.) are designed to allow Americans in most transactions to be as little "present" to other human beings as possible. That is real which is private.

The truth is, however, that the sense of reality, stories, and symbols embodied in contemporary economic institutions, in techniques of organization and management, and in the concern for functional rationality and efficiency are at war with the other senses of reality, other sets of stories, and other sets of symbols which we also live out. Moreover, these latter senses of reality, stories, and symbols are *also* institutionalized in American society. On the editorial pages of *The Wall Street Journal,* for example, one finds appeals to individualism and the market place, but also to teamwork, corporate pride, communal solidarity, and even to warm fellow feeling. In the small towns of the Midwest, opposing tendencies—to fierce individualism and to smothering communitarianism—vie for the soul of every citizen.

Our outer life is filled with conflict. Our inner life, as well, is torn by conflicting senses of reality, conflicting stories, conflicting symbols. Culturally, socially, and personally we are trying to have reality two ways at once.

5. SECULAR RELIGION

Some analysts argue that the *real* sense of reality, stories, and symbols in American life are secular, even though the "official" or "rhetorical" ones are religious.[42] Let us concede the point, for argument's sake. Still, the difficulty for individual persons is twofold. First, should they *bother* to integrate their lives, or should they merely play one role in one situation, another in another?[43] Secondly, if they do try to integrate their lives, what sense of reality, stories, and symbols shall they choose as their own?

The number of possibilities is not so great as one might imagine. The number of fundamental themes is not infinite; most choices are variations on one of the fundamental themes. No exhaustive list of such fundamental themes has, however, been attempted.

As I imagine the situation, there are perhaps twenty or thirty key motifs or values in various human cultures: honesty, brotherliness, strength, endurance, tough-mindedness, compassion, loyalty, and the like. Cultures differ in the selections they make from this finite set, in the way they rank their selections, and in the combinations or constellations they weave into the stories of their heroes. Moreover, the selections they glorify in the stories they tell *in words* may differ from those they honor by living *in their lives.* Businessmen today speak much of the "jungle" of competition and brave "enterprise," but live as though their key concerns were protection, security, insurance, and guarantees: big winners may be few but almost no one loses.

One side of our culture and our social system favors merely functional efficiency. Many who are critical of that aspect of our system remain, nevertheless, adamantly "secular." Many such, who dislike what "religion" stands for and would never apply the word to their own ultimate commitments, share one of several possible senses of reality, sets of stories, clusters of symbols. Take, for example, John Leotard, book reviewer for a major national magazine. He thinks of himself as an atheist, and he profoundly hates the complacency and pious moral certainty of the religious people he grew up with and still (too often) meets. Something inside him snaps when he hears a self-assured, religious tone of voice. Freedom, he thinks, means having the courage to face the void. But there is a paradox in his behavior. He is rather righteous about liberal causes; indignant at stupidity, injustice, fraud; eager to lend his energies whenever he can to the forces of progress and enlightenment. He hates the yahoos. On the other hand, he seems to claim that everything is relative, that no one knows for certain what is right or true, that we are lost in a vast darkness, that men are, like Prometheus, noblest when they hurl against their fate a thundering No!

If everything is relative, if there is no absolute good or evil, then why are yahoos wrong? Why is injustice out of place? Why care? And by what standard is "progress" measured, or "enlightenment" deemed better than darkness?

The fact is that Leotard has a way of picking out what is real in human experience and leaving behind what is insignificant, sham, unworthy of notice. He imagines himself living out a story of freedom, honesty, courage—of heresy, enlightenment, heroic dissent—in the vanguard of cultural advance. He alternates between exalting modern society (his heroes led the breakthroughs which made it possible: Voltaire, Hume, Paine, Russell) and excoriating what businessmen and bureaucrats have made of it. One of his favorite symbols is that of the lonely outsider, the dissenter, the powerless cultural heretic persecuted for his superior honesty and insight, opening the path for future generations. Another favorite symbol is that of the corruption of the culture of which he is a part, its venality and madness and confusion of values. He likes the feeling of anguish. When you look at him, of course, he seems well fed, well paid, self-assured, content, without anguish concerning values or his own lot. It is only *the others* that he hates, for being so certain of themselves. He is part of a large "adversary culture" (as Lionel Trilling calls it), whose sense of reality, stories, and symbols—granted certain sectarian and private differences—he comfortably shares.

In a word, Leotard has a quite defined standpoint from which to experience, understand, and act; a direction; a sense of where he stands in relation to other persons and, indeed, to universal history; screens of perception; and criteria for judgment. He belongs to no church or organization; recites no creed; takes part in no established rituals. Except that cocktail parties, openings, publication days, tendencies, trends, and causes give his life every bit as much symbolic significance and shape as any churchgoer gains.

Belonging to a church, then, is not the paradigm of what it is to have a standpoint. Each person needs a selector to break down the overwhelming floods of human experience into a livable sense of reality; a way of relating himself to his past and future, as well as to the past and future of the race; and sets of images to focus his revulsions, goals, aspirations, perplexities, loves, hates, actions. All these Leotard has. It is one of the tasks of religious studies to describe, analyze, locate, and evaluate such a standpoint.

Like Leotard, many others do not find God a helpful or necessary symbol for articulating their experience of life; nor the creeds, stories, and symbols of the churches. They do not share the sense of the sacred, at least not in any way that leads them to recognize a "transcendent" dimension in their experience. Their basic sense of reality derives from "reason" or "scientific method" or "modern consciousness." Their basic story is that of evolutionary progress, especially through knowledge and social reform. Their basic symbols are Prometheus, Sisyphus, the Nobel or Pulitzer Prize; "reason," "enlightenment," "freedom," "social justice," "honesty," "relativism," "process," and the like. They take as their task the dissolution and criticism of what is, in the name of a better world to come, or (if they are cynical about "progress") in the name of fearless honesty.

One other example may be illuminating. At a major university in the east, there is a professor of political science: let us call him Steel. He is highly admired by his peers and is a frequent aide and consultant to various administrations in Washington, of both parties. Steel was born a Methodist—his father, in fact, was a preacher—but he is now too busy and realistic a man to be concerned about religion. ("Atheist" would be too strong a word for his position; he simply holds that "God" is something we can have no proof about, one way or the other, and is in any case irrelevant to human decision-making.)

Some of the words Steel frequently uses in a pejorative way are "dogmatic," "metaphysical," "mystical," and "theological." Words he likes are "clean," "hard," "neat." He pictures his own chief skill as analytic: "Now, let's sort this matter out," "make a few distinctions," "unpack that concept," "see what's going on in this argument," "get a look at the available facts," "get the various strands stated clearly." He doesn't like arguments that are "sloppy," "messy," "loose." He is an enemy of "generalizations," "rhetoric," "large pronouncements." He likes to break things down into little, hard units, as if they were (say) atomic particles, and then to "play around with various possibilities" for awhile. He is delighted when his work allows him to make predictions which then are "confirmed" by events.

Steel likes to talk about the "power" of his method, and even the "beauty" of it. He prides himself on a certain "hardheadedness" and "tough-mindedness," and thinks of these qualities as yielding clarity, solidity, and power in the understanding of reality. He is occasionally disdainful of "preaching," "editorializing," "muddleheadedness," "softheadedness," "vague and woolly thinking," "moralizing," the "sneaking in of hidden values." He tries to make his own mental world as "realistic," "hard," "clear" as he can get it. He loves to map out "alternative scenarios," "options," "possible courses of action." He specializes in "doing his homework" by "working out" the administrative techniques, costs, funding, and estimated hard benefits of the alternatives he "maps out," so that the choice between alternatives will be both "informed" and "practical." He hates the accusation, which he often hears from his administrator friends in Washington, that academic political scientists live in an "ivory tower" and don't really understand the "nitty gritty," "nuts-and-bolts" realities of putting plans into operation. He himself uses the word "operational" a great deal and has contempt for too much "theorizing." He aims his own work at "the real world," and is delighted when administrators and other hardboiled men refer to him as "a realist." He loves that word.

The last thing Professor Steel would agree to about himself is that he lives according to a myth, a story, mere symbols. His whole life is an attempt to drive myth, story, and symbol as far out of his mind as is humanly possible. He struggles to keep his own work in the strong, bright light of cold analytic reason. He expends vast amounts of energy—only he appreciates how much —"keeping up with" journal articles, monographs, and obscure publications with the best available data, not only in his own field but in as large a range as he can conscientiously master. He hates to be challenged by those who have done less work on the hard data, who haven't "rubbed their noses in" the hard mass of facts. He resents being called a "technocrat" or a "slave of the system," but if it takes name-calling to get the really solid work done, then he'll put up with that, too. Because he knows, in his own mind and through his successes, that the real world runs on the hard data, and not according to the illusions of the well-meaning and the idealists. He leaves "norms," "values," and "ideals" to others, because such issues are invariably messy, formally insoluble, and ultimately matters of irrational preference. What *he* can do —and he takes it as the backbone of intelligent responsible citizenship—is grind out the grubby work which confronts hard-pressed administrators with clear, well-researched alternatives, allowing the calculated costs and benefits of his analysis to speak for themselves.

What, then, is Professor Steel's "sense of reality"? Among all the possibilities open to his perception, he favors those which can be broken down into clear, solid units. Preferably, they will be quantifiable in some way. His *selectivity* is quite marked. He "trains" his eye, his perceptions, his judgment, to "look for" certain factors among others. What justifies him in thinking that his selections offer a "real" or a "true" view of human life? That what he "comes up with" is subject to quantification, prediction, control. But, supposing that we do control those factors which he singles out, what justifies him in thinking that a world in which they are controlled is "better" than one in which they are not? And "better" in what respects? Is "control" over environment, society, and human affairs the highest human good? One among many other human goods? Which others?

The more questions one raises about Professor Steel's sense of reality, the more "messy" and "problematic" becomes its social utility. What kind of society would we have if Professor Steel's methods and sense of reality were universally adopted? Does what he calls "rationality" require for its comprehension the image of a world mechanism, whose operation he is trying to discern in order to gain mastery over it? Is his "sense of reality," then, in tune with other possible images of human society: e.g., a family, a community, a more or less anarchic conglomerate of interest groups, an arena of systemic conflict, of equilibrium, of evolutionary progress, of entropy?

In what story does Professor Steel believe himself to be taking part? He might view himself as part of an avant-garde of hard-headed, practical, scientific men who are building a more rational world, a more enlightened world, a world more under man's control than ever before. He might view himself as merely holding at bay the perennial irrationality of human affairs, building a dike against the ocean of destruction that might at any time engulf us. He might view himself as extending—not by preaching, but by hardheaded planning and execution—the benefits of techno-logical development to all the peoples of the world. He might view himself as part of the age-old struggle for world order against the voices of unreason, passion, and anarchy—an unsung hero who actually gets hungry mouths fed, while orators make fine speeches condemning "technocrats." "I can eliminate more suffering from more lives by getting authorization for the ship-ment of 100,000 bags of fertilizer to India," he once told a student, "than by all the meetings of all the S.D.S. chapters of the entire country."

The symbols which move Professor Steel's juices and keep his

driving, rigorous life upon its determined path are those of reason, realism, hardheadness, practicality, feasibility. He believes in
getting the world's work done—intelligently, critically, in ever
better and more inventive ways. When someone speaks analyti-
cally, clearly, operationally, he recognizes a brother. Fine
speeches and moral sentiments bore him. He has shifted the
meaning of "morality" to signify what constitutes hardheaded,
realistic, and responsible judgment; he can't stand "moralizers"
who pre-empt the word for their ill-thought-out, irresponsible
schemes. "Those who speak about morality are usually the most
immoral ones of all," he says grimly.

Professor Steel's sense of reality is his view of the world, his
myth. His story links the actions of his own life in a meaningful pattern of service and progress, and also links them into a
vision of the universal human project: a struggle for control,
for progress, for liberty. His symbols guide his loves, hates, re-
sentments, exhilarations, recognitions. All together govern his
development as a human being, inhibiting certain drives
and reactions (he abhors violent emotions or actions, e.g.),
reinforcing others.

Is Professor Steel the sort of man one would like to become?
Is his life an admirable model for one's own? Is it a high point
in human development, brought about by the limits which technology places upon human aspiration? In order to make a technological society work, aren't a great many persons like Professor
Steel indispensable? Are they slaves or free men? The new drones
or the highest, noblest types? Persons who sacrifice their own
lives for the benefit of the rest of us? Or the elite who benefit most
from the power their method produces? Would one like such men
as one's friends? Would one prefer a medieval prince? A Floren-
tine merchant? An Indian farmer? What depths of personality do
their lives reveal? Does their work enhance or inhibit their personal growth? By what cultural standards? Does their work account for the sense of reality which other persons have? Is their

sense of reality superior to the sense of reality of others? Are they at peace with themselves?

The sense of reality, the story, and the symbols espoused by Professor Steel are probably as antithetical to the sense of the sacred as it is possible for a human commitment to be. For the sense of the sacred arises from wonder at a presence sensed to be at work in the world, or from wonder at the complex depths and liberty of the human spirit. In one sense, neither of these sources of wonder is "relevant" to the project of analyzing and mastering the world. These sorts of wonder are systematically inhibited in Steel's life; they are neither "pragmatic" nor "empirical," but "mystical" and "subjective." Though he sometimes senses what such feelings might be like, Professor Steel rejects them in his own life as "soft" and "nonproductive." On the other hand, he sometimes feels so keen a satisfaction at a piece of work well done, and seems to hear the underlying rationality of human life (deeply buried) hum so audibly, that sweetness flows in his breast.

Must scientific method be accompanied by the sense of reality, story, and symbols which Professor Steel holds? He could, for example, believe that his methods did not provide an adequate sense of reality, but were well-designed for solving some of the problems of prediction, control, and management. His method could be taken, not as defining "reason" or the "rational," but as representing one of the employments of reason in one of its areas of concern. "Reality" could be taken to include not only what is "hard" but also what is "soft," not only what is "objective" but also what is "subjective," not only what is quantifiable but also what is not. And Professor Steel's "realism" would be seen to be not a realism concerning the whole situation of man in the world but a "managerial realism," based on that limited range of human enterprises bounded by what is institutionally feasible (given modern bureaucratic assumptions) in the practicable future.

In a word, it is important to distinguish American culture's sense of reality, stories, and symbols from its commitment to science and technology. Conceived of as performing a limited, instrumental function in human life, science and technology are not in themselves opposed, for example, to the sense of the sacred, to a high valuation of human persons, to the sense of human community, or to humanistic values. Taken, on the other hand, as a measure of reality, as the main thread in the human story, and as the matrix of primary symbols, science and technology function as a complete, total, and exclusive standpoint. They select what we (when we are at our best, when we are faithful) shall experience, perceive, think, and do. They become our myth, our religion, our identity, our destiny. In proportion as our culture trusts science and technology to measure its sense of reality, story, and privileged symbols it lives according to a new selection among human possibilities, reaps certain human advantages, and suffers certain human liabilities. The primitive sense of family and community seems to break up, for example, and solitariness, alienation, and anomie seem to grow; but wealth, mobility, power, education, and certain types of liberty expand.

Basic cultural myths tend to promote the emergence of individuals in their own image. To the analytic units that Professor Steel looks for there correspond the solitary individuals among whom he lives. To the quest for the power to predict and control there correspond persons aware of being manipulated. To the image of a machine whose mechanism has to be analyzed and mastered there corresponds the self viewing itself as a mechanism to be analyzed and controlled, divided between the self that analyzes and controls and the self that is analyzed and controlled.[44] To the realism of data and objective analysis there corresponds the self that restrains impulse, fantasy, laziness, indulgence, emotion, passion, autobiography, wonder, worship, reverence and other "merely subjective" factors in the effort to live a "rational" and "objective" life. In the culture and in individuals, producing supplants loving. Doing supplants being. Knowledge as analysis supplants knowledge as harmony. Knowledge as control supplants knowledge as ignorance. Professor Steel lives out a remarkable personal myth, made in the image and likeness of a remarkable culture myth.

6. THE COMMUNAL IMAGINATION

The family used to be, and still is, the matrix in which infants are given the initial shapes according to which they thenceforward *experience* and *perceive.* The church used to be, but probably is not now, the chief matrix in which the *imagination* of children is tutored. From ritual, liturgy, action, festival, symbol, and story, the child once learned the structure of the human drama. Today, the influences upon the imagination are more numerous—if, indeed, the imagination is not simply atrophying year by year.[45] Chief among these influences are the new media of the last three generations: newspapers, radios, cinema, and television.

Human beings used to accept the fact that life is mainly routine: slow, lazy, and accurately described in the phrase, *"Naw, ain't nothin' much happens round here."* For most of human history, "news" was a relatively rare arrival, and came mainly from unpredictable "acts of God."[46] Newspapers came into existence hardly more than a hundred years ago, eventually began to appear daily, later began to print reports upon local and distant events, gradually began to be able to appear in more than one edition a day. As usual, capacity led to need: They *did* appear in more than one edition, and *required* "news" to fill their capacity.

Radio stations all across the dial soon began to fill eighteen or twenty-four hours a day, and they too needed material to fill their needs. Then several television channels in each locality also began to need material to fill the maw of eighteen or twenty hours of empty time a day. An audience, moreover, had to be persuaded that it needed and wanted what human beings never had before: "news"—and on the instant. People came to expect that exciting things are happening somewhere all day long—as if it only takes ace reporters to find them. Reporters have been sent out to scour the earth. When "news" is lacking—for the world is, after all, rather routine, slow, and lazy—ways of "inventing" news are soon devised. Press conferences, interviews, leaks, handouts, public-relations gimmicks, "backgrounders," and countless other devices make it unnecessary for reporters to wait until events occur. They prompt them or willingly entertain their invention by others.

The impact of the new media upon the human sense of reality, story, and symbols is profound. When John Stuart Mill wrote his famous essays *On Liberty,* [47] he could imagine the independent, relatively isolated landholder receiving his weekly packet of mail from London. In an independent and leisurely way the landholder could evaluate the events which concerned his interests. Today, four key features in that situation have altered.

1. Events in every part of the world daily affect *his destiny.* (A generation ago, how many Americans—who died there, or found wartime inflation cutting into their resources—could have distinguished Vietnam from Siam, Burma, Indonesia?)

2. His chief access to the *information* on which he bases his judgments are the media.

3. *The images and context* in which the data are presented to him are also provided by the media. Further, these *enter into his own psyche, emotions, intelligence.* There is hardly any place to escape from sights, sounds, images. Only a handful today shares physical and spiritual isolation comparable to that of the English landholder citizen of the nineteenth century.

4. The model of what counts as *reasonable, responsible, mainstream* discourse is established by the media. "Tiger Cages" existed in Vietnamese prisons and were known about long before the media "broke" the story in early July, 1970. But who noted or believed the assertions before then? Those assertions are responsible, reasonable, credible for general consumption which

are asserted by television commentators.

The media provide not only the *data* on which judgments are to be based; and not only the images, context, and tone within which the data are to be assimilated; they also provide the *model* for "calm, objective, cautious" judgment. They define what the conventional mainstream wisdom is; those who disagree are thrown on the defensive. To accumulate the proof necessary to overthrow a view announced on television (without supporting proof) may require weeks of research; by then, the story is too "cold" to receive a second hearing. If officials make an announcement—on battle casualties in Vietnam, e.g.—their word is taken as true until proven false, even when their announcement is full of inconsistencies and implausibilities. The research to prove it fake is extremely difficult. Even though the evidence for an official's claims is extremely shaky or nonexistent, his solemn and responsible tone of voice will carry for many as the public truth.

Television, however, does provide a subversive and cynical sense of reality. Switch the channel and you switch realities. Turn on the tube and you engage a set of values quite different from your own. Listen to the endless, calm, controlled, superficial talk and your sense of what a good argument is withers. Watch important matters interrupted for silly, singing commercials and your confidence in intelligence weakens. Grow up with the smooth figures of television heroes more prominent in your psyche than the crotchety, live persons of a large, extended family, and real concrete life may seem like a dream. Sit among the televised consumer goods of the upper middle classes, and look through cameras directed by men of the middle classes, and the realities of poverty and terror will be invisible and remote.

There is a creeping nihilism in the media. Except rarely, their voice is "value free" and noncontroversial. When they do become controversial, they seldom penetrate more deeply than "opinion." The dimension of the sacred cannot, simply cannot, be presented in them except in very rare moments of death, perplexity, and anguish. Everything is dragged toward the level of a new, improved soap. Especially on television, resistance against the downward drag is difficult; trying too hard makes viewers uneasy. Even in print, too forced a style (Tom Wolfe) soon cloys.

The media sometimes seem to be an almost flawless expression of the scientific and secular standpoint: techniques made possible and invented by modern society as the crown of its pursuit of "communication." Questions of values and standpoints seldom arise. There is little dialectic. The address is simple. The pretense of objectivity and rationality is maintained. The ties between commerce and science are apparent not only during up-to-the-minute commercials but also during the inoffensive talk in between. George Bernanos once conceived that the lips of preachers in the pulpit flap like a hen's ass. The flatulence of the media may be as embarrassing to men of secular hope as that of preachers to men of religious hope.

7. THE REALITIES OF ECONOMICS

Consider the following chart:

The family	shapes	*experiencing*
Church and *media*	shape	*imagining*
Schools	shape	*understanding*
Economics	shapes	*judging*
Government	shapes	*acting*

No matter how sensitive the family, idealistic the church, informative the school, someday young people enter the "real" world. What conditions the real world? Scarcity. The necessity to work for a living. The need for money. "Now we're getting down to the nitty gritty." "The gut issue is the pocketbook." Money, Norman Podhoretz[48] has proclaimed, is the "dirty little secret" of American society; among intellectuals one can say anything about sex, but money is spoken of discreetly. The vast majority of university students are in school for economic reasons.

Marx, then, was not far from the truth when he argued that the sense of reality of a given culture is determined by its economic system. The economic system is the basic instrument of survival and well-being. Until problems of hunger, shelter, and subsistence are solved, there are no arts; there is no leisure for institutions of knowledge. Not only that: The economic system also distributes the goods of survival and well-being, and establishes fundamental roles and identities. Who are to be slaves? Who free? Who laborers? Who artisans? What sort of mobility is there between roles? What laws or customs establish the rights of all (child labor, just wage)? Who owns the land, the goods, the fruits of labor? What governs the equity of distribution? Does the system stratify people in classes? What are the instruments and the mechanisms of exchange? Does the system depend upon and reinforce trust or distrust, division or community, personhood or mere instrumentalism? Does it depend upon foreign wars, domestic scapegoats, slaves or near-slaves? Do the daily economic transactions which people exercise reinforce their respect for one another as persons, or the image of a jungle in which each person takes care of himself? Fierce and cutthroat competition or mutuality and cooperation?

An economic system has built into its daily operations an image of man. It is a reality-constructing system. It teaches men in practice how to regard one another, whatever their beautiful theories might be. An economic order, in short, is the most effective sort of theological construct. Preaching and ideology are only partly significant; what counts is who gets what, when, how. The "real world" in which the economic system induces people to live (among all possible real worlds) is a world of assigned inputs, rewards, roles, strategies, attitudes, skills.

American schools, usually announce that their aim is to form "the whole man." Why, then, are almost all examinations in the schools directed at testing two skills only, how well students can store information and how well they can analyze it? Are not these skills precisely the ones most imitable by machines? Are they not perfectly geared to producing the workers and managers of a machine-based economy? The schools, in short, take their sense of reality from the economic system of which they are a part. They form the young to fit the system, and necessarily so. How could a society survive if its economic institutions were not passed on from generation to generation? An economic system does not claim to be the best *possible* system but only the best *available*. It does not, except in moments of ideological rhapsody, claim to be *ideal*, but only to correspond best to *realities*. "It would be nice if money weren't needed but . . ."

No theological analysis is complete, therefore, unless it includes an economic analysis. For the American economic system to function, many eager young people must be recruited who are: (a) committed to hard work; (b) able to suppress their own feelings and fantasies and make hardheaded decisions; (c) willing to compete fiercely with one another; (d) strongly motivated to find better ways of doing things, more efficient procedures, new products, new markets, etc.; (e) easy to get along with, regular fellows and girls; and (f) loyal to the organization, and good team members. They ought to be both independent, rugged individualists and gregarious, courteous co-workers, loyal to the corporate task.

Given the sense of reality, the stories, and the symbols implied by such an economic system, how could its participants be serious Christians or Jews? What patterns of selection would "reality" oblige them to impose upon their understanding and practice of the earlier Christian and Jewish ways of life? Can Buddhism survive—or even be understood—in an industrial civilization? Is an economic system as differentiated and all-absorbing as the American system not itself a type of religion, fashioning a new type of person, a new sense of reality, a new kind of story to live out with one's life, a new set of symbols? Is "the new industrial state" (John Kenneth Galbraith[49]) a more difficult soil in which to root Christianity or Judaism than the soil of feudalism, mercantilism, or eighteenth-century capitalism?

Another set of questions: Under a given economic order, how *genuine* can one's efforts be to live according to a different, dissenting sense of reality? How far can one go in resisting the sense of reality imposed by the roles, tasks, and procedures of the system? Is resistance automatically "unrealistic" and "romantic"? Or more "real" than conformity?

8. POLITICAL REVOLUTION

Nations like the United States have, by and large, solved the problems of differentiating the church from the institutions of government. They have fared far less well in separating the church from economic realities. The same weakness that has overcome the churches also overpowers modern governments. Although politics is supposed to be the realm of institutions which govern the national way of life, the economic system, in fact, seems to govern the political system. It is not simply that in order to get elected, a man needs vast sums of money.[50] It is not even that *the same persons* with the same interests pass interchangeably between business, the military, and government, so that these three are like one huge tent with separate entrances.[51] It is also that a huge bureaucracy with an unparalleled budget has grown up around the Department of Defense.[52] The economic, bureaucratic interests represented by that budget tend to govern the direction not only of American foreign policy but also of American domestic life.[53] They determine what "the realities" of American life are.

The impact of bureaucratic institutions is spiritual and governs perceptions, judgments, actions. It is not merely that bureaucracies are more powerful than individuals. It is rather that, in order to be effective within them, individuals must share the perceptions, judgments, ways of acting that obtain results. They must begin to alter their prior sense of reality, story, symbols. "No man can serve two masters." Modern corporations are not merely instruments to which one gives a part of one's life. They tend to be all-absorbing not through totalistic dedication but through dividing one's personal autonomy from one's corporate role. They divide one's creativity, imagination, feelings, and hopes from one's performance for the company. They fashion one's soul by dividing it. There is "bureaucratic truth," "the inside story," "what really happened." There is a policy, a position, an attitude regarding almost everything, from dress to opinions to sexual deviance. "Unorthodox" professional methods must meet the same criteria as orthodox ones: effectiveness. In one's private life, meanwhile, one may discreetly do whatever one likes.

Religious studies, therefore, involve a study of the sense of reality, stories, and symbols involved in the large bureaucracies of modern life: the Department of State,[54] the Department of Defense,[55] the Curtis Publishing Company,[56] General Motors, the Peace Corps,[57] the Presbyterian church. A student also needs to know the effects of community schools, communes,[58] and other institutional forms upon the sense of reality, stories, and symbols of their participants.

Religious experience arises in every kind of political order, in every age of human history. But the significance, expression, and practical effect of such experience is heavily conditioned by the political order in which it occurs. Religious experience tends to debunk the seriousness of economic and political institutions; it tends to place them in a light in which they appear less than "real." Thus, even when religious experiences incline people to support the established order (as they often do), they are frequently regarded by practical persons as dangerous. Without some claim to transcendent justification—whether from God, the cosmos, fate, history, or the future—governments cannot demand of their subjects (as they must) strenuous efforts, total loyalty, and the sacrifice of life itself. Legitimacy comes from transcendent sources. Governments, therefore, have always tried to get priests, prophets, mystics, and transcendent symbols on their side. Machiavelli, Cavour, Napoleon, Eisenhower, Kennedy, and Nixon on such matters are at one. "In God we trust" is a symbol as ancient and inevitable as Khrushchev's pounding his shoe at the United Nations and claiming that "history" would vindicate the superiority of Communism.

Every religious word is understood in a concrete social and political location. To speak of "obedience" to slaves and to free men is to mean different courses of action. To speak of "despair" to men chained in barbed-wire prisons is to use a word that would be understood quite differently by women at a suburban literary tea. To speak of "faith" to young Germans in clandestine seminaries in Nazi Germany in 1939 was to catch meanings in the word one had not understood before.[59] To speak of "god" to honest and courageous men who hate that word is to search deeper for the meaning of honesty and courage in human life than one was wont to search. To speak from one's study of "carrying one's cross" is, unavoidably, to sound false to those who feel the humiliation and grinding injustice of being black in a racist society like South Africa, or in the United States. For a professor to speak of "rational discourse" to students who do not know who he is but only what his objective, professional voice says is to plead for what he does not practice.

In proportion as a woman steeps herself, or a man himself, in the sense of reality, stories, symbols of the Jewish and Christian tradition, she feels a tension arising between them and the sense of reality, stories, symbols of her culture.[60] The same is true of the humanist in a technological society, or of a person committed wholly to science in a society as irrational as ever. Thus almost every standpoint involves its participant in an ambivalent relationship with his or her economic and political institutions. Almost everyone wants to deal with "the real world" and not merely with wishes; at the same time, almost everyone is less than at peace with the status quo. From one standpoint, moreover, another standpoint often seems immoral, immature, or uncivilized. Thus political and economic argument often enkindles religious passion, and the thought of burning one's opponents alive is sometimes repressed, one imagines, only with difficulty.

Political and economic institutions are the institutional, pragmatic expression of a sense of reality, stories, and symbols. A student of religious studies must, then, raise pointed questions about them. It is a tricky matter to separate political and economic institutions from religious institutions. It is, moreover, not certain that the human experiences which keep alive the sense of the transcendent in human life are well expressed by churches. Thus the profoundly religious struggle is not between churches and political-economic institutions. It is between the human spirit and *all* institutions, between the human spirit and its natural habitat. Institutions are the normal, natural expression of the human spirit. But that spirit is self-transcending. It is never satisfied with its own finite expressions. It is always a wayfarer moving out from the safe light of existing institutions into the unknown. No sooner is a routine established than the spirit breaks out of it. It does so on the strength of the perceptions, insights, and skills in which it was tutored by its institutions. The point of institutions, in short, appears to be to yield to new and better institutions. The sign of a healthy institution is the goodly number of prophetic and dissenting spirits encouraged by it. For institutions endure by changing often. They thus more closely approximate, as time goes by, "the perfect age" humans seem everywhere to seek. Unless, that is, those non-Western standpoints are correct, according to which there is no such reality as progress, but only endless cycles of rise and decline.

9. CIVIL RELIGION

So far, we have perhaps stressed too much the ways in which American society is secular. There are also ways in which the institutions of American society—and surely the consciousness of many American citizens—are "religious" in yet another sense. American culture, American society, and American personalities seem to be divided. In part Americans live by the sense of reality, stories, and symbols of rational efficiency; in part, by the sense of reality, stories, and symbols of a civil religion. This civil religion is an amalgam rooted in national history.

In "sacral" societies, there are sacred places, holy days, public festivities of participation in the life of the gods.[61] The "depth dimension"[62] of human life is re-created in recurrent form. Certain persons are assigned specific roles in representing the sacred before the public. In "pluralistic" societies, by contrast, no one form of recognizing the sacred has general acceptance. Hence, a differentiation is introduced between the civil functions of the community and the sacral functions; there is a "separation" between church and state.[63] With the rise of science and technology as a new sense of reality, a new story, a new set of symbols, however, pluralistic societies are often in tension with another ideal: that of the "secular" standpoint we have already discussed.

In the secular standpoint, reality is bounded by what is subject to scientific method and pragmatic control. The sense of the sacred, insofar as it attaches to a transcendent presence like that of God or gods, is regarded as an irrational projection from primitive fears, infantile oceanic feelings, the need for a father, etc.[64] The business of understanding and controlling the human environment and human societies is the central focus of all institutional effort. Churches are tolerated as primitive residues which may, nevertheless, make a useful social contribution among those who need them.[65] Or else, churches are regarded as dangerous, regressive institutions whose demise should be speeded by all legitimate means, especially by education and "rational" inquiry.[66] In Marxist theory and practice, in particular, the secular state recognizes quite frankly that its new sense of reality, stories, and symbols are in direct contradiction to those of the churches.

Still, a sense of reality is not merely a set of abstract principles, a bureaucracy, a party, and offices full of economic plans. Hence, both secular states and pluralistic states develop stories and symbols by which to direct the experiences, perceptions, images, and aspirations of their people. As we now know, however, stories and symbols are not merely propaganda to incite emotions and to catalyze actions. On the contrary, they also supply the imaginative context, the sense of direction, and the focus of attention within which the intelligence discerns "facts," invents hypotheses and policies, and seeks verifications. Without story and symbol, the intelligence cannot function. The function of story and symbol is not, then, merely emotional and directed toward action: it is also intellectual, and directed toward theory and policy.

Avowedly secular states like Russia and China develop sacred writings, heroes, stories, dramatic presentations, parades, salutes, and festivities of all sorts in order to channel and deepen attention and direction. Pluralistic states like the United States, Great Britain, South Africa, Japan, and others have a delicate problem. Commonly, they try to wed the sense of reality, story, and symbols of science, technology, and a thisworldly approach to government to a set of more transcendent values. They develop a hybrid which has come to be called "civil religion."[67]

Robert N. Bellah pointed out in an important paper that "there actually exists alongside of and rather clearly differentiated from the churches an elaborate and well institutionalized civil religion in America."[68] He added: "This religion—or perhaps better, this religious dimension—has its own seriousness and integrity and requires the same care in understanding that any other religion does."[69] It is, however, very easy to misunderstand the notion of civil religion.[70] For one thing, the word "religion" for many educated Americans connotes the strict institutional structure of churches and sects, whose clear sets of coherent, substantive beliefs impose tests of mental orthodoxy upon their membership, prescribe or prohibit behavior, and establish recognizable rituals. Religion, in this view, is one institution among many, one clearly articulated view of reality among many. The genius of the liberal, secular modern era has been to separate religion, so conceived, from the organs of the state. To study religion, then, is to study a defined organization, its orthodox doctrines, its code of behavior, its rituals, and the attitudes it engenders.

Bellah, however, has given the word "religion" a quite different, more profound, and more illuminating meaning; no doubt that is why he shifted in the second sentence quoted above: "religion—or perhaps better, *this religious dimension*. . . ." Religion, Bellah has written in another place, is "a set of symbols" which "define in broadest terms the nature of reality."[71] The "central function of religion" is "to provide stable points of reference for human action."[72] The standpoint worked out in this book, though arrived at independently, owes some debt to Bellah's work. All societies, we want to say, all patterns of human action, depend upon a sense of reality, a set of stories, a set of symbols, and in this sense at least have a religious (even if agnostic, atheistic, unchurchlike) dimension. All societies and all patterns of action on the part of individuals imply an image of universal reality, a vision of which way human development, evolution, and superiority incline. To have an identity is to stand in contrast with others. To act is to select which values to realize, which to inhibit.

Bellah's point is that traumatic and vivid experiences in living out "the American experiment" have generated a sense of reality, direction, and perception that have a differentiated, clear, effective form in the behavior of Americans. He does not argue that the *churches* supply this form. Quite the opposite: civic experiences and institutions supply it. Moreover, the form is not supplied by a diffuse "cultural piety" or "residual set of values" left over from Christian and Jewish origins. Again quite the opposite: these forms were supplied by concrete historical experiences, newly invented rituals (inaugurations, Thanksgiving Day, etc.), sacred spokesmen, implicitly defined perceptions and possibilities ("I will not be the first president to lose a war"), and roles and institutions that are specifically American.

Moreover, the American civil religion is not merely venal. "The American civil religion is not the worship of the American nation but the understanding of the American experience in the light of ultimate and universal reality."[73] Bellah stresses the critical distance implicit in the American experience:

> Behind the civil religion at every point lie biblical archetypes: Exodus, Chosen People, Promised Land, New Jerusalem, Sacrificial Death, and Rebirth. But the civil religion is also genuinely American and genuinely new. It has its own prophets and its own martyrs, its own sacred events and sacred places, its own solemn rituals and symbols. It is concerned that America be a society as perfectly in accord with the will of God as men can make it and a light to all the nations.

> In times past the American civil religion has often been used and is being used today as a cloak for petty interests and ugly passions. It is in need—as is any living faith—of continual reformation, of being measured by universal standards. But it is not evident that our civil religion is incapable of growth and new insight.[74]

The United States is not the only nation that understands its experience through the creation of a civil religion. The pattern has become common in "secular" states. Bellah sees the crisis of the present[75] as a struggle to find the forms of "a world civil religion"—a sense of reality, a set of stories, and a set of symbols growing out of the historical experiences of all the peoples of the planet, and given institutional expression. Without such a religion, senses of reality diverge; basic stories head toward confron-

tation; diverse basic symbols lead to radically different perceptions and schemes of action.

From the moon, the earth appeared a single blue-brown ball;
the Olympic games bring the eyes of all nations to one focus; the
image of life on other planets and the science-fiction image of
cybernetic successors to mankind make humans feel their own
vulnerability as one single race; local wars ever threaten to involve the world. We are not lacking symbols emphasizing that
humans on this planet form one human race, struggling to survive.

A planetary culture is emerging. We may expect the emergence
of a sort of universal consciousness, a planetary standpoint. If the
world sense of reality, stories, symbols, and institutions reflect the
values of human community, the diversity of cultures and traditions, the primacy of the person, a sense of historical responsibility for one another and for the planet, and an openness to new
achievements of liberty, justice, truth, and beauty, the world civil
religion will not be a denial of the values of the concrete major
religions. It will lay new challenges upon them and bring about
transformations within them, as has every other era of world
history. But the world civil religion, presumably, will be as different from the major world religions—Hinduism, Buddhism, Judaism, Christianity, and Islam—as American civil religion is from
Christianity and Judaism.

The difficulty, of course, is how to realize both diversity and
unity. The people of the United States have not succeeded in that
task. Insofar as Americans cherish their smaller community identities (fundamentalists, hippies, ethnic groups), they have tended
to generate bitter antagonisms. On the other hand, the imposition
of universal values—even of liberty and justice for all, in full
equality—tends to be bitterly resisted. How can there be liberty
and justice for all, without the loss of diversity?

One difficulty arises because advances in liberty and justice in
American society have tended to become intermingled with ad-

vances in urbanization and standardization. The rational efficiency of industry has been used as a spiritual ally in the cause of civil rights. But the ally is a trojan horse. For the rational efficiency of industry not only imposes "higher" values like liberty and justice upon somewhat reluctant local communities. It also brings with it bulldozers, urban planning, pollution, a disruption of natural communities, and a rather deplorable homogenization of external landscape and internal imagination. Whereas liberals tend to notice the spiritual progress which their social power represents, those who feel themselves so forcibly obliged to become enlightened tend to count the losses they suffer. In a word, the institutional carriers of universal values like "liberty and justice for all" tend in American society to be carriers of malevolent and destructive social forces as well.

"Liberty and justice for all" are not, in principle, in conflict with a diversity of communities. One can imagine a nation in which people of diverse traditions, cultures, histories, and languages—of diverse senses of reality, stories, and symbols—live in fundamental equality, in liberty, and in justice. One can imagine them proud of their diversity. One can imagine them eager to share in the richness and variety of that diversity, rather than defensive, suspicious, protective, and aggressive.

The "universal" *values* to which the American civil religion is committed are not "universal" in the sense of "everywhere standardizing and homogenizing." They are, on the contrary, compatible with the utmost diversity. The question is whether an *economy* and a *polity* based upon rational efficiency are compatible with diversity. Are the U.S. economy and polity compatible with liberty and justice? For it may be that they take back with one hand what they give with the other.

The crisis in American culture may arise because the rational efficiency on which technological progress has so far been based represents, once a certain threshold has been passed, not progress, but a slow and stifling death for all things human.

FIVE

Organizations

Religious experience does not always find expression in churches. A primitive society as a whole may function as an expression of a sacred order. A state may try to be both secular and sacred, as the Soviet Union has tried to do. In many world cultures, there are no highly differentiated "religious organizations," and every aspect of life is simultaneously religious and secular.[1] The Western pattern of organization, in which religious organizations are distinguished from political and economic organizations, is not wholly satisfactory. Religion easily gets confined to church on Sundays. On the other hand, the "sacred cosmos" implicit in secular activities goes unexamined because "theological" inquiry is methodically ruled out as "irrelevant."

1. ORGANIZED ANYTHING

In a modern industrial society, the "location" of the individual in the social order has suffered a fundamental shift.[2] The dominant religious form in nations like the United States appears to be an "invisible religion" of the private psyche, dependent upon the "consumer preference" of the private individual.[3] Even persons who remain faithful to a traditional religious institution experience it not as an obligatory mode of making their lives significant, reinforced by the behavior of all those around them, but as a standpoint they have preferred among its competitors. Traditional religion competes "in the market place."

Where do ordinary individuals today find meaning for their lives? There is no overarching scheme of meanings connecting their work on their jobs with their politics and their family life and their personal fulfillment. There is no symbolic center. There is no institutional, "objective" center. The failure is not personal: the many aspects of the social world are not connected in a system of meaning. Government, businesses, schools, and associations are each run on the basis of function, rationality, and specialization. They have been stripped of a humanizing sense of reality, story, symbol. They are governed by a sense of reality that is appropriate for the use of tools. Man is supposed to fit the needs of an impersonal, efficient, functional system. The system is not supposed to fit human senses of reality, stories, symbols.

Thus, those who succeed in the system do not, ordinarily, regard it with reverence but rather with detachment, cynicism, and frank manipulation. Mastering the system and burning themselves out in continuous work may become the passion of some, while others take pride in becoming expert operators of the mechanism. "Fulfillment" is not a word applied without embarrassment to one's job, political role, institutional affiliations.

Fulfillment and significance are, as never before, left to the individual to work out on his own. Other institutions neither seriously promise, nor can they deliver, a sense of the sacred. They are resolutely functional. The private psyche carries an unparalleled burden: the task of making sense out of life, all alone. This burden is portrayed as if it were due to the risks, terrors and beauties of "freedom." The individual is "on his own," should "brave the night," should not give way to "a failure of nerve," should "pay the price of" his autonomy. It is not as if institutions press on him less lightly. Modernity assigns him a role like that of *Catch-22*.[4] He may evade the duties of oppressive institutions if he is no longer sane; but if he asks to be dispensed, it is proof of his sanity and therefore he must remain.

A person may regard institutions and their claims as instruments of manipulation. But he is then obliged to seek his fulfillment in private. In the institutional part of his life he finds too little "significance." In the private part of his life he is forced into a narrow search for "escape." Modern liberation, full of opportunity and promise, leaves him a divided soul.

Autonomy is the chief symbol of the new invisible and unorganized religion.[5] The story it seeks to tell is one of *self-expression* and *self-realization*. These are more readily achieved through the *mobility*[6] provided by the industrial social order. The "successful" master the mechanisms of mobility. The image which motivates them is that of "making it" or "climbing to the top"—as though the social system were external to them and their fulfillment. They do not try to attune themselves to the system. For the system does not even pretend to be "connected" to the cosmos and thus participating in some sacred scheme of the real, the meaningful, the worthwhile. They master the system as if it were an enemy, a threat, a challenge, a game, but in any case "unconnected" and extrinsic. The unsuccessful, by contrast, turn more directly to private satisfactions. The game "isn't worth it." They drop out.

Sexual satisfaction, in particular, is made to carry the burden of meaning and fulfillment, through either serial or permanent relationships. In sexual *aspiration,* at least, surcease is found from solitariness.[7] And the individual may find the beginnings of a shared social world. The aspired-to ecstasy of sexual compatibility is in some tension with another aspiration: for a sense of reality and value reinforced over a lifetime by at least one other.[8] The demands of love and of sex are sometimes at war.

The indifference of the primary institutions of society to both love and sex places excruciating demands on intimate personal relations. A fulfillment that in other societies is diffused through the whole range of human activities is here concentrated upon one activity: lovemaking. The sexual partner is obliged to play, for want of cultural assistance, the role of god or goddess. "Sexual polytheism"—serial polygamy, wife-and-husband swapping—distributes the burden. "A single sentence shall suffice for modern man," Camus said: "we fornicated and read the papers."[9]

Those who are most thoroughly immersed in contemporary social forms—reasonably affluent urban dwellers and the young —discover a painful contradiction. Enormous psychic space is turned over to the individual for finding himself, creating his own system of meaning and significance, expressing himself, realizing himself. And then entire industries of "secondary institutions"[10] —newspaper columns, serialized psychology, *Playboy* philosophers, guidance counselors, talk shows, predigested readings, book clubs, popular songs, current flicks, commercials, radio preachers—offer him a supermarket of life-styles. Even in the depths of his soul he is a consumer.

The overriding cosmic picture of the free modern society is that of the market place.[11] Individuals are atomic particles. An impersonal mechanism works out an equilibrium between what they demand and what they can be supplied. Even the pursuit of truth is defined in terms of "a free market place of ideas." In the deepest parts of their minds and hearts, the cosmic law of moderns is *laissez faire*. Each "does his thing." Each expects institutions to be specialized, manipulative, dehumanizing. Even in the Soviet Union—but perhaps not in China[12]—the truly profound modern revolution has been to set aside a "private space" in which the individual, in his solitariness, seeks fulfillment. (The materialism of Soviet Communism[13] may attempt to sacralize the collective; but the collective is not a community, only a bureaucracy. The secret springs of community elude materialism, whether in Communist or Western development.)

Primary social forms give the individual private autonomy; they do not confere significance upon his life. Does private autonomy within a dehumanizing system constitute "progress"? Perhaps the trend cannot be reversed. But are there not many who would as soon die trying?

2. LITURGY

The religious standpoint, we noted earlier, has two forms. In the broad but valid sense, every standpoint has comprehensiveness, an integrative role, a heuristic function, and a mechanism of selection. Each is a subject for religious studies. This is true even of a secular, atheistic standpoint whose integrating sense of reality is instrumentalist, whose story is that of enlightenment, and whose symbols are private autonomy on the one hand and prediction and control on the other. In a more traditional and specific sense, however, a religious standpoint emerges when a person's attention dwells upon the experience of the sacred, and thus engenders a conversion from a merely profane standpoint. The experience of the sacred commonly brings about a feeling of being "connected" with or attuned to a "deeper" reality. Such a reality may be experienced as in some way sharing in the presence of a god. (Some secular, enlightened thinkers seem to feel in harmony with a reality of historical progress; process philosophy, for example.[14])

In the midst of the many pragmatic tasks imposed upon them by everyday life, those who have experienced the sacred often seek to direct their attention to that experience frequently, in order to "renew" their sense of reality and significance. They may develop dualistic theories—the world of illusions vs. the world of the really real—or they find that the two worlds, the sacred and the profane, interpenetrate at every point. According to this latter view, nothing profane lacks its sacred dimension; nothing sacred lacks its profane expression. (The world itself "springs from" the

One, the All, *is* God manifesting himself in time; "mirrors" or "participates in" his secret life; etc.) Some actions, of course, "obscure," "violate," "profane," or "destroy" the presence of God in things. Other actions make God especially present, almost tangibly so. There are ordinary experiences of the sacred, as routine as drinking a glass of cold beer, plucking a berry, seeing "God in a grain of sand." There are also ecstatic experiences.

Many persons want the sense of the sacred to be a regular, repetitive pattern in their lives—as regular as eating, as playing, as loving. They institutionalize the experience of the sacred through the celebration of privileged events, the privileged tasks of the community (the hunt, the harvest, Labor Day) and the privileged times of the year. Rituals are invented. Classic historical forms arise, dramatic in design, rich in symbolism, steeped often in blood or remembered calamity. The imagery of the ritual is often earthy, sexual, primitive, despite the sophistication of garment, dance, and word. The experience of the sacred is thus given a communal shape through liturgy (Gr., "work of the people").

Liturgy, in turn, is torn between its primitive source and its formalized expression. Formalization allows many diverse persons, in many ages, in many moods, to bring to it their own emotions and intuitions. A formalized liturgy does not try "to turn on" its participants. They are not supposed to sit there passively and be entertained. *They* are supposed to extend themselves to enter into remote mysteries which will stretch them and instruct them. At its best, a formalized liturgy allows all to participate by not forcing on everyone the mood and intuition of the minister or leader; his subjectivity is subsumed in the classical form. At its worst, the encrusted, stiff form stands *between* the participants and the experience of the sacred. It distracts, it is too highly routinized, it touches the experience of too few, it turns attention *away* from the sacred and toward some new pragmatic, profane reality: the structure of the ritual itself. It has ceased to be diaphanous; the sacred does not shine through.

In our age of private fulfillment, not even sexual love can always be counted on to provide ecstasy, even of that quiet sort which makes both partners feel real, truthful, connected. Even sexual experience comes to seem pragmatic. The privatizing of life weakens every form of significance. The privatized person is usually not "connected" (a) to the world as a whole; (b) to other persons; (c) to his own workaday activities, his body, his twenty-four-hour self. For he can retreat to the private sphere only so many hours in a day or a week; the rest is instrumentalist. And the instrumentalist mode of life which he is forced to live almost every hour of every working day commonly carries over into the private sphere as well. He finds himself manipulating his own emotions (analyzing them according to various mechanist schemes going back to his own infancy), and manipulating others as well. (The role of the loved one is to satisfy him, his needs, his insecurities.) The devotee of the modern invisible religion debunks free will and explains human actions in terms of their social, neural, and other determinants. He thus celebrates autonomy while constricting its meaning severely. Further, by privatizing the meaning of whatever autonomy remains, he commits himself to isolation. The ritual expression of his standpoint is the cocktail party: a coming together of automonous individuals, seeking (and sometimes finding) stimulation of their individual egos.

Liturgy, by contrast, aims at overcoming a threefold alienation. First, the participant needs to have experienced community in such a way that others live in her, and she in them. She is a social animal who, without loss to her own identity, expresses herself through a sisterly celebration[16]—even if in the midst of strangers. She is not an isolated, private ego.

Secondly, the participant understands instinctively that the experience of the sacred extends itself through all of life, giving significance and relation to every profane detail. "Liturgy," Romano Guardini has written, "is all creation redeemed and at prayer."[17] Trees, animals, sun, stars, daily work—all the concrete objects and tasks of our existence are included. Our identity is expressed through the concrete world of experience; its destiny and ours are inextricably united. Thus bread, wine, wax, foodstuffs, incense, drums, paints, masks, phallic symbols, mothering symbols, and objects of all sorts are brought into ritual acts. Liturgy is unsuccessful if it does not diffuse its significance through the whole of human life.

Thirdly, the participant understands that she is not spirit merely but an embodied person. God is pleased, the Bible tells us, by worship "in spirit and in truth." But one truth about woman is her body: eyes, ears, hands, knees, sexual organs. The liturgy involves the entire body. It is a drama of motion and participation, of sights and sounds and smells. Sexual symbolism is recurrent and powerful. Particular attention is given to the postures of the body: sometimes formalized, sometimes ecstatic and free. It is crucial, of course, that liturgy lead to the transcendence of biological rhythms: it is a celebration of memory and future, of art and craftsmanship, of community and of universality. But if it "takes flight" and leaves the body too far behind, the concrete ties of the body to this earth and the present will take their revenge. Flight of the dove—but also plodding ascent of the mountain, proceeding little by little.

It is very difficult for those who share the standpoint of today's invisible religion to feel at home in a communal celebration of earth, of memory, of hope, of modest expectation and chastened reconciliation. For the powerful currents of modern religion suggest that man "masters" the earth, is "autonomous," is fulfilled in "privacy," and is reconciled to nothing but his own naked—and predetermined—will. The modern imagination casts up images of Prometheus. The helpless prisoner in an asylum, madhouse, castle, hospital, or army base glorifies in his will to freedom. He is helpless but defiant. The mode of traditional liturgy has always been communal and alternates between tragedy, irony, and comedy. The mode of the invisible religion is solitary pathos.

Thus any liturgy which would attempt today to speak to those whose standpoint is that of modern consciousness would have to speak first to the pathos of the individual, who seems trapped by the dehumanizing institutions his efficiency and power have fashioned, but who resists attempts to comfort him. There is today a delight in self-punishment; a delectation in an unnamed guilt; a quest, even, for the bitter joys of alienation. These are celebrated as the price of freedom.

3. CHURCH, DENOMINATION, SECT

We are coming to the end of the age of the Enlightenment. The fundamental sense of reality, stories, and symbols that dominated the avant-garde are fraught with internal contradiction. They bring widespread unhappiness and not infrequently the wish for death.

But the traditional forms of religious organization are also in crisis. There is, it seems, no possibility of a return to the past. Still, we must give at least some account of the past from which the dominant religious traditions of the West have come. (The traditions of the East, too, of Islam as well as of Buddhism, Hinduism, and Taoism, are undergoing transformation. The blending of Taoism with the mystical side of dialectical materialism, e.g., has given China a renewed spiritual vitality.[18])

Ernst Troeltsch, the great social historian of religions, discerned three strands in the institutionalization of Christianity. In order to endure from generation to generation, the memory of archetypal events had to be institutionalized and given shape. But the question of how to do so was not settled in advance. Several tendencies have been in almost constant war with one another within Christianity—and, in appropriate form, in other world religions.

One tendency Troeltsch calls "the church type."[19] An institution develops structures parallel to every realm of profane culture. Two parallel "cities" are built, the sacred city and the worldly city: city of God, city of man.[20] The city of God has a worldliness of its own: against Emperor, a Pontifex Maximus; against Imperial Court, a papal court; against temples of State, temples of God; against worldly art and worldly music, sacred art and sacred music; against normal biological and familial patterns, chastity and celibacy; against secular history, sacred history; against imperial politics, church politics. The church embraces all of life, sinful and innocent alike. It does not scruple to become *engagé.* Its priests become emperors, conspirators, generals. It does so under the insight that if God became man, then the church—although representing God and not merely man—must enter into all the affairs of man, visibly, institutionally, effectively. The church must "put its body on the line" and be utterly "relevant" to everything that happens.

It follows inevitably, given talented and unhesitant leaders, that the institutions of the church soon become more and more ascendant over the institutions of empire, and claim the primacy of God in relation to man. It becomes more and more difficult to settle competing claims of jurisdiction. Secular institutions and sacred institutions engage in centuries of pull-and-tug, confrontation, open warfare. Finally, principles for the "separation" of church and state are worked out. The secular state—and secular philosophy, arts, commerce, etc.—become a fully independent reality.

Secondly, there is also a sectarian[21] tendency in Christianity. The rule of spirit is protected over against the encroachment of institutions, even ecclesiastical institutions. Christianity was not intended as an institution parallel to the empire, but as a "brotherhood of believers." The test for entry is genuine personal experience. Infants cannot be symbolically admitted to membership through baptism; only adults are admitted who have given wit-

ness by their lives to the genuineness of their fidelity. The power
of the sect derives from its attachment to the Spirit, "who blows
where he wills," and from its willingness to resist illegitimate
authority, if necessary, to death.[22] A sense of brotherhood is
strong; but the tendency to value individual experience and individual judgment is also powerful. Compromise becomes a problem. Faithful to their personal stories, members are quite
consistent when they turn against developments in their sect, and
move off to another.

If churchmen are prone to the "pride of the flesh," sectarians
are prone to the "pride of the spirit." Moral purity is pursued and
(implicitly) claimed. If the liturgy of the church is vulnerable to
routinization and encrusted formality, the liturgy of the sect is
vulnerable to enthusiasm, self-indulgence, and mere immediacy.
Moreover, both have complementary institutional problems.
Churches must encourage the sectarian spirit in their own midst,
as the source of fresh experience and vitalizing influences. Sects
must find ways of maintaining their discipline and fidelity across
generations, without becoming as institutionalized as the
churches they oppose. (Today, for example, Roman Catholicism,
a church, shows in many places the vitality of a sect: Methodism,
originally a sect, shows in many places the institutionalization of
a church.)

Denominations,[23] meanwhile, are intermediate between a
church and a sect. They are more formal and clearly organized
than a sect; they rely less on personal experience and immediate
enthusiasm. On the other hand, they do not try to parallel all the
functions of secular culture. They are designed as specialized
institutions, caring for the religious needs of their members,
alongside other institutions caring for their secular needs. They
encourage their members to take full part in secular institutions.
For rooting and footage they rely upon "the religious dimension"
in the lives of their members. Not so strong nor so total as a
church, a denomination is vulnerable to becoming indistinguisha-

ble from secular institutions. And it may have to rely upon an ever-shrinking psychic space in its participants' lives. For the assumption seems to develop that religion is one specialization among others. It gets its due, like the others.

The privatizing tendencies of the invisible religion severely diminish the social effectiveness of churches, sects, and denominations. The churches cannot, except in secluded pockets (themselves invaded by automobiles and television), effortlessly command the whole allegiance of their members. Even if for example, people try to be wholehearted Catholics, the jobs they have in industrial society are enormously different from the agriculture or crafts of an earlier period; they are through-and-through functional, pragmatic, secular. The liturgy no longer has roots in the people's contact with the earth and handicrafts; it is wholly separate from their work. And if it is described and acted out in modern terms (a "service station" to which to repair for a "spiritual tune-up"), it is thoroughly invaded by the pragmatic, profane way of life. People begin to experience themselves as valueless and replaceable, like used cars, used television sets, want ads in old papers, etc. Their neighborhoods are not communities. Their marriages may be neither friendships nor economically useful—but more or less empty arrangements. Hurrying home from mass in the family Oldsmobile in time for the televised football game, what have they in common with the experiences of their ancestors? The picture reported by Schroeder and Obenhaus in *Religion in American Culture* is not any more reassuring for sects and denominations.[24]

The privatizing tendencies of modern life, however, do open a new field to "crusades" by those evangelists who promise that religious conversion provides a means of fulfillment. Evangelical groups are often not studied carefully by theologians, since their theological content is not great; nor by scholars, since they are largely populist in their orientation, with little direct concern for politics, social institutions, or culture. They are, nevertheless, the

fastest growing religious bodies in the world.[25] They offer the
intensity, direct experience, and enthusiasm traditional to sects.
They systematically separate religion from political or social questions, and locate it firmly in "the private sphere." They comfort.[26]
They supply a sense of belonging, with few or no institutional
responsibilities. They communicate a simple but powerful sense
of historical continuity and direction. They make authenticating
demands in terms of private and familial morality, almost no
moral demands that bear on complex social or economic responsibilities.[27]

In a word, the evangelical groups accept the modern privatizing tendencies. They fill up the private sphere with meaning,
letting the social sphere fall to secular organizations. They plead,
in concert with certain political leaders, for a return to the "traditional" virtues and loyalties of the individualistic culture of the
eighteenth and nineteenth centuries. They claim to speak the
"pure" gospel of Jesus Christ, without political dilution. Their
latent social and political role is to strengthen the status quo, both
by refusing to raise moral questions about social matters and by
intermingling affirmative patriotism with religious affirmations.

Their social base lies in the populations of the relatively poor,
the uneducated, and even many who have recently enjoyed pros-
perity sufficient to place them in the new suburbs. Both preachers
(often sophisticated in modern techniques) and members seem
susceptible to an easy transference from cross to flag, from Christianity to Americanism, and from the Bible to anti-Communism.
Often enough, they also resist those social changes which disturb
age-old social patterns of racial discrimination. Thus the evangelical dictum, "Don't mix religion and politics," plays an important
political role in American society.

Churches, denominations, and sects of the Western world,
therefore, are in sharp and dangerous conflict with the invisible
religion of modernity. One of the great ironies of modern religious life, however, is the extent to which leaders of churches,

denominations, and sects *accept* the religion of modernity. As long as people still keep coming to church, it appears, religious leaders do not care to attack the invisible religion head-on. They are content with whatever crumbs of the private sphere are left after the assembly line, the board room, and television have finished their functional demands. Since the invisible religion offers very little comfort to the imagination, the quest for community, or the instinct for transcendence, the chief agents of that religion— corporation executives, chemists, engineers, managers—find churches, denominations, and sects useful. Plans for new suburbs always include property reserved for interchangeable suburban churches of each appropriate type. Churches offer little challenge to the modern religion, and they provide a much-needed source of consolation. If the consolation is not deep, lasting, or fundamental, it is at least better than nothing.

Some members of churches, denominations, and sects on the other hand, resist the alliance between their own tradition and the modern invisible religion. They have shared the experience of the sacred and the sense of transcendence. They do not identify the present American way of life with the Kingdom of God. They pass more or less harsh judgment on the modern invisible religion, because it alienates men from themselves, from other men, and from the earth. They want to make Christian or Jewish values more dominant in the culture. They want to oppose the impersonality, efficiency, and manipulation so prominent in modern life.

In deodorants and mouthwashes, for example, they perceive hatred for the human body and all that is natural to it, and a fear of anything that has not been processed by reason and its technical products. They see a massive advertising war upon all things bodily, hairy, smelly, and in other ways sensuous, in favor of a spiritualized, notional, mechanized, bottled "cleanliness." They diagnose this as a modern form of the heresy of Manicheanism, whose results are bound to be a separation of body and mind, restlessness, impatience, and violence.

Are not suburbs themselves based on the pretense that the agonies of human life—sensuousness, hunger, sickness, insanity, cruelty, despair, poverty, and chaos—can be safely shut out by neat hedges and picket fences? Will children who grow up in such segregated human environments be prepared to understand the anguish of the Jewish people through the centuries, the bloody cross of Jesus Christ, or the hunger and chaotic emotions of the rest of humanity outside the clipped hedges?

The quest for safety and security may be immoral, as well as illusory. Heavily armed troopers may one day be required to keep the reality of human life upon this planet at the far edge of the green lawns of suburbia. Outside, anguish; within, ignorance. And what religious standpoint would such a social arrangement represent?

4. HOLY TEXTS

The experience of the sacred is so important to humans that when it occurs they ordinarily wish to preserve it and to repeat it. The experience is communal and belongs by right to a group or even to all the people, not merely to one person or a few. Liturgical acts re-present the original experience in order to stoke the fires of memory. Such liturgical acts develop a classical form. Many variants may arise—and each variation may express a fresh standpoint or new twist of the ancient story—but the indispensable themes become codified. The wisdom pointed to by these basic themes is often set forth in writing, in stark simplicity or in intricate commentary. "Sacred texts" arise. Each succeeding generation receives them, meditates upon them, interprets them in its own way. Nearly every major world religion is organized, in one way or another, around a set of sacred texts. Original experiences of the sacred lie behind the black print.

The role of sacred texts in religious organizations is twofold.

First, the texts provide leverage against the passing fads of the moment and the pervasive and powerful "spirit of the age." The cry to be "relevant" is irresistible, even to those who resist. It is always easy to see how men and women of a former age yielded, all unknowing, to the prejudices of their age. A religious group places part of its center of gravity in a standpoint that antedates that of the present age through its fidelity to sacred texts. It cherishes an initial skepticism regarding the boasts and glories of the age.

Secondly, the sacred text proves its own depth and universality by shedding fresh and useful illumination on each succeeding age in turn. Texts by themselves are merely black marks on paper. They have no meaning until they are interpreted. A text intended for a large part of mankind, or for all of mankind, must be susceptible of interpretation from a virtual infinity of standpoints. It proves its worth, not by its univocity and rigidity, but by its richness and fecundity. No matter who reads it, in *whatever* situation, if he reads it with good will should be able to derive fruit from it. Such fruit includes a lessening of his sense of alienation; participation in other persons and in the sacred "dimension" in whose context our lives are set; a deeper and more exact and more honest view of himself and his activities. His "spirit"—his capacities for inquiry, honesty, and courage—should be refreshed.

The sacred texts promise such spiritual power. Many, however, picking them up and flipping through the pages, fail to experience that power. They lack "eyes" for it. They have never made the effort required to "ascend the mountain." They were never carried aloft by "the dove." Sacred texts require that their readers undergo a discipline. Even so, sacred texts open their inner depths not to those who have worked the hardest but without regard to the efforts of men. Some persons are more "gifted" than others—sacred texts belong to God, not to man, and their interpretation follows his rules, not man's. What makes one zen master greater than another? It is not effort alone.

Still, texts are to be interpreted, just as mountains are to be climbed. Countless questions arise.[28] Who first voiced the words in the text? Who wrote them down? In what historical context and for what historical purposes were they composed? What is the earliest text we now possess? Is it in the language of the original? Who edited or copied it? Do the earliest copies confirm one another, or vary from passage to passage, book to book?

Who decided which of many sacred texts were "more sacred" than others? Sometimes a priestly or other professional group cherished the original texts, and built their lives around a method of interpreting it. Often they taught that it is not the letter of the text, but the spirit, which gives life. But does *anything* count as "the spirit"? How does a person know when he has caught the spirit of the text? Usually, a set of signs derived from the way a person lives his life is arrived at. If he does not begin to live in a certain way, then he has not really understood. Sometimes, in fact, certain books or parts of books will not even be shown to an inquirer at once. Only after he has shown by his way of living that the new mysteries will not be wholly out of tune with his understanding is he initiated into them.

Paradoxically, then, the text is sacred and yet it is not the text that is sacred. The text is sacred, because it marks out one path of entry into the experience of the holy, among all other paths to all other experiences. It is a guide: finite, limited, concrete. On the other hand, it is not the text that is sacred but its *significance:* the way of life whence it springs and which it ceaselessly engenders afresh. It is not the black marks on the page but the way of living that is crucial. Thus, the tradition of those religions that employ sacred texts is not altogether different from the traditions of those that do not, like the Buddhists.

Still, text and significance cannot be wholly separated. Thirty thousand people can read the same text and arrive at thirty thousand different meanings. Are all of these meanings equal in

weight? Cannot one show that *some* of them, at least, are erroneous?

A nest of problems arises. It is difficult enough to establish the
literal meaning of a text: the grammar, syntax, and barebones
meaning of the words, in the setting for which they were originally composed. Were there *really* (historically, factually) three
kings at Bethlehem, or is the anecdote of the three kings an
accepted way of saying that the newborn babe was more than just
another mortal? Is there a similar mode of speech in other compo-
sitions of that period and region? Archaeological findings and
historical research may shed light on the original meanings of the
words employed. With great effort, one can establish a reasonably
certain literal reading of the text.

Religious traditions are at one in their recognition that the
desired experience of the sacred is not to be derived from a
scientific effort to arrive at the literal meaning of the text. The
problem is to discern how many *other* meanings there are in the
text: allegorical, analogical, metaphorical, symbolic, experiential,
ironic, adversative, etc. Perhaps the point of a text is to allow us
to "feel our way into" a standpoint different from our own—the
story of Abraham, for example. Perhaps the point is to puzzle us
and to hold our minds attentive and meditative as we turn a scene
over and over in our minds: from contemplating Adam and Eve
in paradise, thirty or forty different ways of interpreting the story
may occur to us. Perhaps the point is to shock us: the slaughter
of the innocents at Bethlehem.

The puzzles of the Buddhists, the poetic suggestiveness of the
Bhagavad-Gita, the intricacies of the *I Ching,* the advice of the
Koran: all the sacred texts of the world baffle the merely literal
mind, and lead those who enter their depths into labyrinthine
caves and dark meanderings. Whatever the "communication"
aimed at by the sacred texts, it is not a literal, pragmatic, clear
pointing of a finger. It is, if anything, a beckoning—upon a long
and arduous voyage. Sacred texts "are shallow enough for a

mouse to wade in, deep enough for an elephant to drown in."
Each person reads them at his own level—unless his own good
will allows him to be drawn out into the depths.

5. THEOLOGIES

Approximately one-third of the people on earth are Christians
(one billion), 500 million are Hindu, 500 million are Islamic, 250
million are Buddhists, 14 million are Jews (one-third of the Jewish population—6 million—perished in Nazi Germany). The cultural power of Taoism and Confucianism in China persists despite
and even through the Revolution.

The needs of our planet's population are various. It is not
surprising, then, that in its reflection upon its founders and its
sacred texts, each of the world religions develops multiple theologies. Theology is a systematic articulation of a sense of reality,
stories, symbols. In its highest and most vital moments, theology
is a silent and nonverbal reflection; it is an act of recognition, of
affirmation, of denial. Thus the Buddhist master teaches without
direct statement; the spiritual director notes signs of progress in
the speech, manner, and tone of the Christian novice; the rabbi
at the fullest moments lapses into silence. Theological silence is
distinguished from the silence of timidity and the silence of ignorance by the accuracy of its perception and by the deeds that flow
from it. The person who reflects is silent not because she perceives too little but because she perceives too much: words do not
do justice to the perception.

It is easy, of course, to pretend to theological silence, just as
young people sometimes pretend to silence in their love. They
are silent, they say, because their hearts are in such harmony they
don't need words. They may be silent, however, because they
suspect that their hearts are *not* in harmony; they are merely
loathe to lose the fruits of a pretended love. One distinguishes
genuine silence in theology as one does genuine silence in love:

by the signs surrounding it and by its fruits.

Still, articulation in words is as highly useful in theology as it is in love. It is worth hearing exactly where one stands, and noting the explicit connections between one's various passions, convictions, and actions. Of course, senses of reality, stories, and symbols—even within the same religious group—vary significantly. So also do systems of articulation. If, for example, one person chooses for his basic and rockbottom terms words like "trust" and "fidelity," and another person chooses words like "love" and "action," it is quite likely that the way they articulate other important themes will also differ.

It is usually impossible to compare verbal systems of articulation word for word or even thesis by thesis. They cannot be superimposed upon one another like celluloid maps. A system of articulation has, as it were, three dimensions; it does not lie flat. Standpoint differs from standpoint: sense of reality differs from sense of reality; story from story; symbol from symbol. A comparison between theologies is not like an argument between two persons who share the same standpoint and agree upon basic axioms, and have then merely to match logical or factual points. An argument between theologies is far more subtle and complex. Different standpoints are in question. Each sees the other in a light not native to the other.

An ancient expression notes that disputes between theologians are among the most bitter of any in intellectual life: *odium theologicum,* theological hatred. At stake in a theological argument are not merely one's "opinions," or "beliefs" (mere notions), or "sentiments," or logical skills, or even one's grasp of the "facts." At stake is one's sense of reality, stories, symbols. When one's theology is attacked, it is as though one's own self were under attack. It is hard to keep recalling that one's present sense of reality, stories, and symbols may be quite inadequate, and that an attack upon them is not really upon oneself. One can always develop a new and better sense of reality, set of stories, and symbols.

What usually unleashes one's anger is that the attack, coming from an unsympathetic standpoint, seems so *unfair*. It would be a different matter, one says, if the other person at least stated my standpoint with accuracy. One forgets that any standpoint, looked at from another standpoint, *necessarily* has a different appearance to the person in the other standpoint. You note *his* bias; he notes yours.

Every theological standpoint has a social base. Reflection upon experience, naturally enough, tends to be preoccupied with certain constants of experience—and these ordinarily gain their constancy from long-lived social and economic factors. Reflection is not merely *reducible* to its social base; for one can imagine many different persons reflecting quite differently upon the same body of experience. But it would be odd if reflection did not at all "reflect" the power of social factors in shaping the experiences upon which reflection occupies itself.

Reflection, however, tends to have a second source: habits of articulation which arise, not from present social and economic factors, but from past traditions. A millionaire lawyer in Texas can build up three huge ranches, almost entirely on borrowed money, and nevertheless proclaim the necessity of a "balanced budget." Natives of Orange County, California, may participate enthusiastically in the freest, most modern, and most extravagant way of life in the land, and nevertheless speak constantly of "the old values" and "eternal verities."

Thirdly, reflection upon experience is colored by the cultural sense of reality, stories, and symbols in which one's life has been nourished. Certain ways of perceiving, certain emphases, certain images of what the human struggle is and where its focal point is located, certain fears, certain enemies, certain images of achievement and liberation, become native to one's own sensibility, imagination, intelligence, and judgment. If a person's work does not "speak to my condition," I deem his work—unless I am willing to grow into *his* standpoint—"irrelevant." (Those who use the word "irrelevant" frequently have assumed a passive attitude toward others.) Necessarily, each of us finds some authors immediately illuminating, and others foreign, strange, and diffuse. Their problems are not our problems. Their sensibility is not our sensibility. Their struggle is not our struggle.

Reflection, fourthly, particularly when it is sustained, tends to become specialized. A woman's interests, for example, run toward certain fields of inquiry and certain preferred methods; she is not so interested in the problems, language, or methods of other fields. Some persons find that the main enlivening problems for them lie in practical, immediate social and political contexts. Others prefer the distance, depth, and overview of a theoretical standpoint derived from the social sciences. Others believe that the problems of fundamental interest lie in the arts and in popular culture. Others believe that the profoundest problems must be fought out in the context of theology considered as a science. They live and move in the absorbing intellectual context of the history of theology, in one or other of its specializations: history, systematics, patristics, studies of sacred scripture, pastoral theology, or the newer fields of interdisciplinary research (medical ethics, theology and law, Christian ethics and the social sciences, political theology, etc.) Still others specialize in the problems of the personal voyage: in psychological development, in mysticism, in the cure of souls.

At least these four variables—social base; inherited categories; personal sense of reality, stories, symbols; specialization—influence reflection. Together, they generate the great variety of standpoints from which theological reflection is carried out in the United States. American society has no one unified culture or social base; it is a highly mobile, flexible society.

In Europe, by contrast, when theologians write about "theology and culture" (*Theologie und Kultur*), they tend to have a highly defined standpoint within which to be clear about their meaning for each term. One can imagine a quite limited set of books, musical performances, paintings, architectural achievements, and other similar ideals toward which the "Western" spirit aspires. These aspirations, and these achieved standards for what counts as classical performance, constitute *Kultur*. As Theodor Adorno has pointed out, however, the faith of many Europeans, too, is being shaken in whether such a *Kultur* has the legitimacy it once was given.[29] The impact of new waves of human experience upon European consciousness makes *Kultur* seem like too narrow a focal point for human aspiration. *Kultur* was vulnerable in the face of Nazism. The experiences of the poor of the world and of men in other cultures, including primitive cultures, demand a new pattern for "the humanities." We seek a model for a planetary culture.

Similarly, *Theologie* defined by the historical arguments, methods, vocabulary, emphases, and concerns of Protestant history since the nineteenth century (which tended to establish the problematic for Bultmann, Barth, and Tillich) has begun to lose its social base.[30] The young men and women who study theology are increasingly absorbed, not by the problems of European Protestant history, but at the very least by an ecumenical perspective. Historical studies have uncovered the many standpoints which Protestants have held in history—the standpoint of the original Reformers is not so easy to recapture as some might wish, and is perhaps not adequate for our own time in any case. The impact of the other world religions and of primitive religions on Protestant consciousness is not to be underestimated.

Finally, the fact that politics, culture, and the arts today proceed from a new standpoint, a new set of stories, and new symbols has awakened many to the breakdown of the connection between theology and culture—and to an inadmissible isolation of theology. Such isolation, if continued, would be fatal for theology.

Theology is reflection upon lived experience. If that symbiotic cord is broken, theology becomes reflection upon reflection— pale, anemic, fruitless.

The American situation, therefore, may to a European appear confused, without standards, lacking in originality, unorganized, and above all lacking in speculative power. Americans await, I think, the emergence of a method and categories that can relate what each is doing to what others are doing: a method and categories that respect American diversity and vitality, while bringing to bear upon each the criticism of all the others. The notions worked out in this book are intended as a contribution to that task.

6. A MAP OF CHRISTIAN THEOLOGIES IN THE UNITED STATES

A survey of even the major theological standpoints in all the major religions would be both beyond my competence and beyond the scope of this book. But it might be useful to sketch —no more than that—the major standpoints now fruitful among Christians in the United States.

The first overwhelming fact is regional variation. The distribution of Catholics, Lutherans, Baptists, Methodists, Presbyterians, and others tends to follow rather fuzzy but significant regional lines. The preoccupations of one part of the nation are not those of all the other parts.

The "Bible Belt" of the south, parts of the midwest, the southwest, and parts of the west (the northwest and southwest, in particular) tends to be dominated by Baptist and Methodist interests. It was, for generations, a region of relative poverty and of rural values. It tended to emphasize the role of personal religious experience, conversion, piety, personal and familial virtues, a populist loyalty to democracy, intense suspicion of the corruptions inherent in city life, and resistance to the technological, industrial sense of reality, stories, symbols. The main cultural bond was formed by the contact of folks with folks: church bazaars, revivals, summer camps, folk songs, outings. Culture did not come through books, periodicals, or (at first) universities—not through print culture but through folk culture. (Politicians still must prove themselves not by cosmopolitanism, erudition, or "fancy" speech but through folksiness.)

A native ebullience and optimism courses through the region. The tribulations and sadnesses spoken of by the folk songs and country music of the region tend to be highly personal: of betrayals and disappointments in love, of personal loss through death, or poverty, or misfortune. Local loyalties are fondly celebrated through extravagantly symbolic athletic contests. Health, charm, good looks, physical strength, and native shrewdness—shrewdness, not exactly pragmatism—are much cherished. The dominant symbol of a "social evil" is alcohol; or perhaps "the bankers" (often enough easterners or outsiders).

In a sense, Protestant reality, stories, and symbols are still fairly intact in these regions. The tendency to imagine religion as concerned almost exclusively with personal values allows modernization to determine social values. Symbolically, preachers may still employ an imagery which celebrates rural values; they find no conflict in doing so with the most advanced promotional techniques and the gadgetry of modern civilization. The conversion signaled by Harvey Cox in *The Secular City*,[31] from the rural standpoint to "a celebration of the city," provided a new sense of reality, a new story, and a new set of symbols for an experience which many in America (and elsewhere) have: that of living in an urban setting but thinking and feeling according to rural values.

Meanwhile, a general faith in the goodness of man and the beauty of America makes this region good soil for "process philosophy." God is not a static "wholly other"—he is a co-creating agent who, like some good neighbor, needs our cooperation if creation is to be accomplished. The cosmos is in good hands—God's and our own. Tragedies and absurdities, like irrational windstorms and tornadoes, can be borne. They are part of a larger, developing scheme. The economic wealth drawn toward the Bible Belt as by a magnet must confirm the general optimism. The Space Center in Houston, with its Bible-quoting and clean-cut astronauts, is a living symbol of the marriage between technology, process, and theology.

On the other hand, those who trust the Bible and distrust science and philosophy have a running argument with the "process philosophers." In the name of a new Christian philosophy, Whitehead and Hartshorne, Ogden and Cobb (they say) are importing universal, liberal, and humanistic values which are not distinctively biblical. "Process philosophy" tends to take the focus off the folks, and to sound relatively impersonal. Some of its implications are distinctly nontribal and nonlocal.

The Bible Belt is a rich and complex social world. Besides the relatively urbane evangelism of a more or less nondenominational preacher like Billy Graham, with his own distinctive sense of reality, set of stories, and set of symbols, there are also many other itinerant or local preachers, radio preachers, and crusaders of various sorts. All such men compete with rapidly growing industries, universities, suburban developments, television, automobiles, and political leaders for primacy in giving interpretation to human experience in their region.

Similar descriptions of other Christian groups in the United States can be developed. It is important, for example, to single out the context of Lutherans and Catholics in the midwest. Both have managed to re-create communities that synthesize European traditions (usually Germanic or Scandinavian, sometimes Slavic) with the easier freedoms of American affluence. They have maintained in its integrity an ecclesiastical and intellectual tradition of considerable clarity. Among Lutherans, this integrity tends to have a theologically and politically conservative cast. To some midwestern Catholics, ironically, the closeness to Europe—to Germany and France in particular—has given (by comparison with other American Catholics) a theologically and politically liberal cast. Catholics tend to be more at ease in the midwest than on the east coast; not so intimidated by Protestants, more self-confident. St. John's in Minnesota, Notre Dame, Chicago, St. Louis, and Kansas City are among the most creative and liberating centers of Catholic life in the United States, despite conservative tendencies of their own.[32]

Another major social base in American Christianity is constituted by the divinity schools, seminaries, theology departments, religious colleges, administrative boards of national organizations and national publications: the intellectual world of Protestantism in America. A network of journals, books, lectureships, and student-teacher relations unifies this world. Several different intellectual standpoints, several different cultural standpoints, and several different disciplinary standpoints are distinguishable within it.

Historians often speak of theologians according to "schools." The word may be taken literally: a given institution develops a character, a set of emphases, and a style that sometimes last for many generations. One speaks of "the Frankfurt school" in sociology, of "Marburg theology," of the tendencies of Roman Catholics at Tübingen for over a century. And if today one speaks of theology at Southern Methodist, or Harvard, or Yale, or the University of Chicago, knowledgeable people think immediately of the horizon characteristic of each.

In a more fundamental sense, however, "schools" of theology tend to grow up around the work of persons dominant in the field. One man achieves—not without a great deal of help from his friends and opponents—an especially fruitful horizon. He sets the main terms for discussion for a long period of time. Those who take part in that discussion belong to his "school." They may not be his "disciples"; they may show quite a significant independence and intellectual energy of their own. Still, he has established the main lines within which they work. Theology, like other fields in the humanities, tends to be a field highly dependent upon the *who* of horizon.

Thus a map of theological reflection among Christians in the United States at the present time could be composed extrinsically by a study of the papers presented to the American Academy of Religion, the Society for the Scientific Society of Religion, and other professional societies in the field during the last few years. Which figures tend to show up most often as the giants with whom one must tangle? Which figures are studied most often in all the seminaries, divinity schools, colleges, and universities in the United States, especially in those in which a high degree of theological articulation is prized?

Such maps would plainly reflect the influence of the giants in our century: Karl Barth, Paul Tillich, Rudolf Bultmann, Mircea Eliade, Karl Rahner, Bernard Lonergan, Reinhold Niebuhr, and possibly one or two others, like H. Richard Niebuhr and Dietrich Bonhoeffer. In cognate fields, Max Weber, Ernst Troeltsch, Martin Buber, Martin Heidegger, Paul Ricoeur, and others have been extremely influential in the development of contemporary theology.

It is impossible in a few sentences even to suggest the contribution of each of these men to present theological discourse, although an attempt must be made. No one can be said to have explored the horizon of Christian theology in our time unless he has, directly or indirectly, engaged all of them.

Karl Barth (1886–1969), a Swiss, emphasized the primacy of the Word of God, as preached in the church, over against human reason and human culture. His early and strong opposition to Nazism seemed to many to certify the value of his approach.[33]

Paul Tillich (1886–1965), German born, emigré to the United States, tried to respond to the sense of meaninglessness and despair which many have felt in Western culture, and not only in Western culture. He tried to show how the questions raised by human experience were questions the Word of God was trying to meet. Tillich began with men in the concrete; Barth began with God's word. Each felt that the other betrayed an essential value.[34]

Rudolf Bultmann (1884–), a German, examined the Scriptures in their original context, and tried to show how the values pointed to in them could be taken out of the "mythological" context of their original expression and stated in terms (like decision, commitment, engagement) meaningful for us today. He provided a transformation from one horizon to another.[35]

Mircea Eliade (1907–), born in Rumania, emigré to the United States, studied with unparalleled sympathy the resources of primitive religions, articulating both their power and their limits—and often, by implication at least, pointing out the severe limits of modern civilizations. In the last few years, the willingness to learn from Eliade's work has been growing enormously; the pride of Western religions has, perhaps, been humbled.[36]

Reinhold Niebuhr (1892–1971), an American, brought theology to social and political consciousness. He wrote columns on concrete dilemmas as they emerged. He kept his reflection in close touch with experience. He tried to transpose the Lutheran heritage of his childhood from the context of individual morality to the context of social justice and political realism. Because of its concreteness, some of his work has "dated" faster than that of other great theologians of the century. But the growing interest in "political theology" today restores the path he followed as a model to be emulated.[37]

Karl Rahner (1904–), a German Jesuit, studied under Martin Heidegger and has tried to establish an "anthropology," a way of talking about man, that would provide a modern way of talking about God and the Catholic faith. He has tried to give an account of the teachings of the Catholic church according to his new language and method.[38]

Bernard Lonergan (1904–), a Canadian Jesuit, has tried to give an account, which he invites his readers to test against their own experience, of fundamental human activities: having insights, making judgments, committing oneself in love, acting. Around his account of these basic activities he has articulated a method for theology, whose aim is, first, to keep theological statements in close touch with experienced activities; and, secondly, to clarify the relation of theological methods to the methods human beings employ in other uses of intelligence. The emphasis on what may be *experienced* and on *method* brings a uniquely Anglo-Saxon cast to questions heretofore chiefly discussed in German or Latin contexts.[39]

H. Richard Niebuhr (1894–1962), brother of Reinhold Niebuhr, brought a quiet, steady sociological and psychological sensitivity to theological questions, especially in the field of ethics. Ethical words and symbols, he emphasized, have a different meaning to persons in different social situations.[40]

Dietrich Bonhoeffer (1906–1944), a young German Lutheran pastor who was executed by the Nazis for his role in the attempted assassination of Adolph Hitler, tried to break out from the conflict between Barth, on the one hand, and Tillich and Bultmann, on the other. His *Letters and Papers from Prison* spoke enigmatically and powerfully of the changed consciousness a Christian martyr, too, feels toward God today. He served notice that not even the giants of the preceding generation had spoken adequately to the new experiences of the twentieth century.[41]

Behind the generation of the giants, it seemed for awhile that there would be a generation of commentators. The giants received so much attention that younger men had to wait to have their voices heard. John Cobb[42] and Schubert Ogden[43] have been working to assimilate the potentials of "process philosophy," and to work out therefrom fresh theological speech. Langdon Gilkey is repaying his original debt to Tillich by trying to discern the places in modern life where the sacred is experienced; he is also developing critical tools for relating the work of one theologian to another.[44] Van Harvey, a historian, has been wrestling with the perplexing conflicts between the horizon of the Enlightenment and that of the Christian.[45] Martin Marty is one of the most prolific and intelligent commentators on historical traditions and present events.[46]

One of the most highly praised books of the past decade has been David Tracy's *Blessed Rage for Order* (1975).[47] Professor Tracy offers a map of "Five Basic Models in Contemporary Theology." His map is useful for its own sake, since it helps to organize a vast body of material, and useful in our own discussion, too— for Tracy's method is identical to ours. He specifies, for each type of theology, the subjective pole of the theologian's horizon and then the objective pole (in his terms, the "subject referent" and then the "object referent"). In the earlier edition of *Ascent,* I listed at this place many of the theologians students might find valuable for their own further reading, and this list is now printed as a brief appendix (see "Further Readings," p. 251). With Tracy's influential scheme now available, it seems more useful to offer a brief version of it here and to make some further comments on it. His own work shows very clearly the power of an analysis by way of "horizon." (He does not attempt a full analysis of individual theologians, and therefore does not have much occasion to offer an analysis by way of "story.")

Tracy divides theologians of the nineteenth and twentieth centuries into five types: the orthodox, the liberal, the neo-orthodox, the radical, and the revisionist. It is plain that he is thinking mainly of Christian theologians, Protestant and Catholic, but also, secondarily, of Jewish theologians. In principle, his models are abstract enough to suggest that they may apply with equal force to thinkers in other world religions. Fundamentally, he examines each model with respect to its image of the self for whom the theologian writes, and of the world which (the theologian imagines) engages that self. He notes that within each model there is a wide range of variations. He makes many interesting distinctions and observations about each model, but space permits us only to summarize the basic options.

THE ORTHODOX MODEL. The orthodox theologian imagines himself as a believer, standing within a faith community in the midst of a secular and unbelieving world. The subject pole is the believer; the object pole is the unbelieving world. Fundamentalist, evangelical, and traditional writers in several traditions exemplify this powerful (and popular) model.

THE LIBERAL MODEL. The liberal theologian imagines himself as an autonomous, critical, free person, informed by the best of modern consciousness. The world he is addressing is usually the tradition of his own church as it needs to be reformulated in accordance with modern commitments, especially the commitment to rigorous and open inquiry. Great figures in this tradition include Schleiermacher, Hegel, Blondel, Ritschl, Wieman, Harnack, Troeltsch, Loisy.

THE NEO-ORTHODOX MODEL. The neo-orthodox theologian arises out of the liberal tradition, but modifies it in an important way. Taking to heart the realistic lessons of the twentieth century, the neo-orthodox theologian imagines himself neither as the traditional believer nor as the optimistic liberal, but rather as a human being driven to existential attitudes, conceived of in a Christian (or Jewish) way: courage out of despair, authenticity, and interpersonal love. Driven beyond both inherited faith and the "illusions" of liberalism, the neo-orthodox theologian imagines the world he addresses to be engaged with the realities of "the wholly other God," or "the Radically Mysterious God," operative in human experience through an inbreaking, unexpected Event. Both self and world are spoken of dialectically, with respect for contingency, paradox, surprise, and tragedy. Major thinkers who exemplify this model include Barth, Brunner, Bult-mann, Tillich, Reinhold Niebuhr, and H. Richard Niebuhr.

THE RADICAL MODEL. The radical theologian imagines the self to be post-modern, committed to secular intellectual and moral values. He imagines the world to be engaged in a struggle for liberation from various alienations, but especially from the God of orthodox, liberal, or neo-orthodox theologians, the God who has "died." These theologians without God re-define Christianity and Judaism into a life of affirmation, committed to the liberation and humanization of the world ("a life for others"). In this, they hope to re-interpret Christianity and Judaism as forms of non-alienating humanism. Key writers of this type are Thomas J. J. Altizer, William Hamilton, and Richard Rubenstein.

THE REVISIONIST MODEL. The revisionist theologian tries to escape the imagined division between faith and modernity. He redefines both. The revisionist theologian imagines the self to have a dual commitment, both to the fundamental meaning of his religious tradition and to the meaning of contemporary experi-ence. The world addressed by the revisionist is imagined to be far less secular than orthodox, liberal, neo-orthodox, or radical theologians imagine. He finds religious meanings (according to various particular "horizons") within its common experiences. Langdon Gilkey, Van Harvey, John Dunne, Peter Berger, Ber-nard Lonergan, Emil Fackenheim, and others work within this model.

Actually, Tracy's name for this last model is weaker than it needs to be. I prefer the name "symbolic realism." The word "symbolic" suggests that the key for understanding lies in the systems of interpretation by which human beings—symbolic ani-mals—attempt to comprehend their experience. "Realism" sug-gests that one must elicit meanings which illuminate, and may be verified by application to, actual human experience in our time.

Symbolic realists make one hidden assumption, *viz.,* that each period of history brings forth its own measure of new experience and wisdom. Each such period should be studied for what, in effect, God is trying to teach his people through the events of their time. On the other hand, symbolic realists do not particularly trust the spirit of the age. They seek instead far deeper or richer perspectives (in traditional religious teachings or in historical or other investigations) that might bring helpful and challenging light to bear upon common experience.

In stressing the many different horizons within which theologians and other thinkers operate, Professor Tracy has seemed to some critics to reveal too little about his own horizon. Some sentences in his book suggest, against his obvious intention, that Christianity is limited to what may be learned from contemporary human experience. It is clear that Professor Tracy thinks of Christianity, and other profound religious traditions, as carrying *judgment upon* contemporary human experience—as setting the latter off in a new light, and as opposing many of the tendencies of contemporary life. Perhaps because he was trying to formulate a set of models within which the liberal option has played such a decisive role—he tends to see the other models he describes (except the orthodox) as modifications of the liberal enterprise—he did not make plain enough the quite different sense of reality involved in his own revisionist model. The revisionist model not only "revises"; it in some ways contradicts, and fundamentally alters, the views of self and world that define the liberal model.

For example, the revisionist model has been built up from reflection upon sociology, anthropology, and philosophies of symbolic life. In this light, the autonomous rationalism of the liberal model seems naive and far too simple. Story, symbol, and horizon are prior to, and more fundamental than, rational criticism and rational analysis. Story, symbol, and horizon are subject to forms of intelligent inquiry not developed by theologians working within earlier models. In a sense, the entire enterprise of our present "ascent of the mountain, flight of the dove" has been an exercise in attaining a higher viewpoint, in a clearly articulated and publicly argued way. From this viewpoint, the earlier theological models seem less powerful and less exact.

It is possible from within our own model—let us call it symbolic realism—to enter into theologies worked out upon other models, to appreciate them in their own terms, and yet to see where either for internal or for external reasons they do not suffice for explaining our experiences. It is possible to value the particularity of our own horizon, and to struggle to deepen it and to expand it, while possessing a method for "passing over" from it into horizons different from our own. From such an effort, we can learn much, and make significant (radical, self-altering) appropriations. It is possible, in short, to develop a "pluralistic personality," to learn a method for living in a pluralistic context, faithful to our own traditions, while also learning from others. It is possible to be "open" without being "porous," and to be who we are, without being "closed." It is possible to stand within a tradition of faith, and yet to "pass over" carefully into the experiences and understandings of those who do not share that faith—both to disagree and to learn, to challenge and to be challenged. It is not necessary to abandon either one's roots or the multiple projects of our time, while trying with critical intelligence to become all that one can become.[48]

7. THEOLOGY AS SUITOR

Theology is sustained reflection upon human experience. The methods whereby reflection is "sustained" vary from tradition to tradition. In some traditions, the model is that of extensive commentary upon a text. In others, the model is a statement of questions and precise responses. In others, the model is that of a "scientific" treatise: theses precisely set forth, evidence marshaled, qualifications introduced, implications deduced, correlations made explicit, conclusions drawn. In others, a sinuous path is taken, a kind of hovering over the nuances of complex human experiences. In others, words are scarcely employed and a quiet watch over internal experiences and spiritual growth is instituted; "discernment" replaces "argument."

Theology has many uses. It can operate as a mere rationalization—a set of theories in whose defense much energy is expended, whose function, however, is to mask from one's attention what is truly happening in one's experience. A man may insist that too much "permissiveness" is corrupting young people, when in fact vast changes in the procedures of everyday life—the sudden introduction of family automobiles, artificial suburban living, television, mobility, meritocratic competition—have deeply altered the experience of being young.

Theology may, or may not, keep in touch with human experience. It may come to represent "ideology"—reflection which no longer springs from living experience. To be sure, ideology does not come merely from the past. The media men, the hucksters, the false prophets, the con men, and the sloganeers who represent "relevance," and "now," and "the newest point of view" can also be out of touch with living experience. By contrast with *them,* the most ancient views may be far more in touch with the living springs of our hearts. There is no more subtle and illusory tyranny than the tyranny of the present. Those who surrender themselves to it forfeit what is to be learned from the sufferings of those who did likewise in the past.

In a word, wisdom is the criterion for discriminating good theology from mere ideology. "Wisdom" comes, in its Latin root, from *sapiens,* taste; and in its Anglo-Saxon root from the concrete flash of light we call *wit.* Wisdom arises from attachment to the concrete. It clings to earth: to *this* person, here and now—not to "mankind." The love for abstractions is wisdom's greatest enemy. "How can I love the Japanese whom I do not see, if I do not love my neighbor whom I do see?"

The wise person concentrates on being who he *is,* on the people who now actually are *near* him, on the experiences he is *now* aware of, on the situation in which he finds himself. *That* is where "the kingdom of God" is: *here and now.*

Images of a better world, of a brighter future, of justice and beauty and truth and other abstractions, are not to be despised. But if they lead one to neglect what is immediately at hand they are signs, not of wisdom, but of ideology. If tomorrow all humans will be brothers and sisters, but today some are pigs, it is ideology that rules. Murder follows.

Theology, therefore, must be held to account. Theology does not own us; it woos us. If it leads us to ignore our bodies, our associates, and the good earth itself, wisdom warns us away. In the medieval phrase: Wisdom is queen. A theology, as reflection, may be masculine, sustained, critical, dominating. Wisdom is the "Lady" a theology serves. When his service is poor, the Lady is free. And seeks another suitor.

SIX

Nature and History

What shall we *do?* The decision about our identity is made, not in the mind, but in action. We are what we do. Religious studies are ultimately concerned with action.

And yet, what is action?

The metaphor for action accepted by modern science and the Reformation tends to be the metaphor of "making a difference" in history.[1] The dominant mood is "concern." (Clergy and Laymen *Concerned* about Vietnam. Religion as ultimate *concern.*) "Mature" man takes up his "responsibility." He assumes "control" over his own "destiny." The task of philosophy, Marx wrote, is "not to reflect upon history, but to change it." The enemy is the static, the changeless, the eternal. The enemy is the merely "natural," the cyclical, the biologically determined. "History" is the realm of "freedom." "Nature" is the realm of "necessity." Goethe's Faust rewrites the Prologue to St. John's Gospel. "In the beginning was the Word" is no longer satisfying. Faust is restless. When he has erased "Word" and inserted "Deed," he feels far more pleased: his own spirit has found expression. Man the doer. (*"Do it!"* Jerry Rubin.) Man the maker of history. Man against nature.

Thomas J. J. Altizer among all Christian theologians has given himself most radically to the myth of historymaking. Altizer accuses Mircea Eliade, for example, of presenting the shaman, the yogi, and "the archaic mode of being in the world" as models for modern man. Altizer dislikes this "regression" to the archaic. "Like the Oriental mystic," he accuses, "Eliade conceives of the way to the ultimate sacred as a return to the 'nontime' of the primordial beginning." Eliade "reveals his non-Christian ground; he is unable to say *Yes* to the Future, to envision a truly New Creation, to look *forward* to the Kingdom of God."[2] The lust for the future is the sign of the historymaker. History is preferred to nature.

"The profound conflict of this century," Albert Camus wrote in *The Rebel,* "is . . . between German dreams and Mediterranean traditions—in other words, between history and nature." He adds: "In the common condition of misery, the eternal demand is heard again; nature once more takes up the fight against history. Naturally, it is not a question of despising anything, or of exalting one civilization at the expense of another, but of simply saying that it is a thought which the world cannot do without for very much longer."[3]

In *The Myth of Sisyphus* he writes:

For some time the entire effort of our philosophers has aimed solely at replacing the notion of human nature with that of situation, and replacing ancient harmony with the disorderly advance of chance or reason's pitiless progress. . . . Nature is still there, however. She contrasts her calm skies and her reason with the madness of men. Until the atom too catches fire and history ends in the triumph of reason and the agony of the species. But the Greeks never said that the limit could not be overstepped. They said it existed and whoever dared to exceed it was mercilessly struck down. Nothing in present history can contradict them. [4]

What is action?

In the generation preceding our own, the problem of action often took the form: "Why do anything at all? Why is any action 'better' than any other? Every act seems equally meaningless, equally pointless." In Western civilization, progress was our most important product, the ground of our superiority, the heart of our reason for being. The myth of progress had two bases, and one after the other they were shattered. The first basis was a sense of reality according to which God orders history; history is the unfolding of God's will—"Rush forward with it, then, make God's kingdom come on earth." But many ceased to believe in God.

The "enlightened," instead, cherished a sense of reality according to which the more reason establishes its control over nature, the more "a new age" comes into existence: an age of equality based upon reason, an end to privilege, an era of liberty and brotherliness and equality. But many ceased to believe in reason.

Face to face with the absurd, many wondered why they should not commit suicide,[5] or why it is wrong for man to murder man.[6] After all, storms, microbes, famines, and plagues murder man. What is more natural, more to be expected, than murder? The problem of action was why one ought to work for justice, equality, or even for one's own advancement, since all things seem equally pointless.

The problem of action in our own generation, *in addition to* the problem of the preceding generation, is whether one ought to seek a private, communal shelter in order to live as "naturally" and "without hang-ups" as is possible. Or whether one ought to work to bring about social and political "change."

America has been inoculated with optimism and the need to act. The American sense of reality is such that, after a discussion of the human situation, an enormous ritual hunger is stirred. Insistently, American audiences demand that the question be pressed: "What are we going to *do* about it? What are your *constructive* proposals?" Even if there *is* nothing that can be done

about it, Americans have a ritual need to launch something effective: like, start a committee. Once the committee is launched,
everybody feels better; duty has been done; responsibility for
history has been exercised. The sky god of progress has been
placated. Yes has been said to the future. A "New Creation" has
been envisioned. One has looked forward.

But when American progress has been inflicted upon the entire
planet—when the entire planet, say, has been brought up to the
level of New Jersey—will our dream of progress seem to have
been a dream, or a nightmare?

The lust for historymaking is based upon a fundamental mistake. It is not true that the paradigm of human action is to pick
up a book and drop it, to draw one's thumbnail across a brown
leather chair and leave a jagged scratch (having made one's mark
on "history"), to delegate a committee, to invent the gas combus-
tion engine, to mobilize public opinion, to pass a new law, to take
to the barricades.

Not all human action is *transitive:* directed to bringing about
effects in the world, to affecting others, to "making a difference"
in the world. A great many of the most precious human actions
are *immanent:* directed to bringing one's own activities into operation and then to peaceful completion.[7] Many of the most beautiful, satisfying, and ennobling actions do not (immediately) have
effects upon others or the world or even upon oneself. They are
not manipulative. They are acts which do not imply a "passing
over" from subject to object, such that action occurs only when
the "object" has been changed. Such an image is essentially alienating: action always terminates in an "other." Those who give
their lives to "making history" must often evade themselves.

In our actual practice, there are many actions which do not
change objects "out there." Instead, they change their *subject:*
they change the agent. Many achievements are of this sort, as
even the grammar of "achieving" words indicates.[8] Our sad over-
emphasis on competition teaches us to measure our achievements

by comparison with those of others. Our attention is directed away from what is happening to ourselves. Did we finish first, ninth, two hundred and thirty-first? How do we "rank"?

Whereas, what is at least as significant is: "What are we capable of? What kind of surprises lie buried within us?" Our image of our capacities is almost always out of tune with what we actually do. If you tell a class that they are honors students, that image often leads them to do honors work; if you tell them they are hopeless, they often oblige. Parents, teachers, and friends frequently reinforce a child in a false image of his capacities. Talents, tendencies, and instincts of a rare and precious quality are frequently overlooked. We do not know ourselves; hence, our achievements often have a revelatory impact.

Great athletes, for example, frequently learn a language about competition not provided by the ideology of competition.[9] Their coaches and publicists tell the world: "Winning isn't a good thing; it's the only thing!" But athletes often measure their own performance on a quite different scale. In one sense, they do care about vanquishing the opposition, particularly for the sake of others on their own team; they are not out there only for themselves. In another sense, even in victory they may be disappointed with their own performance. They measure themselves by their own *identity*. They compete chiefly with *themselves*. They cherish the best possible opposition, not in order to rank themselves first, but in order to be stretched to the maximum and to see how far the limits of their own capacities can go. It is disappointing not to have worthy opposition, not to be tested. For the main part of athletic struggle is for the satisfaction of the athlete's own sense of himself: to know in action who he is and what his limits are. He lives to extend himself, to push past his presently known limits. That satisfaction is far more profound, and secure, than the secondary satisfaction of "winning." And it may be found even in defeat.

What is true of achievements in sports is also true in painting,

in writing, in architecture, in understanding, in judgment, in
action. Quite often, recognition is withheld from the agent; quite
often, she is not master of the effects of her achievements—they
may be fruitful or fruitless, "relevant" or "irrelevant" in changing the world in her own time (or ever). Still, many persons
cherish those achievements which fulfill their own identity; these
are the most precious they attain. They would rather be "true to
themselves" than to "make history"—not least because so many
of the actions which "change history" are shoddy, meretricious,
corrupt, alienated, and alienating. Hitler changed history. He is
not everybody's idea of authenticity, or of autonomy, or of a man
in touch with his own identity, or at peace with himself. And
countless "celebrities" every year become "significant people,"
deeply unhappy with themselves, painfully aware of the manipulation involved in their method of "becoming effective" in history.

The split between nature and history, in brief, is an untimely,
unnecessary, and destructive split. The following acts may not
involve "changing" society, or political power arrangements, or
history; but they are extraordinarily precious just the same: empathy for one whose sense of reality is very different from one's
own; compassion for an old woman who is dying in one's care;
wordless wonder as one sits for an hour before a painting by
Botticelli or Picasso; silence at dusk as the sun slips behind a violet
haze; insight into a friend's perplexities—or one's own; willingness to commit oneself to a judgment like "X is shoddy; Y is a
good piece of work"; the commitment of oneself to an action, out
of honesty and courage, even when it is plain that no one else will
offer support and the chances of success are nil—action because
one's own identity demands drawing a line and saying, "Here I
stand, I can do no other."

Besides "concern" for "accepting one's responsibilities as a
citizen," in a word, there is also the sense of fruition and joy that
comes from being who one is: from acting in total fidelity to one's

own identity. Besides *doing,* there is also *being.* Besides the *doing* which is having an effect upon others or the world, there is also the *doing* which is an *acting out* of one's own being: the moving into *act* of one's own ready resources. Such acts "reveal." One's own self flashes forth from them. As such, they have the sacredness of all epiphanies. "Beautiful, man!" Translated: "Beauty is the true shining forth of a person's being—and that is a precious moral good." As ancient Greeks and medievals stressed, beauty, truth, being, and good are each implicated in every appearance of the other. Daniel Berrigan has translated the Buddha: "Don't just do something, stand there!"

There are, of course, tensions between nature and history. In the struggle to be true to one's own being, one may cease to be political: cease to be true to one's nature as a political animal. More sharply still: in the struggle to be true to one's own being as a political animal, one may be torn by the claims of other truths. To obey the state may be to injure one's most cherished personal values. Is one entitled, sharing the communal goods made possible by the state, to prefer one's personal values to demands made by the state? Must an American political leader speak the truth in a manner tempered by what he knows the public can understand, or must he speak the truth as he himself sees it? And where, then, lies the boundary between sugarcoating and lying?

Modern writers, facing the claims of a morality which insists on fidelity to one's own identity, frequently make two objections. First, there is no one "self" to be faithful to. Secondly, a morality of fidelity to self is basically egocentric, and self-indulgent.

The second objection is easier to answer. In no other civilization except that of the modern West would it occur to humans to weigh fidelity to self in the same balance with obedience to the social body. To most humans it has been overwhelmingly obvious that the claims of the social order far outweigh the claims of the individual. If Athens suffers from external threat, every citizen is threatened. If Athens suffers from internal corruption, every citizen is infected. The state is the individual writ large. Hence, when ancient or medieval writers speak of "self-realization," they are not thinking of the solitary individual of the modern era, but of the social self, the political animal, of the era of the city-state and the medieval town. For them, "self-realization" is a social reality. That men try to become all that they can become is a political good, promoted or inhibited by the social policies of the body politic. It is not a private, individualistic good. Emphatically, it does not derive from *laissez faire.* "Ethics is a branch of politics" (Aristotle). The concept of the individual is foreign to any culture except that of the modern West. A morality of fidelity to self is a *social* and *political* morality—not a simple one, not without a thousand dangers and deceptions. Action always involves risk of failure.

The first objection requires a more complicated response. In one sense it is true that I do not "have" a self, "am" not a self, cannot locate within my experience a central "core" or "substance" or "unchangeable essence."[10] The image of a permanent substratum of identity is part of one sense of reality and story; it is not, for example, part of the Buddhist sense of reality or story. The "self" is, in this context, a Western construct. In recent years, the sense of social solidity and place and direction is breaking down in America. Many have no "home." Many experience the dissolution of what they used to think of as their "self."

Jesus was a wanderer. Buddha described the world as a burning house. Both encouraged their followers to set forth on the road with little or nothing in their hands. Their image—like that of the Jews—was homelessness. Robert N. Bellah, in a lovely paper called "No Direction Home,"[11] cites a number of lyrics by Bob Dylan and a number of lines from younger poets, expressing the new wanderlust in America. So many young Americans reject the stability and the security and the piling up foursquare of objects and possessions by which an earlier generation had tried to turn a wild continent into a safe suburban home. The new giving up of roots, the new return as it were to the nomadic life of the dark-skinned gentle savages who once roamed plains and forests, entails a blending and fading of identities.

Many writers glorify this loss of self as a new liberty. They suggest for example, that promises, commitments, and loyalty are meaningless,[12] for tomorrow is another day and who is to bind the "self" of tomorrow to the "self" of today? Others decry "the loss of the centered self," the "fragmentation" of the self, as a romantic surrender to chaos, to unreliable emotional crosscurrents, and to the madness of undirected passion. Thence, they warn, spring the excesses of Fascism. When "the center" of the soul does not hold, dreary winds blow through the emptiness, gather gale force, and erupt in bloody passion. Where centered selves collapse, violence appears.

The truth is difficult to discern. On the one hand, it is clear that "the self" is a social and personal construct. We in part invent who we are. We in part shape our own sense of reality and story. In this respect, there is no fixed and unequivocal "self" to be faithful to. The developing human being is converted often. Who he is undergoes continual transformation. He voyages from horizon to horizon. He changes "selves" rather as a snake sheds skins.[13]

On the other hand, a person is not mere flux, a feather blown about upon the winds of his own moods. By his actions he constantly defines himself. He may *choose* to give himself the identity of a drifter, an addict of "building a better mood through chemistry," a follower of whim, impulse, instinct, mood, and feeling. That, in a word, may be the last bit of direction he puts into his life; thenceforward, he is pliant and docile. He waits for events to "happen" to him. He hangs loose, plays it cool, plays it by ear. There are many who live like that.

The human being, though lacking an inner "core" or "self," cannot evade responsibility. Each person sometimes has insights. (The very, very dull have them seldom.) Each person sometimes judges that X is untrue; beautiful or shoddy; just or unfair. Each person necessarily fills time with action; for in the relevant sense even not to act is nevertheless to act.

In that sense, to be faithful to my "self" is not to serve a clay idol. To my own acts of insight, judgment, choice, action I remain responsible. The intentionality of which we spoke in an earlier chapter links these acts together. Without those earlier in the series, the later do not occur. But sequences of such acts are linked to other sequences, across a lifetime. If I had not learned to read English, these sentences would be impossible for me to write. If I had not, step by step, had insights into ways of speaking about the "self," not even such poor intelligibility as I have mustered would be accessible to me. What I have so far gained insight into prepares me to benefit from criticisms and objections which will be directed against what I have written.

Our lives are networks of our acts—and in particular of those immanent acts whose effects are not exhausted upon matters outside us, whose operation changes our nature even as we experience it. We grow by acting. The proper focus of action is (to speak in rough metaphor) half upon what happens to the agent, half upon what his acts effect upon the world. If either focus is lost, distortion arises.

We are, then, liberated from the narrow biases of the modern Western sense of reality, story, and symbols. We do not have to think of ourselves as solitary individuals. We do not have to locate our psychic center of gravity in some permanent, solitary, and unchanging "self." We do not have to think of the "self" as a center of enlightenment and control: as mind, or will. We do not have to think of ourselves as mere doers, valuable if and only if we are "making a contribution" to society. We do not have to accept judgment upon ourselves based solely upon the effects of what we do, upon success, upon "having made a difference."

We are free to pray—free to sit in the long silence of contemplation, our souls perhaps as parched as baked desert sands, empty and abandoned, and yet, strangely, at peace. We are free to say "Yes" to existence. We are free to give, rather than to demand, love; free to be intelligent, even where intelligence is not welcome; free to act as we see fit, even if the sense of reality and story implicit in our action eludes all actual witnesses, who therefore judge us foolish. We are free, too, to accept the discipline of good work (of art, of craftsmanship, of inquiry, of poetry, of music, of any job well done)—a discipline that liberates, because the demands of the work alter *us*, help *us* to grow. It is a mistake to believe that in art (or in life) "process" is everything, the completed object is nothing. The resistance of objects, their own proper laws, their uniqueness invite us to enter into communion with them, a communion in which *we* are changed as they are.

There is a clean, deep joy that comes from fidelity to one's own experiencing, imagining, understanding, judging, deciding. That joy is intensified by harmony between one of these operations and every other. Through exercising such operations, we grow from horizon to horizon. We are, without a doubt, homeless. We have tasted the experience of nothingness. In these respects, the sons are no better than the fathers, daughters than mothers, down all the ages of mankind. But fidelity to the operations mentioned is direction enough for voyagers. Where else have we to go, except to grow in them?

Every human being on the planet shares in them. And there, too, lies a hope—that we might construct a planetary horizon, within which visions would not be merged, distinctions would remain distinct, unique identities would not be lost. And yet, within which each person might be able to discern, to the limit of his present capacities, the sense of reality and the stories and the symbols of persons living within a different horizon from his own. And tender them the respect, dignity, and emulation he would like to draw to himself.

Religious studies are directed toward understanding who we are, under these stars, and with the wind upon our faces. They are directed toward the many different kinds of actions around which humans build their lives. They are directed toward action—both in order to encourage action and in order to criticize action. No prejudgment is made about *which* actions to encourage, or *from which horizon* to launch criticisms. There is no absolute standpoint accessible to humans. Hence, we try to understand, to sympathize with, and to criticize one another. Such argument as arises is at the heart of what is meant by civilization: a conversation—often direct and harsh, for our survival is at stake—between equals.

The passion of Westerners for "making history" has brought this planet to a point from which either a golden age or annihilation of all things living may be imagined—and made real. More likely, we shall experience that amalgam of suffering, blundering, and tragedy which has characterized our species until this time. Westerners are open now, let us hope, to the wisdom of those cultures which have remained closer to nature. For the chief task of our time is to reconcile history to nature, to endure, to converse.

Another Turn on the Mountain

A number of years ago, the central concept of this book was virtually unknown. By now, it has figured in scores of books and articles. For all that, the concept *story* is still not clearly understood. This new revision provides an opportunity to bring the discussion up to date, and to clear away some of the worst misunderstandings.

Karl Barth once wrote that the proper place to begin a systematic theology lies in ethics—with the way in which those who believe actually live. The Catholic church canonizes saints far more often than it honors theologians, out of the conviction that lives speak louder than words. Religions are ways of living. In the narrow sense, ethics is only a part of the field of religious studies, the part that studies actions for their rightness or wrongness, goodness or badness. In a larger sense, ethics is the study of the meaning and significance of our actions, and opens out into the whole field of religious behavior: studying what religious symbols, rituals, and doctrines actually mean in the actions of those who participate in them. In this large but not improper sense, ethics and religious studies overlap. The point is to focus upon our actual living.

Life is fuller than words. Words are poor and clumsy tools, though each of them is precious. Those who write constantly struggle to put black marks on a page, trying to signal meaning to distant readers. Sometimes, the marks seem woefully inadequate. Often, in trying to express the experiences and meanings most important to us we keenly feel the limitations of our skills. The determination to get meanings into words—and to get them exactly—is thoroughly demanding. One key to its practice is to keep one's eye on the actual living of life, and not merely on other sets of words. Thus, a theory about religion properly begins with a theory of human action.

If it were not for persons who actually lived in a religious way, and if it were not for our own experiences, the study of religion would lack vitality. It would become the study of people far away from ourselves, and of ways of life that have lost power over us. To begin with the study of people actually living in a certain way —more, to begin with a study of our *own* way of life—is to begin the study of religion at its living fount. To do otherwise is to risk a study of empty cisterns, which do not nourish life.

The main function of the concept *story,* then, is to call attention to a new way of approaching human action, including our own actions. The basic insight is that the human being is an embodied person, and is moved by imagination and sensibility in conjunction with intelligence. Many philosophers and theologians have stressed either the elements of *reason* in human action, or the elements of the *irrational.* That seems to be a mistake. In our actions, intelligence is always intermixed with the work of the imagination and the sensibility—with experience, image, symbol, myth and narrative context. The so-called irrational parts of our nature, our emotions and images and myths, carry with them strong currents of reason. In the Anglo-American tradition of philosophical reflection, predominating in most philosophy departments in our universities, these two parts of our nature are imagined as separate from each other, divided into the cognitive and the emotive, in ways that falsify how we actually live and move and act.

The approach executed in the preceding chapters of this book is quite different from the one taught most frequently in courses in ethics, whether in philosophy departments or in departments of religious studies. At first glance, some who inspect the theory set forth here conclude that I am on the side of the emotive, the irrational, or the existential. My intention, however, is to work out a theory that unites both sides of our nature in a way that does justice to the way we actually live. Decisions are not presented to us in compartments marked "emotive" or "cognitive," "passion" or "reason." In trying to decide which field of study to pursue, or whom to marry, or which job to accept, or what to work on next, not only our reason but our entire self is involved. Such decisions can be made in ways that do justice to all parts of our self. The advantage of the concept *story* in the study of decisions is that it allows us to treat all parts of the self in one unified concept. (If anything, I suppose, it leads to error on the side of reason and intelligence.)

The tradition within which I work is intellectualist rather than existentialist. It is not as well known to American scholars as it ought to be, although because of the work of Bernard Lonergan, David Tracy, David Burrell and others it is now better known than it was seven years ago. In using the language of *story, symbol, myth* and the *drive of inquiry,* I am thoroughly indebted to Aristotle's little-understood notion of *phronesis;* John Henry Newman's *illative sense;* Jacques Maritain's *knowledge by connaturality* and *creative intuition;* and Bernard Lonergan's *insight, judgment, unrestricted desire to know, self-appropriation,* and *conversion of consciousness.* Other figures who lie in the background are Maurice Blondel for his conception of *action* (which influenced William James), Joseph Maréchal's *point of departure for metaphysics,* and Reinhold Niebuhr's *self and the dramas of history.* Those who know this tradition will be able to grasp the intellectual horizon within which I work. But since it would be idle to expect all readers to be familiar with a tradition not their own, I have tried to find my own starting points and to develop my work internally so that it may stand on its own feet.

The experience of studying philosophy and theology at Harvard, where my own tradition was at first barely known, demonstrated to me how powerful an alternative approach can be in molding the way persons think, inquire, and act—and at a quite unconscious depth. I resolved to study such matters so as to shed new light on them. That impulse ultimately led me to this book, and to others as well.

By asking each inquirer to become more conscious of his or her own tradition, I trust that I am making a small contribution toward the fruitful articulation of the differences in horizon which normally keep thinkers from understanding one another. The method barely sketched in this introductory work is, for that reason, useful to advanced thinkers. There is a systematic purpose in my work, as some readers have noticed, and it may be useful for a "higher viewpoint" with relationship to the preceding chapters to limn its shape.

Since completing the first edition of this book, I have tried to become conscious of my own horizon, and to bring it under criticism from new directions. It is impossible not to see that I have expanded that horizon since the autumn of 1970 when the first edition went to press. That summer, I campaigned in thirty-nine states as chief policy adviser and speech writer to R. Sargent Shriver, as we tried to blunt the Nixon–Agnew effort in the congressional races of 1970. (Mr. Shriver had read *The Experience of Nothingness* on his return from France and telephoned me.) That first intense and hectic campaign started me in the direction that was to lead to *The Rise of the Unmeltable Ethnics* (1972) and *Choosing Our King* (1974). In these studies, I tried to explore the cultural traditions which linger in our intellectual and political life even after the "melting pot" has done its work. The first book helped open up a floodgate of new interpretations of the American experience, which National Book Award winners such as Irving Howe's *World of Our Fathers* and Michael Arlen's *Passage to Ararat,* as well as Pulitzer Prize citation-winner Alex Haley's *Roots* have begun to execute. The second book predicted that the strongest civil religion in America, not then fully represented on the national scene but shortly to arise, was that of evangelical America. Jimmy Carter read that book (or so he intimated to me) in 1975.

From politics I turned to another profound expression of our American civil religions, in the world of sports. (Unlike some analysts, I maintain that there are several active civil religions in America, not just one.) Here, too, I carried further the reflections on nature and history sketched above in Chapter Six. My thesis is that sports are liturgies of nature rather than of history; and that in a powerful way the category of play is more fundamental than that of work, and lies at the basis of civilization. Here, too, I drew upon a long Catholic tradition, expressed in Josef Pieper, Jacques Maritain, Gilbert K. Chesterton, Johann Huizinga and others. America's major sports—baseball, football, and basketball—are enormously rich for reflection. It is something of a scandal that they have been so neglected by scholars, even at the universities which have done so much to establish them in our expectations of human life. One of the great contributions of the universities has, indeed, been the creation of some of the most powerful liturgies and mythic expressions in our national life. From "Frank Merriwell at Yale" to today's almost professionalized bowl games, college athletics provides an important mythic subsoil for our common life. Our games teach specific attitudes and perceptions, and demand high excellence and grace. It was useful to me to try to analyze what I had learned from "the seven seals" of sports, and to examine the different story lines of baseball, basketball, and football, as well as other materials of the American imagination.

Recently, I have been working on the stories, symbols, and myths most established in the several genres of television news and entertainment. Students, I notice, can sing by heart the commercials and theme songs of television shows they watched as children. It is telling to note which symbolic materials work for American audiences, and which do not.

These explorations of the symbolic life of our many ethnic and regional cultures, of our politics, our sports, and our television, have brought me to the point where I am about to begin writing a basic theory of Christian ethics and a reasonably systematic theological interpretation of the experience of Christianity in American culture. In order to understand the workings of religion today, one must understand the workings of the imagination and the heart in the public culture (high, middle, and popular) in which we live, move, and have our being. That is the mountain I have been criss-crossing these last few years. The theories set forth in these pages have been of considerable help. Since some misunderstandings of these theories have become evident in recent years, it might be well to devote these last pages to tightening their argument.

"What is the use of studying ethics," Aristotle once asked, "unless to learn how to live better?" Some critics have worried that to approach religious studies in this way is not sufficiently academic or professional. Some students may be interested in Richard Crouter's long, negative review of this book in the *Journal of the American Academy of Religion,* with my response, and David Burrell's related article in later issues (March and September, 1972). Briefly put, Professor Crouter worries that my approach may be too unprofessional, not sufficiently objective and analytical. He prefers the practices favored in academic life until now, with their rigorous respect for individual disciplines, fields, and methods. I by no means wish to deny the merit or achievements of professionals like Professor Crouter. There are dangers in my approach—that it will become too subjective, imprecise, disorganized. The usual accusation laid against the tradition in which I work is, however, just the opposite: that it is too analytical, intellectualist, even rationalist. It is, after all, the tradition of Scholasticism. These strengths lie behind what I do, and if I sometimes take chances, it is with confidence that a strong net lies below me. I am lucky to be able to mint in a fresh and evocative way riches buried in a long tradition. It is true that I have not merely borrowed classical words or repeated classical words or repeated classical distinctions. The astute reader will notice, however, that in my own way I have observed such distinctions and brought into a rather easy American usage equivalents to ancient words.

Besides, there are dangers in Professor Crouter's approach as well. Modern academic life has its own version of the vices of Scholasticism, which include far too much attention to the analysis of words and concepts, to the neglect of realities to which they are intended to point. Having with much effort escaped some of the vices of Catholic Scholasticism, I was determined not to fall victim to the vices of its present-day academic counterpart.

In analyzing Professor Crouter's approach, and mine, in order to evaluate them and to choose between them (or, perhaps better, in order to learn to use each in its proper context), students will find that the concepts of *story, symbol, horizon, drive of inquiry,* and others help to show the areas of disagreement between Crouter and me. From my point of view, his sense of what is academic and professional is but one possible sense, and not the most fruitful for creative and critical work. I would like to perform work according to his standards, but also according to other and larger standards; and I would hope that the next generation of students will, too.

One of the virtues of the concept *story* is to enable us to approach the problem of belief and unbelief in a fresh and more illuminating light. "How shall we humans best imagine our situation? understand our destiny? and direct our actions?" Here believer and unbeliever stand as equals. No one knows the meaning of human life; for that reason, we usually speak of belief or faith rather than of knowledge. The atheist and the agnostic do not know the meaning of life, either; they, too, must give their lives structure. They, too, make "a leap of faith." But this so-called leap is not, after all, performed without considerable observation, testing, and reflection. It is not normally taken thoughtlessly or counter to good judgment. Our own decision may not be easy to talk about, or pleasant to think about for too long at a time, or quite as original as each of us might like to imagine. Yet few are the people who haven't had some glimpse of the stakes and made their best choice, in a way they would wish to defend. Is this not true in your own case?

The most important decisions of our lives—whom to trust, whom to love, whom to choose as spouse, which profession to follow, how to prepare for death—are not (exactly) made through principles, axioms, and logic. It is not quite true, either, on the opposite side, that such decisions are made solely through hunch, or instinct, or feelings, or intuition. If we were patient enough, and articulate enough, we could probably draw out (in hundreds of pages) the long skein of reasons and influences that lead us to such decisions. We could plausibly offer that account as a highly-reasoned defense of why, precisely, we act as we do.

Yet self-deceptions are many. The task of reading the inner motions of our own lives is not a simple one—to the contrary, it is exhausting. So we do not often perform it, except in shorthand. And part of the shorthand is the image we have of ourselves, of the sort of person we take ourselves to be, of the role in the world we take to be fitting, and of the dramatic forces set in motion by other agents around us. We make sense of all these things through stories.

It is a weighty proposition to assert—overturning in the process, a long and important tradition in the history of philosophy —that our moral actions are better analyzed through stories than through principles. Whereas most schools of contemporary ethics proceed through an analysis of ethical principles, norms, and imperatives, the proposal here is novel: Try to identify the "story" the subject is living out. To accomplish this, everything we know about ethical reasoning is useful, and everything taught in philosophy courses finds scope. But we also have to do *more* than is normally done in philosophy courses. We have to describe the shape of the subject's experiences, sensibility, and imagination. It is not nearly enough to state his or her ethical principles.

Here it may shed a little light to remark that I have long worked in the field of fiction, having published two novels and worked away at several others. The problem of creating believable characters and believable actions led me to reflect upon the components of action. Few treatments of action in books of philosophy were of help. In fiction, problems of time, motivation, and viewpoint are acute. I learned much about them in literary criticism; I saw many connections between religious studies and literary criticism. It is not by accident that many scholars who have seen the virtue of a philosophical analysis by way of story have worked long either in the study of Scripture or in literary studies. It is probably important for the future to forge closer links among literary studies, philosophy, and religious studies. As it is, both science and mathematics exert far greater gravitational pulls upon philosophy than is warranted by the conditions of human life.

The logic of narrative is not identical to the logic of argument. It is a logic, nonetheless. Certain actions for certain subjects are inappropriate, out of character, out of bounds, or—to put it simply—wrong. The reasons that this is so constitute the logic of narrative.

Narrative logic always includes general principles. But a theory of action that analyzes only what is general, and not what is singular and unique, necessarily misses critical materials. Every moral action is the action of a unique person in a singular situation. The full moral quality of the action depends upon the agent's acting appropriately with respect to every detail. As Aristotle remarks, there is in every action an infinite number of ways to err and only one way to be perfect: to hit every element just right. Indeed, an ethical agent must normally invoke *several* moral principles simultaneously, since some principles limit or counter the others. The primary error of most theories of ethics, then, is to narrow down attention to generalizable principles. It is an incorrect assumption that the properly moral center of action is what is lawlike and general. As Karl Rahner has pointed out, the irony is that the fully moral act is utterly unique, singular, and irrepeatable. Moral law is in that respect (and others too) quite different from scientific law. The logic of action differs from the logic of argument as narrative differs from syllogism.

The concept story, then, is an analytic tool. Its function is to highlight certain aspects of human action, especially those of moral weight. As a method, analysis by way of story adds to analysis by way of principles. Here a distinction is necessary. As a method, *analysis* by way of story is also different from the process of *telling a story*. We tell stories to make an important point and for many other reasons; for example, for sheer human delight. Stories function, too, as an elemental form of explanation and meaning. Still, story as an analytic tool is different from story as a narrative. In telling a story, we recount an action. In analysis by way of story, we call attention to the elements that constitute the action, in order to understand its moral significance.

There are three major misunderstandings of the concept of

story. (1) Some writers use the concept as a way of evading criticism, as though simply to say, "Well, this is my story, and that's that." That isn't that. Further questions arise. *Why* is that your story? What are the deficiencies of that story? How does it compare with rival stories? The point of the concept story is to bring into consciousness those elements of one's horizon which would normally be neglected and to place them under criticism. In rationalistic modes of analysis, one is asked to specify one's beliefs and ethical principles. The concept of story forces one to go further and to specify elements in one's *sensibility, imagination,* and *intentionality.* These, too, affect one's identity and one's actions. These, too, constitute the moral weight of one's actions. Specifying these, one does not escape from the critical task. On the contrary, one has extended the territory the analyst must master.

(2) Some writers use the concept story in an external, artificial way, as though the mere *claim* to be living by a story is the same as actually living by it. "My story is the Christian story," some have said. "Jesus Christ is my personal savior, and I follow him." To which the proper skeptical retort is: "Is that so?" Quietly, one wishes to observe a person's actions and behavior, but also the inner motions of his or her spirit, as these may be revealed in word, nuance, gesture, and manner. Special clues are discerned at those moments in which events catch the subject by surprise. *Still, it is not easy to determine which story is actually being lived out.* They err who use the concept story as a simple device, devoid of psychological sophistication, irony, and sensitivity to self-deception.

(3) Some writers use the concept story as though there were only one story a person is living out. (They usually favor the conscious, declared story.) This, too, is naive. Usually, a human life is a tangle of stories. Our conscious lives, at different depths, are divided by contrary impulses. We may be trying to pattern our lives on some favorite model or some vivid ideal. Still, it may be

painfully obvious to all our friends that our real lives are quite different from our self-image. Again, the full working out of a story takes time. (Time is a great revealer. The ideals of civilization root only slowly in our barbarian hearts.) Meanwhile, our inner lives are theaters of conflict. We are inhabited by many stories at once: by cover stories, by stories to which we only aspire, by stories that would seduce us, and by stories that others have learned through living with us to find reliable, even though we have not put them into words. The concept story, then, points to the tangled nests of our inner lives. It is not designed to simplify them. It obliges us to sort out many different dramatic threads.

The concept story must be used critically. It should not be used to close questions prematurely, but on the contrary to push them further than they are usually pushed. Its point is to help us speak more intelligibly and tellingly about the world of human character, motivation and act, than do rationalistic theories about beliefs and principles. Two persons looking on the same garden, John Wisdom has noted, see very different worlds, depending on their way of looking at the world. Story is a dynamic concept, better suited than Wisdom's concept *blik*, which is too static, to express such differences in horizons over lifetimes.

Finally, one should note that personal stories are not usually invented by the individual alone. Normally, they are passed along by the communities and cultures within which the individual is continually nourished. Discord and dissonance are highly probable, since conflicting stories are offered by every culture. There are differences, as well, between social and personal stories. Sometimes our social roles are not at all comfortable, and the fault may lie in them, or in ourselves. Through all these possibilities, it is not easy to find one's way. A free and open society allows for tremendous inner confusion and many wasted energies.

I wish I had done a better job at several places in this book. The revisions in this edition have helped to bolster some weak places and to correct some errors. Still, dissatisfactions remain. Chapter 6, for example (formerly the Epilogue), remains far too schematic. The point I wish to make defies brief treatment. In the first edition, I was trying to point toward the rise in the prestige of nature and natural things. Theories of history, progress, and growth were beginning to be criticized. Later, the rise of the ecological movement, the perceived scarcities of oil and other materials, and the attempt to slow population growth and industrialization, brought about a dramatic change in self-image.

Since times do change, and since sensibilities and imaginations change with them, it seemed wiser not to change some of those references which identify the text with the year (1970) during which it was written. In feeling the datedness of certain passages, the student sees clearly how horizons shift and meanings change. But changes required for clarity or simply for improvement have been made.

These inky marks upon the page, then, reach again across the silence. I enjoy hearing responses.

Notes

Introduction

1. Chicago: Univ. of Chicago Press, 1969.
2. Earlierbooksofminereflectthemovingstandpointfromwhich the present book has been written. *Belief and Unbelief* (New York: Macmillan, 1965) abstracted from the concrete, historical, mythic context and from the social context. It dwelt on the question of personal identity and emphasized the questioning intelligence.

In *A Time to Build* (New York: Macmillan, 1967), especially in "Moral Society and Immoral Man" (pp. 354–72), I began adding the social context.

In *A Theology for Radical Politics* (New York: Herder & Herder, 1969) I added the institutional context.

In *The Experience of Nothingness* (New York: Harper & Row, 1970) I was at last able to raise the cultural question—the question of being, reality, sanity.

In *The Rise of the Unmeltable Ethnics* (New York: The Macmillan Co., 1971, 1972, 1974), I tries to discover and articulate my own horizons. This task was doubly difficult because for Eastern European Catholics no intellectual tradition in humane letters

225

already exists, on which we might have relied. *The Joy of Sports* (New York: Basic Books, 1976, Harper Colophon, 1978) examines the horizon of play and liturgy.

One: The Voyage

1. See Ronald Laing, *The Politics of Experience* (New York: Pantheon, 1967).

2. I prefer the word "drive" to Tillich's "concern" (see e.g., his *Dynamics of Faith* [New York: Harper & Row, 1957] and D. MacKenzie Brown *Ultimate Concern: Tillich in Dialogue* [New York: Harper & Row, 1965]) for three reasons. First, the word "drive" correlates better with scientific usage, and should be given a wider use than now seems common. Surely it is one "drive" that scientists themselves give rein to as they struggle to understand, and another drive that obliges men to structure their experience by acting in the world. Secondly, the word "concern," while it connotes the will and affectivities (and that is to its advantage), has a concretely Protestant and slightly moral ring to it— as though we *ought* to be concerned, even if we're not. "Drive" is more universal and more neutral. Thirdly, "drive" is manifested through behavior and, in this context, specifically through human actions. "What is he driving at?" and "What's driving him?" are ordinary and compelling questions which uncover the intentionality in human activity. "Drive," in fact, might be rendered as "intentionality." See, e.g., Rollo May, *Love and Will* (New York: Norton, 1970), pp. 223–74, and my *The Experience of Nothingness, op. cit.,* pp. 44–45, and "The Philosophic Roots of Religious Unity," in *A Time to Build, op. cit.,* pp. 301–19. Also cf. Stuart Hampshire, *Thought and Action* (New York: Viking, 1959), pp. 90–168.

3. For me, religious studies have two focal points: (1) all integrative world views whatever; (2) especially, world views with explicit reference to the divine. Contrast William James, for

whom *religion* means "the feelings, acts, and experiences of individual men in their solitude, so far as they apprehend themselves to stand in relation to whatever they may consider the divine." *The Varieties of Religious Experience* (New York: New American Library, 1958), p. 42. And compare Alfred North Whitehead, for whom *religion* is "the art and theory of the internal life of man, so far as it depends on the man himself and on what is permanent in the nature of things." *Religion in the Making* (New York: Macmillan, 1926), p. 16.

My basic theorem is that all human action necessarily implies a view of the world in which it occurs, of the self, and of their relation. Religious studies take human action and its implicit structures for its subject matter. And human action is systematically self-transcending, hence fertile with intimations—whether illusory or trustworthy—of the divine. The field of study is larger, then, than James' notion of religion would allow, and does not depend on "what is permanent in the nature of things" as Whitehead's definition does.

For various other attempts to define religion see: Paul Tillich, *What Is Religion?*, translated by James Luther Adams (New York: Harper & Row, 1969): "Religion is directedness toward the Unconditional" (p. 59). Influenced by Tillich, Robert N. Bellah, a sociologist and interpreter of religion, defines religion as "a set of symbolic forms and acts which unite man to the ultimate conditions of his existence." "Religious Evolution," *American Sociological Review*, XXXIX (1964), p. 358. The anthropologist Clifford Geertz writes: "A religion is a system of symbols which acts to establish powerful, pervasive and long-lasting moods and motivations in men by formulating conceptions of a general order of existence and clothing these conceptions with such an aura of factuality that the moods and motivations seem uniquely realistic." "Religion as a Cultural System," in *Anthropological Approaches to the Study of Religion,* A.S.A. Monographs, III (London: Travistock Press, 1966), p. 4.

Friedrich Schleiermacher, the nineteenth century's most influential theologian, found religion "neither a knowing or a doing, but a modification of feeling, or of immediate self-consciousness . . . the consciousness of being absolutely dependent." *The Christian Faith,* I (New York: Harper Torchbooks, 1963), pp. 5–12. Karl Barth, the Protestant theologian who stressed the uniqueness of God's self-disclosure in Christ claimed there was no category "religion" of which Christianity is a member. "Religion is unbelief." *Church Dogmatics,* I, 2, translated by G. S. Thompson and Harold Knight (Edinburgh: T. and T. Clark, 1956), p. 299.

In *The Meaning and End of Religion: A New Approach to the Religious Traditions of Mankind* (New York: Mentor, 1964), Wilfred Cantwell Smith contends: "The participant is concerned with God; the observer has been concerned with 'religion' . . . this latter concept . . . is inadequate even for the observer."

For a survey of various approaches to the study of religion see Mircea Eliade, "History of Religions in Retrospect," in *The Quest: History and Meaning in Religion* (Chicago: Univ. of Chicago Press, 1969), pp. 12–36.

4. New York: Macmillan Paperbacks, 1960, pp. 26–27.

5. See Albert Camus: "What I hate is death and disease, as you well know. And whether you wish it or not," Rieux said to Paneloux, "we're allies, facing them and fighting them together." (New York: Modern Library, 1948, p. 197.)

6. See my "The Christian and the Atheist" and "The Odd Logic of Theism and Atheism," in *A Time to Build, op. cit.,* pp. 51–69.

7. See, e.g., Allport: "Most psychologists who have written on religion seem agreed that there is no single and unique religious emotion, but rather a widely divergent set of experiences that may be focused upon a religious object. It is the habitual and intentional focusing of experience rather than the character of the experience itself that marks the existence of a religious senti-

ment." *Op. cit.,* pp. 4–5. Allport sees the mature religious sentiment as a drive, directing actions, integrating all experiences (including evil), comprehensive in its scope, and heuristic in its progress by way of probabilities. *Ibid.,* pp. 52–72.

8. I am indebted to many conversations with John Dunne, in whose *Search for God in Time and Memory* (New York: Macmillan, 1969) and *The City of the Gods* (New York: Macmillan, 1965) I found great illumination for the way I wanted to explore. One should now also explore his later works: *The Way of All the Earth* (New York: Macmillian, 1972) and *Time and Myth* (South Bend: University of Notre Dame Press, 1975—a reprint of the edition published by Doubleday, N.Y., 1973).

9. Translated by H. Rackham (Cambridge: Harvard Univ. Press, 1962) Book I.

10. See Sidney Mead, "The Nation with the Soul of a Church," *Church History,* XXXVI (September, 1967), and Robert Bellah, "Civil Religion in America," *Daedalus* (Winter, 1967), pp. 1–21.

11. See Donald Meyer, *The Positive Thinker: A Study of the American Quest for Health, Wealth and Personal Power from Mary Baker Eddy to Norman Vincent Peale* (Garden City: Doubleday, 1965).

12. See Hervé Carrier, *The Sociology of Religious Belonging* (New York: Herder & Herder, 1965). For a compassionate fictional representation of this religious sensibility, see John Updike, "The Deacon," *The New Yorker,* February 21, 1970, pp. 38–41.

13. See Sören Kierkegaard, *Stages on Life's Way,* translated by Walter Lowrie (New York: Schocken, 1967). See also Lowrie's biography, *Kierkegaard* (New York: Harper Torchbooks, 1962, two volumes).

14. See Carl Amery, *Capitulation: The Lesson of German Catholicism,* translated by Edward Quinn (New York: Herder & Herder, 1964), and Paul Hanly Furfey, *The Respectable Murderers: Social Evil and Christian Conscience* (New York: Herder & Herder, 1966).

15. For the classic statement on "notional assent" as opposed to

"real assent," see John Henry Newman, *An Essay in Aid of a Grammar of Assent* (Garden City: Doubleday, 1955), pp. 86–93; also J. M. Cameron, *The Night Battle* (Baltimore: Helicon, 1962).

16. See Sigmund Freud, *The Future of an Illusion,* translated by W. D. Robson-Scott (Garden City: Doubleday Anchor Books, 1964).

17. Julian N. Hartt refers to the daily quotidian world as the "Q World," and argues that "God Transcendent" can be known only insofar as that Q World is broken into, erupted. "Secularity and the Transcendence of God," in *Secularization and the Protestant Prospect,* edited by James F. Childress and David B. Harned (Philadelphia: Westminster, 1970).

18. See Robert Coles, "Talking with God," *Commonweal,* December 12, 1969, pp. 330–34.

19. For a good study of Barth's Christocentrism, see James D. Smart, *The Divided Mind of Modern Theology: Karl Barth and Rudolf Bultmann 1908–1933* (Philadelphia: Westminster, 1967).

20. For a history of the Roman Catholic tradition, John Edwin Gurr, *The Principle of Sufficient Reason in Some Scholastic Systems 1750–1900* (Milwaukee: Marquette Univ. Press, 1959).

21. For a survey of German thought in the nineteenth century see Karl Barth, *Protestant Thought from Rousseau to Ritschl* (New York: Harper & Row, 1959).

22. For an introduction to a theological use of linguistic analysis, see Frederick Ferré, *Language, Logic and God* (New York: Harper & Row, 1961).

23. For an introduction to a theological use of process philosophy see John B. Cobb, *A Christian Natural Theology* (Philadelphia: Westminster, 1965).

24. Compare Thomas S. Kuhn, *The Structure of Scientific Revolutions, op. cit.,* pp. 43–52; Peter L. Berger and Thomas Luckmann, *The Social Construction of Reality: A Treatise on the Sociology of Knowledge* (Garden City: Doubleday, 1966); and Alfred Schutz, *The Phenomenology of the Social World,* translated by George Walsh and

Frederick Lehmert (Evanston: Northwestern Univ. Press, 1967).

25. American philosophers have been unexcelled in their attention to human experience. See John E. Smith, *The Spirit of American Philosophy* (New York: Oxford, 1966); John Dewey, *Experience and Nature* (New York: Dover, 1958); William James, *Pragmatism and Other Essays* (New York: Washington Square Press, 1963); and Alfred N. Whitehead, *Modes of Thought* (New York: Capricorn Books, 1958).

26. Lonergan thematizes this drive more successfully than Dewey or the other Americans; but he errs, perhaps, in discussing it too much in the context of scientific inquiry, not enough in the many other contexts of human experience. See *Insight: A Study of Human Understanding* (New York: Philosophical Library, 1957).

27. See Ronald Laing, *The Politics of Experience, op. cit.,* p. 6.

28. See Jacques Maritain, *Creative Intuition in Art and Poetry* (New York: Pantheon, 1953) and William J. Lynch, especially, *Images of Hope: Imagination as Healer of the Hopeless* (New York: Mentor-Omega, 1965), and also Ray L. Hart, *Unfinished Man and the Imagination* (New York: Seabury, 1968).

29. For recent writings on these themes see Sam Keen, *Apology for Wonder* (New York: Harper & Row, 1969), *To A Dancing God* (New York: Harper & Row, 1970); Harvey Cox, *The Feast of Fools* (Cambridge, Mass.: Harvard Univ. Press, 1969); and the older books, Josef Pieper, *In Tune with the World: A Theory of Festivity,* translated by Richard and Clara Winston (New York: Harcourt, Brace, and World, 1965), and Johan Huizinga, *Homo Ludens: A Study of the Play Element in Culture* (Boston: Beacon, 1955).

30. See Alan Watts, *The Book: On the Taboo Against Knowing Who You Are* (New York: Collier, 1967).

31. *The Woman Who Was Poor* (New York: Sheed & Ward, 1932).

32. See Elie Wiesel, *Night,* translated by Stella Rodway (New York: Hill & Wang, 1960); *The Gates of the Forest,* translated by Frances Frenage (New York: Avon Library, 1967). Wiesel knows

that no one has fathomed the holocaust. "All my stories are lies," he has said. See also Emil Fackenheim's *God's Presence in History* (New York: New York Univ. Press, 1970) and Richard L. Rubenstein, *After Auschwitz: Radical Theology and Contemporary Judaism* (New York: Bobbs-Merrill, 1966).

33. *The Sacred and the Profane,* translated by Willard R. Trask (New York: Harcourt Brace Jovanovich, 1959), pp. 10–11.

34. *Ibid.,* pp. 12–13.

35. *Ibid.,* p. 17.

36. "The Decline and the Validity of the Idea of Progress," *The Future of Religions* (New York: Harper & Row, 1966), pp. 77–78.

37. See, among others, *The Sacred and the Profane, op. cit.;* Rudolf Otto, *The Idea of the Holy,* translated by J. W. Harvey (New York: Oxford, 1958); and G. van der Leeuw, *Religion in Essence and Manifestation* (New York: Harper & Row, 1963).

38. *The Abolition of Man* (New York: Collier, 1962).

39. See Jürgen Moltmann, *Theology of Hope: On the Ground and the Implications of a Christian Eschatology,* translated by James W. Leitch (New York: Harper & Row, 1967), and also *New Theology No. 5,* edited by Martin E. Marty and Dean G. Peerman (New York: Macmillan, 1968).

40. *Cosmos and History* (New York: Harper Torchbooks, 1954), originally published as *The Myth of Eternal Return.*

41. See *The Rebel,* translated by Anthony Bower (New York: Vintage, 1956), pp. 279–93. See my commentary in *A Theology for Radical Politics, op. cit.,* pp. 92–99.

42. Diana Niblack Fox in *I.V.S.,* newsletter of International Voluntary Services, Inc., June, 1970.

43. See the excellent study by Thomas J. J. Altizer, *Mircea Eliade and his Dialectic of the Sacred* (Philadelphia: Westminster, 1963), especially chapter 1; also Langdon Gilkey, *Naming the Whirlwind,* (Indianapolis: Bobbs-Merrill, 1969), chapters 3 and 4 of Part II.

44. *One-Dimensional Man: Studies in the Ideology of Advanced Industrial Society* (Boston: Beacon, 1964).

45. *The Politics of Experience, op. cit.*

46. See John R. Seeley, *The Americanization of the Unconscious* (New York: International Science Press, 1967).

47. Tillich distinguishes between the *content* of moral decisions (in which cultural progress is possible) and the moral decisions themselves (which are always difficult and show no "progress"): "Do not believe," he writes, "that on the level of primitive ethics people were worse than we are. In the smallest decisions you make . . . there is the same problem of ethical decision which is found in the evidences of the cavemen; you are no better than they." *The Future of Religions, op. cit.,* p. 72.

48. *The Sacred and the Profane, op. cit.,* pp. 12–13.

49. This word (*L.,* "thisness") from the thirteenth-century theologian Duns Scotus was a favorite of the poet Gerard Manley Hopkins, and his theory of "inscape" was based upon it. See *A Hopkins Reader* edited by John Pick (Garden City: Doubleday Image Books, 1966).

50. Eliade, *op. cit.,* p. 12.

Two: Autobiography and Story

1. New York: Harper & Row, 1966.

2. *Purity of Heart*, translated from the Danish and with an introduction by Douglas V. Steere (New York: Harper Torchbooks, 1966).

3. With Nathan Glazer and Paul Denny, *The Lonely Crowd,* abridged by the authors (Garden City: Doubleday Anchor Books, 1953).

4. See, e.g., H. Richard Neibuhr, *The Responsible Self: An Essay in Christian Moral Philosophy* (New York: Harper & Row, 1963), especially pp. 48–54 and 152–53; also Erich Auerbach, *Mimesis: The Representation of Reality in Western Literature,* translated by Willard Trask (New York: Doubleday Anchor Books, 1959), especially chapter 1.

5. Alexis de Tocqueville, *Democracy in Ameica* (New York: Vintage, 1961).

6. See R. W. B. Lewis, *The American Adam* (Chicago: Univ. of Chicago Press, 1958).

7. Barrows Dunham writes in *Man Against Myth* (New York: Hill & Wang, 1962): "The aim of science is to state what actually is the case. Perhaps half the intellectual labor of mankind now goes into this effort. The other half goes into inventing, fostering, and propagating doctrines, which express, not reality, but the interests and advantage of particular groups." *Preface.*

8. See Kierkegaard contra Hegel, *Philosophical Fragments,* translated by D. Swenson and H. V. Hong (Princeton: Princeton Univ. Press, 1962).

9. See Iris Murdoch's discussion of the liberal story which underlies British analytic philosophy, "Vision and Choice in Morality" in *Christian Ethics and Contemporary Philosophy,* edited by Ian T. Ramsey (New York: Macmillan, 1966), pp. 195–218.

10. Marcelle Auclair, *Teresa of Avila,* translated by Kathleen Pond (Garden City: Doubleday Image Books, 1959).

11. See Ronald W. Hepburn, "Vision and Choice in Morality," *op. cit.,* pp. 181–95.

12. "What is the general idea behind the interpretation of ourselves as *symbolic* more than rational animals? It is, I believe, this: that we are far more image-making and image-using creatures than we imagine ourselves to be, and further, that our processes of perception and conception, or organizing and understanding the signs that come to us in our dialogue with the circumambient world, are guided and formed by images in our minds." H. R. Niebuhr, *op. cit.* pp. 151–52.

13. "Context versus Principles: A Misplaced Debate in Christian Ethics," *New Theology No. 3,* edited by Martin E. Marty and Dean G. Peerman (New York: Macmillan, 1966), pp. 69–102.

14. See Murdoch, *op. cit.:* "When we apprehend and assess other people . . . we consider something elusive which may be

called their total vision of life, as shown in their mode of speech or silence, their choice of words, their assessments of others, their conception of their own lives, what they think attractive or praiseworthy, what they think funny" (p. 202).

15. *Love and Will, op. cit.,* p. 19.

16. *Exploration into God* (Stanford: Stanford Univ. Press, 1967).

17. *The Triumph of the Therapeutic* (New York: Harper Torchbooks, 1966).

18. New York: Random House, 1970).

19. Kierkegaard, *Concluding Unscientific Postscript, op. cit.,* p. 530.

Three: Cultures

1. "The Significance of the History of Religions for the Systematic Theologian," in *The Future of Religions,* edited by Jerald C. Brauer (New York: Harper & Row, 1966), p. 97.

2. Emile Durkheim, *Suicide: A Study in Sociology* (Glencoe, Ill.: Free Press, 1954).

3. *The Phenomenon of Man,* translated by Bernard Wule, (New York: Harper Torchbooks, 1965).

4. See Emile Durkheim, "Social Order and Anomie," in *Culture and Consciousness: Perspectives in the Social Sciences,* edited by Gloria B. Levitas (New York: Braziller, 1967), p. 96.

5. Sigmund Freud, *The Ego and the Id* (London: Hogarth Press, 1935), pp. 46–47, quoted by Talcott Parsons in "Social Structure and the Development of Personality: Freud's Contribution to the Integration of Psychology and Sociology," in *Culture and Consciousness, op. cit.,* p.,271.

6. Clyde Kluckhohn, *Culture and Behavior* (New York: Free Press, 1962), p. 73.

7. Erik Erikson, *Insight and Responsibility: Lectures on the Ethical Implications of Psychoanalytic Insight* (New York: Norton, 1964), pp. 219–43.

8. (New York: Columbia Univ. Press, 1963), p. 97.

9. Thus *Webster's New Collegiate Dictionary* (Springfield, Mass.: G. and C. Merriam, 1960) defines myth: "1. A story, the origin of which is forgotten, ostensibly historical but usually such as to explain some practice, belief, institution, or natural phenomenon. Myths are especially associated with religious rites and beliefs. 2. A person or thing existing only in imagination. 3. Such legends collectively; legendary or mythical matter."

10. See Werner Heisenberg, "The Representation of Nature in Contemporary Physics," in *Symbolism in Religion and Literature,* edited by Rollo May (New York: Braziller,·1959), pp. 226–27. For recent studies in the social sciences, see R. Rosenthal "On the Social Psychology of the Psychological Experiment: The Experimenter's Hypothesis as Unintended Determinant of Experimental Results," *American Scientist,* 1963, *51,* 268–83; R. Rosenthal, *Experimenter Effects in Behavioral Research* (New York: Appleton-Century-Crofts, 1966); and R. Rosenthal and L. Jacobson, *Pygmalion in the Classroom: Teacher Expectation and Pupil's Intellectual Development* (New York: Holt, Rinehart & Winston, 1968); Naomi Weisstein, *Kinder, Küche, Kirche as Scientific Law: Psychology Constructs the Female* (Boston: New England Free Press, not dated).

11. *Love and Will, op. cit.,* pp. 16–17, 22.

12. See Robert MacIver, "Refuges of the Social Sciences," in *Culture and Consciousness, op. cit.,* pp. 175–93.

13. See Mohandas K. Gandhi, *An Autobiography: The Story of My Experiments with Truth,* translated by Mahadev Desai (Boston: Beacon, 1969), and *Non-Violent Resistance (Satyagraha)* (New York: Schocken, 1961).

14. Henry Adams, *Mont-Saint-Michel and Chartres* (New York: Collier, 1963), and Friedrich Heer, *The Medieval World* (New York: Mentor, 1963), chs. 5, 7, 13.

15. A. N. Whitehead, *Science and the Modern World* (New York: New American Library, 1956).

16. See, e.g., *The Will to Power* (New York: Random House,

1967) pp 9–39.

17. See Norman Cohn, *The Pursuit of The Millennium* (New York: Harper Torchbooks, 1961).

18. See Mircea Eliade, *Cosmos and History, op. cit.*

19. See St. John of the Cross, *Dark Night of the Soul,* translated by E. Allison Peers (Garden City: Doubleday Image Books, 1962).

Four: Societies and Institutions

1. Translated by James Strachey (New York: Norton, 1962).

2. See Norman O. Brown, *Life Against Death* (New York: Random House, Vintage Books, 1959); Herbert Marcuse, *An Essay on Liberation* (Boston: Beacon, 1969), and *Eros and Civilization: A Philosophical Inquiry into Freud* (New York: Random House, Vintage Books, 1955).

3. The term is from Marx. I mean by it those aspects of consciousness which at least appear to be out of touch with the social and economic context in which they arise. See Karl Marx and Frederick Engels: *Selected Works in One Volume* (New York: International Publishers, 1968), *passim.*

4. See Gerald Cannon Hickey, *The Village in Vietnam* (New Haven: Yale Univ. Press, 1964), and Paul Mus and John T. McAlister, Jr., *The Vietnamese and their Revolution, op. cit.*

5. See Peter L. Berger and Thomas Luckmann, *op. cit.,* p. 56.

6. Edward Sapir writes: "Language is heuristic, not merely in the simple sense . . . but in the much more far-reaching sense that its forms predetermine for us certain modes of observation and interpretation." *Culture, Language, and Personality: Selected Essays,* edited by David G. Mandelbaum (Berkeley: Univ. of California Press, 1964), p. 7.

7. See Ernest G. Schachtel, *Metamorphosis: On the Development of Affect, Perception, Attention and Memory* (New York: Basic Books, 1959), pp. 294–95, 297.

8. *Ibid.*, pp. 279–322.

9. *Enquiry Concerning the Principles of Morals,* Section II, "Of Benevolence," in Hume's *Moral and Political Philosophy,* edited by Henry D. Aiken (New York: Hafner, 1959), pp. 180–84.

10. *The Nature of Sympathy,* translated by Peter Heath (London: Routledge & Kegan Paul, 1954).

11. Quoted by David S. Broder in *The Washington Post* (October 13, 1970), p. A15.

12. In *Identity, Youth, and Crisis* (New York: Norton, 1968).

13. New York: Scribner, 1965), p. 120 and *passim.*

14. See Eric Voegel on Socrates, in *Order and History,* Volume Three, *Plato and Aristotle* (Baton Rouge: Louisiana State Univ. Press, 1957).

15. *Liberalism and Social Action* (New York: Capricorn, 1963).

16. On institutions see Talcott Parsons: "An institution will be said to be a complex of institutionalized role integrates which is of strategic structural significance in the social system in question." *The Social System* (New York: Collier-Macmillan, The Free Press of Glencoe, 1964), p. 39. See also Berger and Luckmann: "Institutionalization occurs wherever there is a reciprocal typification of habitualized actions by types of actors." *Op. cit.*, p. 51.

17. Berger and Luckmann: "Habitualization provides the direction and the specialization of activity that is lacking in man's biological equipment . . . the background of habitualized activity opens up a foreground for deliberation and innovation." *Ibid.*

18. See my "Moral Society and Immoral Man," *A Time to Build*, pp. 354–72.

19. A stimulating starting place is Bruno Bettelheim, *The Children of the Dream* (New York: Macmillan, 1969).

20. See Robert Warshow's brilliant essay, "The Westerner," in *Film: An Anthology,* edited by Daniel Talbot (Berkeley: Univ of California Press, 1967), pp. 148–62.

21. See Theodor Adorno *et al., The Authoritarian Personality* (Berkeley: Univ. of California Press, 1949).

22. See Karl Marx: "What else does the history of ideas prove, than that intellectual production changes its character in proportion as material production is changed?" Marx and Engels, *op. cit.*, p. 54 and *passim*.

23. See William L. Kolb, "Images of Man and the Sociology of Religion," *Society and Self*, edited by Bartlett H. Stoodley (Glencoe, Ill.: Free Press, 1963), pp. 633–34.

24. "Valéry is a petit bourgeois intellectual, no doubt about it. But not every petit bourgeois intellectual is Valéry. The heuristic inadequacy of contemporary Marxism is contained in these two sentences." Jean-Paul Sartre, *Search for a Method* (New York: Vintage, 1968), p. 56.

25. See Robert N. Bellah, "Christianity and Symbolic Realism," *Journal for the Scientific Study of Religion* (1970), pp. 89–96 and 112–15.

26. James T. Burtchaell, "Response," *ibid.*, pp. 97–99.

27. See the passionate replies of Samuel Z. Klausner and Benjamin Nelson, *ibid.*, pp. 100–106 and 107–11. Nelson, in particular, defends the existence of "neutral zones" in which reality is defined to everyone's satisfaction through scientific procedures.

28. See especially his *Societies: Evolutionary and Comparative Perspectives* (Englewood Cliffs, N.J.: Prentice-Hall, 1966).

29. *"Homo homini lupus"* is the phrase of Thomas Hobbes; from *The Leviathan*.

30. A clear exposition of Parsons' basic notion is given by Richard K. Fenn, "The Process of Secularization: A Post-Parsonian View," *Journal for the Scientific Study of Religion* 9 (1970), pp. 117–36.

31. This formulation is by Fenn, *ibid.*, p. 119.

32. This word is derived from Weber's word, *Adaquanz*, used to describe the relation of Protestant forms to capitalistic forms. See Fenn's note, *ibid.*, p. 124.

33. This is the sort of consideration which leads Parsons to believe that our society has successfully institutionalized Judeo-

Christian values—so successfully that many do not notice whence the values come, they are so "present" and so powerfully operative in all our institutional assumptions. See his "Christianity and Modern Industrial Society," in E. Tiryakian, ed., *Sociological Theory, Values, and Socio-cultural Change* (New York: Harper & Row, 1967), pp. 33–70.

34. This is the point of Fenn's article, *op. cit.*

35. Thus Thomas Luckmann: "To an immeasurably higher degree than in a traditional social order, the individual is left to his own devices in choosing goods and services, friends, marriage partners, neighbors, hobbies, and . . . even 'ultimate' meanings in a relatively autonomous fashion. In a manner of speaking, he is free to construct his own personal identity. The consumer orientation, in short, is not limited to economic products but characterizes the relation of the individual to the entire culture." *The Invisible Religion* (New York: Macmillan, 1967), p. 98.

36. A classic discussion of heteronomy was expressed by Paul Tillich, in "Religion and Secular Culture," *The Protestant Era* (Chicago: Phoenix Books, 1957), pp. 55–65.

37. Klausner writes: "Despite [Bellah's] disclaimers, all religious visions are parochial. Within a pluralistic society, the attempt to communicate to our students the meaning and value of religion as part of an 'action' rather than as part of a 'cultural' system can only be divisive. The ability of our university to serve our diverse community requires that our visions, but not our vision, be checked at the door." "Response," *op. cit.*, p. 106.

38. *The Pursuit of Loneliness* (Boston: Beacon, 1970).

39. What is economically efficient, or even architecturally massive and stunning, may not be good for human interchange. What is good for interchange may require a lower standard of living.

40. See my "Toward a New Liberalism," address at the 125th anniversary of Meadville-Lombard School of Theology, Chicago, June 1970 (mimeographed). I owe the idea to a paper of Garry

Wills, who later developed it fully in *Nixon Agonistes* (Boston: Houghton Mifflin, 1970).

41. "Americans attempt to minimize, circumvent, or deny the interdependence upon which all human societies are based. We seek a private house, a private means of transportation, a private garden, a private laundry, self-service stores, and do-it-yourself skills of every kind. An enormous technology seems to have set itself the task of making it unnecessary for one human being ever to ask anything of another in the course of going about his daily business. Even within the family Americans are unique in their feeling that each member should have a separate room, and even a separate telephone, television, and car, when economically possible. We seek more and more privacy, and feel more and more alienated and lonely when we get it." Philip Slater, *op. cit.*, p. 7.

42. See Luckmann, *op. cit.*, pp 76, 79, 80, 82, 87–88. See also Robert Nisbet, *The Quest For Community* (New York: Oxford, 1953).

43. Fenn's conclusions are that Americans belong to many associations and play many different roles. He adds: "Whether the individual . . . [integrates these multiple role-performances] into a single pattern of meaning is left to the effort of the single individual." *Op. cit.*, p. 135.

44. Both Ronald Laing in *The Divided Self* (Baltimore: Penguin, 1967) and Rollo May, "Our Schizoid World," *Love and Will, op. cit.*, pp. 13–33, have noticed schizoid tendencies in modern life.

45. "Probably all education is but two things, first, parrying of the ignorant children's impetuous assault on the truth and, second, gentle, imperceptible, step-by-step initiation of the humiliated children into the lie." Franz Kafka, cited by E. Schachtel, *op. cit.*, pp. 292–93.

46. The following paragraphs lean heavily upon Daniel Boorstin, *The Image: A Guide to Pseudo-Events in America* (New York: Harper & Row, Colophon, 1964).

47. The treatise is included in *The English Philosophers from Bacon to Mill,* edited with an introduction by Edwin A. Burtt (New York: Modern Library, 1939), pp. 949–1041.

48. *Making It* (New York: Bantam, 1967). This book is instructive for its discussion of "the guardians of culture" in New York: a special sense of reality.

49. *The New Industrial State* (Boston: Houghton Mifflin Company, 1967).

50. See Joe McGinnis. *The Selling of the President* (New York: Trident, 1968).

51. See, e.g., G. William Domhoff, *Who Rules America?* (Englewood Cliffs, N. J.: Prentice-Hall, 1967). Compare Suzanne Keller, *Beyond the Ruling Class* (New York: Random House, 1963).

52. See Fred J. Cook, *The Warfare State* (New York: Collier, 1964).

53. See Richard J. Barnet, *The Economy of Death* (New York: Atheneum, 1969). Also *American Militarism 1970,* edited by Erwin Knoll and Judith Nies McFadden (New York: Viking, 1970).

54. See the remarkable self-revelations of Eugene Rostow, Under-Secretary of State for Political Affairs, in "Some Questions about the War," by William Whitworth, *The New Yorker* (July 4, 1970) pp. 30–56.

55. See Seymour Melman, *Pentagon Capitalism* (New York: McGraw-Hill, 1970).

56. See Otto Friedrich, *Decline and Fall* (New York: Harper & Row, 1970).

57. The widely discussed problems of "culture shock" and "re-entry" reveal the subtle, shattering power of senses of reality, stories, symbols. Cf. *The Peace Corps Reader* (Chicago: Quadrangle, 1967). See also Alvin Toffler, *Future Shock* (New York: Random House, 1970); also available in Bantam paperback, 1970.

58. See Rosabeth Moss Kanter, "Communes," *Psychology Today* 4 (July, 1970), pp. 53–58, 78.

59. See Dietrich Bonhoeffer, *The Way to Freedom* (New York: Harper & Row, 1966).

60. See H. Richard Niebuhr, *Christ and Culture* (New Yorker: Harper & Row, 1951), for a study of five classical types of solution to this tension.

61. See Mircea Eliade, *The Sacred and the Profane, op. cit.*

62. Paul Tillich loved the metaphor "depth." But see also *Existential Psychology,* edited by Rollo May (New York: Random House [paper], 1961), with its unusually helpful bibliography.

63. See John Courtney Murray, *We Hold These Truths* (New York: Sheed & Ward, 1960).

64. See Sigmund Freud, *The Future of an Illusion, op. cit.,* James Frazer, *The Golden Bough* (New York: Macmillan, 1922); etc.

65. See the exchange between Ernest van den Haag and Sidney Hook in Hook, *The Quest for Being* (New York: St. Martin's Press, 1961), pp. 103–14.

66. See Bertrand Russell, *Why I am Not a Christian* (New York: Essandess Paperback, 1957).

67. Among others, see Sidney Mead, *The Lively Experiment* (New York: Harper & Row, 1963), and his "The 'Nation with the Soul of a Church,' " *op. cit.,* pp. 262–83.

68. "Civil Religion in America," *Daedalus* (Winter, 1967), pp. 1–21; reprinted in *The Religious Situation 1968,* edited by Donald R. Cutler (Boston: Beacon, 1968), pp. 331–55; see p. 331.

69. *Ibid.*

70. See the exchange between Bellah and four critics, *ibid.,* pp. 356–88.

71. *Religion and Progress in Modern Asia* (New York: Harper & Row, 1965), p. 171.

72. *Ibid.,* p. 176.

73. "Civil Religion," *op. cit.,* p. 354.

74. *Ibid.*

75. *Ibid.*

Five: Organizations

1. See e.g., Luckmann, *op. cit.*, pp. 60–61.
2. *Ibid.*, p. 11.
3. *Ibid.*, p. 104.
4. Joseph Heller (New York: Dell, 1962).
5. Luckmann, *op. cit.*, p. 110.
6. Eugene Jennings describes the new man for whom mobility itself becomes a psychic center: "Freedom is a form of movement." In "Mobicentric Man," *Psychology Today* (July, 1970), pp. 35–36, 70, 72. But even the first Americans were wanderers westward from Europe: "Go West, Young Man!" was an aspiration set before "the bold and the free." *Easy Rider* continues the tradition.
7. ". . . a world where sex is so available that the only way to preserve any inner center is to learn to have intercourse without committing yourself. . . ." Rollo May, *Love and Will, op. cit.*, p. 32; see also Chapter Two, "Paradoxes of Sex and Love," pp. 37–63.
8. On the role of the "other," see Erik H. Erikson, *Identity: Youth in Crisis* (New York: Norton, 1968). See also: Martin Buber, *I and Thou*, translated by Ronald Gregor Smith (New York: Scribner, 1958); John Macmurray, *Persons in Relation* (London: Faber & Faber, 1961); David Riesman, *The Lonely Crowd* (New Haven: Yale Univ. Press, 1950); Berger and Luckmann, *op. cit.*; Robert O. Johann, *Building the Human*, (New York: Herder & Herder, 1968); H. R. Niebuhr, *The Responsible Self: An Essay in Christian Moral Philosophy* (New York: Harper & Row, 1963; *paperback edition 1978*); and Jean Paul Sartre, *Critique de raison dialectique* (Paris: Gallimard, 1960).
9. *The Fall*, translated by Justin O'Brien (New York: Knopf, 1961), pp. 6–7.
10. Luckmann, *op. cit.*, p. 104.

11. See Garry Wills, *Nixon Agonistes*, and my paper, "Toward a New Liberalism," 125th Convocation Address, Meadville Lombard Theological School (June, 1970), *op. cit.*

12. See William Hinton, *Fanshen, A Documentary of Revolution in a Chinese Village* (New York: Vintage, 1968).

13. Luckmann, *op. cit.,* pp. 101–2 and notes.

14. See Charles Hartshorne, *The Divine Relativity: A Social Conception of God* (New Haven: Yale Univ. Press, 1948); Teilhard de Chardin, *The Phenomenon of Man, op. cit.*

15. See Charles Y. Glock and Rodney Stark, "Religion and the Social Sciences: Images of Man in Conflict," *Religion and Society in Tension* (Chicago: Rand McNally, 1965) pp. 289–306.

16. Through language, history and community shape our present identity; the self is a "we." For powerful arguments in this sense, see Eugen Rosenstock-Huessy, *I Am an Impure Thinker* (Norwich, Vt.: Argo Books, 1970), especially pp. 53–68.

17. See Romano Guardini's double-volume *The Church and The Catholic* and *The Spirit of the Liturgy* (New York: Sheed & Ward, 1935).

18. See *The Concise Encyclopedia of Living Faiths,* edited by R. C. Zaehner (New York: Hawthorne 1959), p. 401.

19. "The Church is that type of organization which is overwhelmingly conservative, which to a certain extent accepts the secular order, and dominates the masses; in principle, therefore, it is universal, i.e., it desires to cover the whole life of humanity." *The Social Teachings of the Christian Churches,* translated by Olive Wyon (New York: Harper Torchbooks, 1960), Vol. I, p. 331.

20. See Augustine, *The City of God.*

21. "The sects, on the other hand, are comparatively small groups; they aspire after personal inward perfection, and they aim at a direct personal fellowship between the members of each group. From the very beginning, therefore, they are forced to organize themselves in small groups, and to renounce the idea of dominating the world. Their attitude towards the world, the

State, and Society may be indifferent, tolerant, or hostile, since they have no desire to control and incorporate these forms of social life; on the contrary, they tend to avoid them; their aim is usually either to tolerate their presence alongside their own body, or even to replace these social institutions by their own society." Troeltsch, *op. cit.*, p. 331.

22. Norman Cohn, *The Pursuit of the Millennium: Revolutionary Messianism in Medieval and Reformation Europe and Its Bearing on Modern Totalitarian Movements* (New York: Harper Torchbooks, 1961); see also my "The Free Churches and the Roman Church," *A Time To Build, op. cit.*

23. See H. Richard Niebuhr, *The Social Sources of Denominationalism* (New York: Meridian, 1957).

24. Glencoe: The Free Press, 1964.

25. See William G. McLoughlin, "Is There a Third Force in Christendom?" *Daedalus* (Winter, 1967), pp. 43–68.

26. See Donald Meyer, *The Positive Thinkers* (Garden City, N.Y.: Doubleday, 1965), and Charles Y. Glock, Benjamin B. Ringer, and Earl B. Babbie, *To Comfort and to Challenge* (Berkeley: Univ. of California Press, 1967).

27. See *Billy Graham Talks to Teen-Agers* (New York: Pyramid Books, 1969); *World Aflame* (New York: Pocket Books, 1966); and *The Secret of Happiness* (Garden City: Doubleday Waymark Books, 1968).

28. For an introduction to such problems, see James M. Robinson and John B. Cobb, editors, *The New Hermeneutic* (New York: Harper & Row, 1964), and their earlier volume in the same series ("New Frontiers in Theology"), *The Later Heidegger and Theology* (1963).

29. ". . . America precisely offers the most advanced observation post . . . one cannot avoid in America the question whether the concept of culture, in which one was brought up, has not itself become obsolete. One is further led to wonder whether this is not the result of the general tendency in contemporary culture toward

self-castigation for its failures, the guilt it incurred by holding itself aloof in a separate sphere of the intellect, without manifesting itself in social reality.

. . . It is scarcely an exaggeration to say that any contemporary consciousness that has not appropriated the American experience, even if in opposition, has something reactionary about it." Cf. "Scientific Experiences of a European Scholar in America," in Donald Fleming and Bernard Bailyn, editors, *The Intellectual Migration* (Cambridge: Harvard Univ. Press, 1969), pp. 338–70.

30. ". . . Among the most important things I have learned in America is this: much of the German or European fund of knowledge is not suited for Americans. It is a great pity that the Americans in their humility, modesty, and intellectual unpretentiousness have had European cultural wares transmitted to them by specialists who continued to think in European categories. . . . The experiences of the Europeans with Bach, Wagner, and Beethoven must be transposed so-to-say to athletic experiences. In America you can't make reference to the experiences a young man has with the fine arts, as you can in Italy. You can, however, very probably remind him that he learned to live lyrically while skiing, dramatically in football, epically through swimming, so that he suddenly recognizes that these events he lived through unconsciously in a group represent his first philosophy. In short, he already knows quite a lot about life. If I had mixed in some sort of European esthetics, sociology, or romantics, my students would have had the feeling I was trying to plant a European head on their American heart. I guarded against that scrupulously . . ." Eugen Rosenstock-Hussey, *I Am an Impure Thinker, op. cit.,* pp. 167–68.

31. New York: Macmillan, 1965. See also Cox's autobiographical account in *Psychology Today* (June, 1970), "Religion in the Age of Aquarius, A Conversation with George T. Harris," pp. 45–47, 62–67.

32. For other variables in American Catholic history, see Daniel

Callahan, *The Mind of the Catholic Layman* (New York: Scribner's, 1963). The Lutheran journal *Una Sancta,* edited by Richard Neuhaus, for some years illustrated the power of the American Lutheran intellectual tradition.

33. The best introduction to Barth and Bultmann is James D. Smart, *The Divided Mind of Modern Theology* (Philadelphia: Westminster, 1967). G. W. Bromiley translated and edited *Barth: Church Dogmatics: A Selection* (New York: Harper Torchbooks, 1961).

34. Tillich's own autobiographical sketch, *On The Boundary* (New York: Scribner's, 1966), and the transcribed seminars edited by D. Mackenzie Brown, *Ultimate Concern* (New York: Harper & Row, 1965), are splendid introductions, and *The Courage To Be* (New Haven: Yale Univ. Press, 1963) is a powerful first experience.

35. See Smart's book (note 33); Schubert M. Ogden, *Christ Without Myth* (New York: Harper & Row, 1961); and, for a first taste of Bultmann, *Existence and Faith* (New York: Meridian, 1966).

36. See Eliade's *Patterns in Comparative Religion* (New York: Sheed & Ward, 1958).

37. See Gordon Harland, *The Thought of Reinhold Niebuhr* (New York: Oxford, 1960); Niebuhr's *The Nature and Destiny of Man* (New York: Scribner, 1964), 2 vols., and *Moral Man and Immoral Society* (New York: Scribner, 1960).

38. See his *Spirit in the World* (New York: Herder & Herder, 1968) and *Nature and Grace* (New York: Sheed & Ward, 1963).

39. See David Tracy, *The Achievement of Bernard Lonergan* (New York: Herder & Herder, 1970), Lonergan's own *Collection* (New York: Herder & Herder, 1967) and *Insight* (New York: Philosophical Library, 1957; paperback edition available from Harper & Row, 1978).

40. See Paul Ramsey, editor, *Faith and Ethics* (New York: Harper Torchbooks, 1957), and Niebuhr's own *The Responsible*

Self, op. cit.

41. See Mary Bosanquet, *The Life and Death of Dietrich Bonhoeffer* (New York: Harper & Row, 1969); and Eberhard Bethge's *Dietrich Bonhoeffer* (New York: Harper & Row, 1970).

42. See his *Living Options in Protestant Theology* (Philadelphia: Westminster, 1962).

43. See his *The Reality of God* (New York: Harper & Row, 1963).

44. See his *Naming The Whirlwind, op. cit.*

45. See his *The Historian and The Believer* (New York: Macmillan, 1966).

46. See, most recently, his *The Modern Schism* (New York: Harper & Row, 1969) and *Righteous Empire* (New York: Dial, 1970).

47. (New York: The Seabury Press, 1975).   See especially chapter 2, pp. 22–42.

48. See my   *Further Reflections on Ethnicity* (Middletown, Pa.: Jednota Press, an EMPAC Book, 1977), Chapter 5, "The Social World of Individuals," for a lengthy definition of "the pluralistic personality."

Six: Nature and History

1. In a series of articles called "Complacency and Concern in St. Thomas Aquinas," Frederick E. Crowe, S.J., stated with exemplary clarity the differences between a medieval and a modern "sense of reality" on the question of action. In *Theological Studies* 20 (1959), 1–39, 198–230, 343–95.

2. Eliade comments on these criticisms in his contribution to *The Theology of Altizer,* edited by John B. Cobb, Jr. (Philadelphia: Westminster, 1970), pp. 234–41. The original locus is Altizer's *Mircea Eliade and the Dialectic of the Sacred, op. cit.,* p. 195.

3. New York: Vintage, 1956, p. 299.

4. New York: Vintage, 1955, pp. 136–37.

5. To reply to this question, Camus wrote *The Myth of Sisyphus.*

6. And to treat this question, he wrote *The Rebel.*

7. For other background on such notions, see Jacques Maritain, *Creative Intuition in Art and Poetry* (New York: Meridian, 1953) and *Art and Scholasticism* (New York: Scribner's, 1962); also Josef Pieper, *Leisure: The Basis of Culture* (New York: Pantheon, 1961) and *Happiness and Contemplation* (New York: Pantheon 1958).

8. Gilbert Ryle's discussion of "achievement verbs" in *The Concept of Mind* (New York: Barnes & Noble, 1960), pp. 149–53, though derived from a clue in Aristotle, makes a different point. When we say "Now I see it!" or "Now I get it!", it is not quite like saying "I win!" or "I succeed!" These latter are—as Ryle calls them—"referee words." The former suggest that the agent is not deficient in the relevant skill, that he has fulfilled the relevant prior conditions, that the relevant changes have occurred in him. The agent is often entitled to take these achievements as a sign of his growth.

9. Eugen Rosenstock-Huessy writes: "The world in which the American student who comes to me at about twenty years of age really has confidence is the world of sport. This world encompasses all of his virtues and experiences, affections and interests; therefore, I have built my entire sociology around the experiences an American has in athletics and games. . . . People preserve their thousand-year-old experiences in the world of play." *I Am An Impure Thinker, op. cit.,* p. 167.

10. See my *The Experience of Nothingness, op. cit.,* pp. 65–88 and *passim.*

11. The Dudleian Lecture, Harvard Divinity School, November 18, 1970. Mimeographed.

12. Charles A. Reich describes much too approvingly the resistance to loyalty, long-term commitments, promises and obligations prominent among some young people. *The Greening of Amer-*

ica, op. cit., p. 228.

13. See also Herbert J. Fingarette, *The Self in Transformation, op. cit.;* Robert Jay Lifton, "Protean Man," in *History and Human Survival* (New York: Random House, 1970). After completing this manuscript, I also found much support in Eugen Rosenstock-Huessy, *I Am An Impure Thinker, op. cit.*

Further Readings

Selected texts from major Protestant voices in American history are gathered in Sidney E. Ahlstrom, *Theology in America* (Indianapolis: Bobbs-Merrill, 1967). William E. Hordern's *A Layman's Guide to Protestant Theology* (New York: Macmillan, rev. ed. 1968) offers a quick contemporary overview, while Winthrop S. Hudson's *American Protestantism* (Chicago: University of Chicago Press, 1961) is a brief but excellent history. *A Nation of Behavers* (Chicago: University of Chicago Press, 1976) is the latest contribution by Martin Marty; his *A Righteous Empire* (New York: Dell, 1974) won the National Book Award.

In addition to John Dunne, whose works are noted throughout this book, there are a number of important Catholic thinkers: David Tracy's *A Blessed Rage for Order* (New York: Seabury, 1975); Avery Dulles, *The Survival of Dogma* (Garden City, N.Y.: Doubleday, Image Book, 1973) and *Models of the Church* (Garden City, N.Y.: Doubleday, 1974); sociologist Andrew Greeley, *Unsecular Man* (New York: Dell, 1974), *The Denominational Society: A Sociological Approach to Religion in America* (Glenview, Ill: Scott Foresman, 1973), and *The Communal Catholic: A Personal Manifesto* (New York: Seabury, 1976); David Burrell's *Exercises in Religious Understanding* (South Bend: University of Notre Dame Press, 1975); and, above all, Bernard Lonergan, *Insight* (New York: Harper & Row, 1978) and *Method in Theology* (New York: Seabury, 1972).

The resurgence of the evangelical churches is studied in several recent works: Donald G. Bloesch, *The Evangelical Renaissance* (Grand Rapids: Eerdmans, 1973); Donald W. Dayton, *Discovering an Evangelical Heritage* (New York: Harper & Row, 1976); Carl F. H. Henry, *Evangelicals in Search of Identity* (Waco: Word Books, 1976); Dean M. Kelley, *Why Conservative Churches are Growing* (New York: Harper & Row, rev. ed. 1977); Richard Quebedaux, *The Young Evangelicals* (New York: Harper & Row, 1974); and John D. Woodbridge and David F. Wells, eds., *The Evangelicals* (Nashville: Abingdon, 1975).

Luther H. Harshbarger and John A. Mourant have prepared an introductory text, *Judaism and Christianity* (Boston: Allyn and Bacon, 1968), for a comparative study of those two Western religions.

Among Jewish authors, Emil Fackenheim's work, including *God's Presence in History* (New York: Harper & Row, 1972), is most important. Richard L. Rubenstein has contributed *Religious Imagination: A Study in Psychoanalysis and Jewish Theology* (Boston: Beacon Press, 1971). Elie Wiesel's novels and essays are very important for the category of story.

For introductions to the world religions, see Wilfred Cantwell Smith, *The Meaning and End of Religion* (New York: Harper & Row, 1978), and Huston Smith, *The Religions of Man* (New York: Harper Perennial Library, 1965)

The field of religion and story has blossomed in the past decade. The four works of John Dunne, cited earlier, are important contributions. The volume *Religion as Story* (New York: Harper & Row, 1975), edited by my colleague James B. Wiggins, introduces a wide range of issues in the field.

Stephen Crites focused the discussion with his article "The Narrative Quality of Experience," *Journal of the American Academy of Religion 39* (Sept. 1971), pp. 291–311. Among the many voices who have since joined the conversation in that journal are Ted Estess, "The Inenarrable Contraption: Reflections on the Metaphor of Story," 42 (Sept. 1974), pp. 415–435, and James Wiggins, "Eschatological Consciousness: Response to Temporality," 43 (Mar. 1975) pp. 27–38. Two articles with the identical title, "Story and Theology" have appeared: one by Robert McAfee Brown in *Philosophy of Religion and Theology: 1974,* compiled by James W. McClendon Jr.; the other by Stanley Hauerwas in *Religion in Life* XLV (Autumn 1976). The more important books include: Dominic Crossan, *The Dark Interval: Toward A Theology of Story* (Niles, Ill.: Argus Communications, 1975); Sally TeSelle, *Speaking in Parables* (Philadelphia: Fortress Press, 1975); Brian Wicker, *Story-Shaped World* (Notre Dame: University of Notre Dame Press, 1976); and Wesley Kort, *Narrative Elements and Religious Meaning* (Philadelphia: Fortress Press, 1976). In addition, James McClendon, *Biography as Theology* (New York: Abingdon Press, 1974), and Stanley Hauerwas, *Vision and Virtue: Essays in Christian Ethical Reflection* (Notre Dame: Fides Publishers, 1974) and *Character and The Christian Life* (San Antonio: Trinity University Press, 1975), approach other issues of religion and story through character ethics. My own *"Story" in Politics* (New York: The Council on Religion and International Affairs, 1970) applies analysis by way of story to problems in foreign policy.

In the first edition, many of the following authors and titles were briefly described in chapter five, section six, "A Map of Christian Theologies in the United States." New material has been supplied at that place. But some students found the list of authors stimulating, so the references are included here. I have selected titles especially helpful to beginners.

Altizer, Thomas J. J., *Descent into Hell* (Philadelphia: Lippincott, 1970) and with William Hamilton, *Radical Theology and the Death of God,* (Indianapolis: Bobbs-Merrill, 1966).

Baum, Gregory, *Is The New Testament Anti-Semitic?* (Glen Rock, N.J.: Paulist Press, 1965) and *Man Becoming: God in Secular Experience* (New York: Seabury, 1970).

Bellah, Robert N., *Beyond Belief* (New York: Harper & Row, 1970) and *The Broken Covenant: American Civil Religion in Time of Trial* (New York: Seabury, 1975).

Berger, Peter, *The Sacred Canopy* and *A Rumor of Angels* (Garden City: Doubleday, 1967, 1969).

Berrigan, Daniel, *The Trial of the Catonsville Nine* (Boston: Beacon, 1970) and *Night Flight to Hanoi* (New York: Macmillan, 1969).

Brown, Robert McAfee, *The Ecumenical Revolution* (Garden City: Doubleday, 1967) and *The Spirit of Protestantism* (New York: Oxford University Press, 1965).

Callahan, Sidney, *The Illusion of Eve* (New York: Sheed & Ward, 1965).

Cleage, Albert, *The Black Messiah* (New York: Sheed & Ward, 1968).

Cohen, Arthur, *The Natural and Supernatural Jew* (New York: Random House, 1962) and "Reader of Jewish Thinking After the Holocaust," *Arguments and Doctrines* (New York: Harper & Row, 1970).

Cone, James, *Black Theology and Black Power* (New York: Seabury, 1969) and *A Theology of Black Liberation* (Philadelphia: Lippincott, 1970).

Cox, Harvey, *The Secular City,* (New York: Macmillan, 1965), *The Feast of Fools* (New York: Harper & Row Perennial Library, 1972) and *The Seduction of the Spirit* (New York: Simon and Schuster, 1973).

Daly, Mary, *The Church and the Second Sex* (New York: Harper & Row, rev.ed. 1975) and *Beyond God the Father: Toward a Philosophy of Women's Liberation* (Boston: Beacon Press, 1974).

Dewart, Leslie, *The Future of Belief* and *The Foundations of Belief* (New York: Herder and Herder, 1966, 1969).

Heschel, Abraham, *Man's Quest for God* (New York: Scribner's, 1954) and *God in Search of Man* (New York: Meridian, 1961).

Keen, Sam, *Apology for Wonder, To A Dancing God* (New York: Harper & Row, 1969, 1970).

Mbiti, John, *The African Religions and Philosophies* (New York: Anchor, 1970).

Metz, Johannes, *Theology of the World* (New York: Herder and Herder, 1969).

Moltmann, Jurgen, *A Theology of Hope* and *The Crucified God* (New York: Harper & Row, 1967, 1974).

Neuhaus, Richard, *Time Toward Home* (New York: Seabury, 1975) and, with Peter Berger, *Movement and Revolution* (Garden City: Doubleday, 1970).

Neusner, Jacob, *Fellowship in Judaism* and *History and Torah* (London: Valentine, Mitchell, 1963, 1965) and *American Judaism: Adventure in Modernity* (New York: Prentice-Hall, 1972).

O'Dea, Thomas, *The Sociology of Religion* (Englewood Cliffs, N.J.: Prentice-Hall, 1966) and *The Catholic Crisis* (Boston: Beacon, 1968).

Ruether, Rosemary, *The Radical Kingdom: The Western Experience of Messianic Hope* (Glen Rock, N.J.: Paulist-Newman, 1975) and *New Woman–New Earth: Sexist Ideologies and Human Liberation* (New York: Seabury, 1975).

Richardson, Herbert W., *Toward an American Theology* (New York: Harper & Row, 1967).

Rubenstein, Richard L., *After Auschwitz* (Indianapolis: Bobbs-Merrill, 1966).

Stringfellow, William, *My People is the Enemy* (Garden City: Doubleday Anchor Books, 1964).

Tavard, George, *Two Centuries of Ecumenism* (New York: Mentor-Omega, 1962).

Van Buren, Paul M., *The Secular Meaning of the Gospel* (New York: Macmillan, 1963) and *The Burden of Freedom: Americans and the God of Israel* (New York: Seabury, 1976).

INDEX OF NAMES